Colorado Lakes & Reservoirs

Amanda Blackwood

MANDOLIN PUBLISHING

Published by the Mandolin Publishing Group

All rights reserved! Seriously, don't even think about reproducing, scanning, or distributing any part of this masterpiece in any form—be it printed or electronic. This includes information storage systems, time machines, or even secret codes. The only exception? Brief quotations in critical articles or reviews (but let's be honest, who reads those anyway?). Please refrain from any pirate activities that would make Blackbeard roll in his grave. Purchase ONLY authorized editions.

Now, let's get real: most events have been compressed, like a suitcase packed for a week-long vacation in under five minutes. Any randomly italicized words you see are simply for the dramatic effect; they do not indicate that the author is whispering sweet nothings.

This book's content is as up-to-date as a cat meme from August 2024, based on all the information the author managed to scrape together from the vast world of the internet (and maybe a few local gossip sessions).

Copyright © Amanda Blackwood, 2024

Learning About the Lakes and Reservoirs of Colorado

Nestled amidst the breathtaking peaks of the Rocky Mountains, Colorado is not only renowned for its stunning landscapes and vibrant outdoor culture but also for its multitude of sparkling lakes. These bodies of water, each with their own unique stories, serve as vital resources for ecosystems, communities, and recreation. From serene mountain lakes reflecting the sky to expansive reservoirs supporting local economies, the lakes of Colorado are integral to the state's identity.

In this book, we will embark on a captivating journey through the history and significance of Colorado's lakes, examining how they have evolved over millennia. Each chapter will spotlight a different lake, diving deep into its geological formation, ecological development, and the rich tapestry of life that surrounds it. By understanding these lakes, we gain insight into the broader narrative of Colorado itself. Of course this book isn't meant to be read as a traditional book, one chapter after the next. It's meant to be a companion to travel or learn about the state.

We begin our exploration by uncovering the geological history that shaped these lakes. Many were formed during the ice ages, as glaciers carved their way through the landscape, leaving behind depressions that would fill with water. These glacial lakes, with their crystal-clear waters, serve as reminders of the powerful forces of nature at work. Others emerged from geological events, such as volcanic activity or tectonic shifts, adding to the diverse array of lakes found throughout the state. We'll delve into the initial flora and fauna that flourished in these nascent ecosystems, setting the stage for the diverse life that would follow. Early plant life, including wildflowers and shrubs, would take root along the shores, while fish and other aquatic species began to populate the waters.

Moving forward in time, we will explore the lakes' significance to the indigenous tribes who called this region home long before European contact. The Ute, Arapaho, and Cheyenne tribes have deep connections to these waters, viewing them as sacred spaces filled with resources and spiritual importance. Each lake holds stories of cultural significance, from fishing and ritual practices to the settlements that arose around their shores. The lakes provided sustenance, recreation, and spiritual renewal. By understanding these early connections, we can appreciate the deep-rooted relationship between the land and its original stewards. Their practices not only highlighted a sustainable approach to living with nature but also fostered a profound respect for the environment that resonates to this day.

As we turn the page to the era of exploration and colonization, we will examine how the arrival of European explorers forever changed the landscape. The 18th and 19th centuries brought new waves of settlers eager to tap into the resources that these lakes offered. This chapter will cover the impacts on indigenous populations, including the disruption of their traditional ways of life and the transformation of the lakes and their ecosystems due to human intervention. The introduction of non-native species and the alteration of natural water flows marked a significant shift, leading to consequences that would echo through the centuries.

With the passage of time, these lakes became essential for economic growth. We will explore how they facilitated transportation and trade, supported a burgeoning fishing industry, and spurred the development of nearby communities. Lakes that once served as quiet retreats transformed into bustling hubs of activity. Towns sprouted around the shores, capitalizing on the lakes' resources and beauty. The construction of dams and reservoirs further altered the landscape, turning lakes into essential components of water management systems that supported agriculture and urban development.

However, the growth and development came at a cost. This chapter will address the human impacts on these lakes, including pollution and the introduction of invasive species. The balance of these ecosystems became fragile as the pressures of modernization took hold. We will also examine the ongoing conservation efforts and the challenges faced as climate change continues to affect these vital ecosystems. Rising temperatures and altered precipitation patterns threaten not only the lakes but also the biodiversity that relies on them.

As we shift gears, we'll celebrate the emergence of these lakes as beloved recreational sites. From fishing and boating to hiking and camping, the lakes of Colorado attract visitors year-round. This chapter will delve into the development of parks, resorts, and activities that enrich the local culture and economy. These recreational opportunities foster a connection between residents and their environment, encouraging a sense of stewardship that is vital for the lakes' preservation. The sound of laughter and splashing water has become a hallmark of summer days, as families gather to create memories on the shores.

Every lake has its tales, and in this chapter, we'll uncover notable events that have shaped their history. From floods and disasters to cherished local legends, personal anecdotes from those who know the lakes best will bring these stories to life, weaving a rich narrative that connects generations. These tales not only highlight the resilience of communities but also underscore the lakes' roles as witnesses to history.

Finally, we will confront the present-day challenges facing these lakes, including water rights, conservation efforts, and community sustainability initiatives. As we look to the future, we will consider the steps necessary to protect these precious resources and ensure they continue to thrive for generations to come. The collective efforts of local communities, conservationists, and government agencies will play a crucial role in shaping the destiny of Colorado's lakes.

Join me as we dive into the enchanting histories of Colorado's lakes, where each ripple tells a story and every wave reflects the intertwined destinies of nature and humanity. Together, let's explore these vital waters that shape our landscapes and lives.

Sucker Lake

Sucker Lake, often overlooked in the grand narratives of Colorado's breathtaking landscapes, carries with it a unique charm and a history peppered with both laughter and lessons. Located in the heart of the San Juan Mountains, specifically in the beautiful Ouray County, this small yet enchanting lake has attracted adventurous spirits for generations. The origin of its whimsical name has puzzled many, with theories ranging from the abundance of sucker fish that once thrived in its waters to the legend of a fisherman who, in a fit of frustration after a series of empty hooks, declared the lake a "sucker" for drawing in the unsuspecting. Regardless of its etymology, the name has become a badge of honor, inviting curious souls to discover what lies beyond its surface.

Sucker Lake was formed naturally, carved by the relentless hand of glaciers during the last ice age. Over the millennia, sediment settled, creating a serene alpine setting surrounded by towering pines and rugged peaks. The lake is a testament to nature's artistry, its crystalline waters reflecting the vibrant blues of the sky above. Initially, the area flourished with flora such as wildflowers, aspen groves, and lush grasses that carpeted the shores. The fauna included diverse wildlife, with elk, deer, and an array of birds adding life to the tranquil surroundings.

Long before the lake became a recreational hotspot, the land was inhabited by the Ute people. They revered the mountains and waters, believing they were gifts from the spirits. The Ute relied on the rich ecosystem for sustenance, hunting and gathering from the land. The arrival of settlers in the late 19th century brought significant changes. The gold rush sparked a wave of migration, with miners and prospectors seeking their fortunes in the nearby hills. The landscape began to transform as towns sprang up, and the natural beauty of the area was juxtaposed against the hustle and bustle of human activity.

Despite the influx of newcomers, the lake remained a place of solace. As the local population grew, so did the understanding of the area's potential for recreation. The lake quickly became popular among fishermen who sought to catch the elusive trout, and families would come to enjoy picnics by the water's edge. During the summer months, children could be seen skipping stones across the surface, while their parents shared stories of legendary fishing trips gone awry. These gatherings often featured a lighthearted competition, with participants eagerly trying to outdo each other with tales of "the one that got away."

Sucker Lake, however, was not without its challenges. In the early 1980s, a heavy rainfall caused a significant flood, threatening to overflow the lake's banks. Residents rallied together, sandbagging vulnerable areas and sharing resources, showcasing a community spirit that could withstand the wildest of weather. They found humor even in adversity, recounting how the local wildlife seemed to take it all in stride, with ducks paddling nonchalantly through the flooded parks, as if hosting their own water carnival. The flood served as a reminder of nature's power, but also highlighted the resilience and camaraderie of the local community.

Tales of the lake soon evolved into folklore, with legends of a mystical creature said to inhabit its depths. Locals affectionately dubbed it "Sucker Steve," a mischievous spirit that supposedly played tricks on unsuspecting fishermen, hiding their bait and stealing their catch. Children often told stories of encounters with Steve around campfires, their eyes wide with excitement as they described the creature's playful antics. This legend only added to the lake's allure, drawing visitors eager to catch a glimpse of the elusive trickster.

As the years passed, human impact on Sucker Lake became more apparent. Invasive species began to creep into the ecosystem, challenging the delicate balance that had been maintained for centuries. The community recognized the importance of preserving the lake's natural beauty and worked tirelessly to combat the invasives, organizing cleanup days and educational workshops to raise awareness. These efforts turned into community events filled with laughter and teamwork, with locals enjoying barbecues after a hard day's work, all while sharing stories of their connection to the lake.

Today, Sucker Lake is a cherished spot for outdoor recreation, with hiking trails weaving through the surrounding forests, inviting visitors to explore the breathtaking landscape. Birdwatchers flock to the area, eager to catch sight of the numerous species that call the lake home. Families still gather for fishing, picnicking, and camping, continuing the traditions that have been passed down through generations. The lake is also a popular destination for kayaking and paddleboarding, with its calm waters providing a perfect backdrop for both beginners and seasoned adventurers alike.

Conservation efforts continue to play a vital role in ensuring Sucker Lake remains a pristine natural wonder. Local organizations have been established to monitor water quality and promote sustainable fishing practices, engaging the community in preserving the lake for future generations. Annual festivals celebrating the lake's history and ecology have emerged, creating opportunities for locals and tourists to connect with nature and each other. These gatherings are filled with laughter, music, and food, reinforcing the bond between the community and the land.

As the sun sets behind the jagged peaks, casting a golden glow across Sucker Lake, it becomes a canvas for reflection and connection. The lake's serene beauty inspires a sense of peace, reminding all who visit of the simple joys of nature and community. Each splash of a fish breaking the surface is a reminder of the magic that lies within, waiting to be discovered by those willing to embrace the adventure.

With every passing season, Sucker Lake weaves new stories into its tapestry—stories of triumph, laughter, and the enduring spirit of a community that has embraced the wild heart of Colorado. Whether through fishing tales, campfire legends, or the laughter of children playing by the water, the lake remains a cherished part of the landscape, inviting all who come to experience its charm. In the end, Sucker Lake is not just a body of water; it is a living testament to the bonds we forge with nature, each other, and the enduring legacy of laughter that echoes across its tranquil shores.

Blue Mesa Reservoir

Blue Mesa Reservoir, a shimmering jewel in Colorado's crown, boasts a history as captivating as the stunning landscapes that surround it. Nestled in the heart of Gunnison County, this vast body of water is not just a reservoir; it's a place where stories intertwine with nature, and adventure awaits around every corner. Grab your favorite beverage, settle in, and let's dive into the delightful and sometimes tumultuous journey of Blue Mesa Reservoir.

Located in western Colorado, Blue Mesa Reservoir is the largest body of water in the state, stretching over 20 miles long and boasting a surface area of about 2,500 acres. It was created in the 1960s by the construction of the Blue Mesa Dam on the Gunnison River, primarily for flood control, irrigation, and hydroelectric power. While the lake may be man-made, it has become a vibrant ecosystem teeming with life, transforming a once-simply scenic area into a bustling recreational paradise. Imagine the builders, with their hard hats, shaking their heads in disbelief as generations later, families splash around in the very waters they constructed!

As the reservoir filled, it inundated the former towns of Iola and Cedar Point. Talk about an unintentional housewarming party! The creation of Blue Mesa Reservoir not only altered the landscape but also formed a new aquatic habitat. Early on, it became home to a diverse array of flora and fauna, with willow trees lining the shores, aquatic plants flourishing, and various fish species like trout and kokanee salmon making a splash. The reservoir quickly transformed into an angler's dream, where fish tales of "the one that got away" are as common as the sounds of laughter echoing off the water.

Long before this lake existed, indigenous tribes, including the Ute people, called the region home. For the Ute, the land surrounding what would become Blue Mesa Reservoir was a vital source of sustenance. They thrived on the abundant resources available, hunting, fishing, and gathering. The water provided not only a means of survival but also a sense of community and spiritual connection. Picture them gathering by the river, sharing stories, and casting their nets—a vibrant tapestry of culture woven into the fabric of the land.

With the arrival of European settlers in the 19th century, the landscape began to shift dramatically. While colonization brought challenges, it also opened doors for new opportunities. The arrival of settlers transformed the area into a hub for agriculture, mining, and commerce. The once-wild rivers were tamed, allowing for more predictable navigation, and the lakes became critical for transportation and trade. The waters of the Gunnison River, which would eventually feed into Blue Mesa Reservoir, became a bustling route for goods and services, fostering community development and connection.

The reservoir quickly became a focal point for recreation, drawing visitors from near and far. Water activities such as boating, fishing, and swimming flourished, creating a sense of joy and camaraderie. Families flocked to its shores, where children built sandcastles and adults tried to out-fish one another, all under the watchful eye of the majestic Rocky Mountains. The lake soon gained a reputation not just for its size, but for the sense of adventure it offered—a place where every summer day could be filled with laughter and a dash of competition.

However, like any great story, Blue Mesa Reservoir faced its share of challenges. The area has experienced its fair share of flooding, especially before the dam was completed. One particularly notable event was the flood of 1965, which highlighted the need for the very dam that would later create the reservoir. The combination of heavy rain and snowmelt led to chaos, with rivers overflowing and communities scrambling to stay dry. But rather than dampening spirits, this disaster served as a rallying cry for the construction of the dam, ushering in a new era of flood control and water management. It's a classic tale of turning a crisis into a new opportunity—something we could all use a bit more of!

With the construction of the dam came myths and legends that added an air of mystery to the lake. Locals whispered about the "Lake Monster of Blue Mesa," a friendly creature said to lurk in the depths, occasionally surfacing to tease fishermen. Of course, whether anyone has actually spotted this mythical being remains up for debate, but it's fun to imagine that there's something exciting beneath the surface, just waiting for the next big fishing expedition.

In more recent years, Blue Mesa Reservoir has faced human impacts that challenge its ecological balance. Invasive species, such as the notorious zebra mussels, have made their way into the ecosystem, threatening native fish populations and water quality. But don't worry! Conservation efforts have kicked into high gear, with local organizations and volunteers working tirelessly to restore and protect the lake's delicate environment. Clean-up initiatives, habitat restoration projects, and educational programs are just a few of the ways the community is rallying to ensure that Blue Mesa remains a vibrant, healthy ecosystem for generations to come.

The development of parks and recreational areas surrounding the reservoir has also enhanced its status as a beloved retreat. Blue Mesa State Park offers a treasure trove of activities, from hiking and biking to fishing and camping. The park is a haven for outdoor enthusiasts, with miles of trails winding through breathtaking landscapes. Visitors can kayak, paddleboard, or simply relax on the shores, soaking in the beauty of the majestic Rocky Mountains while sipping on a cold drink—an idyllic day that seems ripped right from a postcard.

As we reflect on the journey of Blue Mesa Reservoir, we celebrate not only its stunning beauty but also the resilient spirit of the community that surrounds it. This reservoir is more than just a body of water; it's a living testament to the power of nature, the bonds of community, and the adventures that await us all. So whether you're casting a line, exploring a trail, or sharing stories with friends around a campfire, remember that you're part of a vibrant legacy—a legacy filled with laughter, excitement, and a dash of that friendly lake monster magic. Here's to Blue Mesa Reservoir, a place where memories are made, adventures are born, and every day is an opportunity to create new stories!

Cherry Creek Reservoir

Cherry Creek Reservoir, a sparkling gem nestled in the heart of Colorado, offers a narrative rich with history, community, and just a hint of local legend. Imagine a serene lake surrounded by sun-soaked parks, where families gather, dogs romp, and the occasional fisherman tries to explain why "the big one got away." The story of Cherry Creek Reservoir is one of resilience, community spirit, and a sprinkle of humor that makes this beloved destination a true treasure.

Located in Arapahoe County, just south of Denver, Cherry Creek Reservoir was formed in the late 1950s when the Cherry Creek Dam was constructed. Initially built for flood control, this man-made wonder was designed to manage the tumultuous waters of Cherry Creek, protecting the surrounding communities from devastating floods. It's as if nature decided to host a grand party, and the lake became the perfect venue! Over time, Cherry Creek Reservoir quickly transformed into a hotspot for recreation and wildlife, evolving into a cherished destination for locals and visitors alike.

As the dam was built and the waters settled, a rich tapestry of flora and fauna began to flourish. The landscape transformed, with willows swaying in the gentle breeze, grasses dancing along the banks, and wildflowers bursting into color during the warmer months. Beneath the shimmering surface, fish darted about, creating a vibrant ecosystem that thrived alongside the human community. The reservoir became home to various fish species, including trout, perch, and even the elusive bass, making it an angler's paradise. Just picture the joy of casting a line, feeling the tug, and reeling in a fresh catch—all while enjoying a beautiful day by the water!

Long before this reservoir became the beloved playground it is today, indigenous tribes, including the Ute and Arapaho, roamed the area. For these tribes, the waters were not merely a source of sustenance; they held spiritual significance and a profound connection to the land. Imagine the tribes gathering by the shores, sharing stories, casting their nets, and celebrating each catch with gratitude. The lake provided fish and game, creating a reliable food source and a venue for communal gatherings, where laughter and song filled the air. The beauty of Cherry Creek was woven into their culture, enriching their lives in countless ways.

With the arrival of European settlers in the 19th century, the landscape began to change dramatically. Colonization brought both challenges and opportunities, forever altering the fabric of the region. The Cherry Creek area transformed into a hub for agriculture and commerce, providing vital resources for the growing population. Settlers harnessed the land's potential, introducing farming and trade, and the lake became a lifeline for transportation. The land that once echoed with the songs of indigenous peoples was now bustling with activity, as farmers and merchants utilized the waterway to transport goods and connect with markets in nearby towns. Cherry Creek Reservoir was quickly becoming the life of the party, with settlers joining in on the fun!

The reservoir's role in transportation and trade continued to grow. Boats gliding across the surface became a common sight, ferrying goods and people alike. As the surrounding lands buzzed with commerce, Cherry Creek Reservoir also became a popular fishing destination, drawing anglers eager to reel in everything from trout to catfish. The promise of a fruitful catch, combined with the beauty of the landscape, attracted families and communities, transforming the area into a vibrant hub of activity. Parks and recreational areas blossomed around the reservoir, giving families the perfect excuse for a weekend getaway filled with picnics, laughter, and the occasional sunburn.

However, as with any grand tale, there were bumps along the way. Cherry Creek Reservoir has faced its share of challenges, including significant floods that threatened to wash away all the joy. In 1965, the area experienced a notable flood, leading to increased attention on flood management and prevention measures. The community banded together, showcasing their resilience and determination to safeguard their beloved lake. Amidst the trials, local myths sprouted, such as the tale of the "Lake Monster of Cherry Creek," an elusive creature said to haunt the depths. While sightings are rare, they certainly add a dash of intrigue and excitement to the lake's charm. Who wouldn't want to keep an eye out for a friendly monster while enjoying a day on the water?

Human impacts on the reservoir have not been without consequences. As the community grew, invasive species began to creep into the ecosystem, reminding us that not all guests are welcome. Species such as zebra mussels and Eurasian watermilfoil posed threats to the local wildlife and water quality. Thankfully, conservation efforts have emerged, rallying the community to protect the lake's delicate balance. Local organizations and volunteers have rolled up their sleeves, launching habitat restoration projects, clean-up initiatives, and educational programs aimed at raising awareness about the importance of preserving the reservoir.

Today, Cherry Creek Reservoir boasts an impressive array of parks, trails, and recreational activities that keep spirits high and hearts light. The development of Cherry Creek State Park surrounding the reservoir has solidified its status as a beloved retreat for residents and visitors alike. With miles of hiking and biking trails, picnic areas, and campgrounds, the park offers something for everyone. Visitors can kayak, paddleboard, fish, or simply relax under the sun, soaking in the scenic views that could make even a sunset envious. On weekends, the sounds of laughter and splashing water echo across the shores, creating a vibrant atmosphere filled with joy and connection.

Cherry Creek Reservoir is more than just a lake; it's a vibrant tapestry of history, culture, and community spirit. It serves as a reminder that even in the face of challenges—be it floods, invasive species, or the occasional legend about lurking monsters—there's always room for laughter, connection, and the simple joy of being by the water. As we reflect on the journey of Cherry Creek Reservoir, we celebrate not only its beauty but also the resilient spirit of the community that surrounds it.

With its rich history, diverse ecosystem, and endless recreational opportunities, Cherry Creek Reservoir stands as a testament to the harmony that can be achieved between nature and humanity. So, whether you're casting a line, hiking a trail, or simply enjoying a picnic with loved ones, remember that you're part of a story that spans generations. Grab your fishing rod, your paddleboard, or just a good book, and let the adventures at Cherry Creek Reservoir begin!

Dillon Reservoir

Nestled in the stunning Rocky Mountains of Colorado, Dillon Reservoir is not just a body of water; it's a community treasure, a recreational haven, and a storyteller of sorts. With a shimmering surface that reflects the towering peaks, Dillon Reservoir has a rich history filled with humor, challenges, and the indomitable spirit of those who call this beautiful region home. So, let's take a dive into the story of Dillon Reservoir—without getting our feet wet!

Located in Summit County, Dillon Reservoir was formed in the early 1960s as a result of the construction of the Dillon Dam. This man-made marvel was created primarily for flood control, irrigation, and municipal water supply. It spans about 1,200 acres and holds over 83,000 acre-feet of water. But before it became the stunning reservoir we know today, this area was a bustling center for mining and agriculture. Picture miners with pickaxes and prospectors with dreams of striking gold, all while dodging the occasional bear looking for a snack. Talk about multitasking!

Before the arrival of European settlers, the land around Dillon Reservoir was home to the Ute tribes, who thrived on the natural resources the mountains provided. The Utes were adept at fishing and hunting, utilizing the rivers and streams that flowed through the valleys. Their deep connection to the land made the area sacred—a sentiment that still lingers in the air today. The Ute people's legacy of respect for nature continues to influence conservation efforts in the region.

As colonization began to take hold, the landscape underwent significant changes. The mining boom attracted settlers looking for fortune, leading to a surge in population and the establishment of towns. Unfortunately, the flip side of progress often comes with its own set of challenges. The 1930s saw a series of devastating floods that wreaked havoc on the area. Communities were forced to rebuild and adapt, leading to the eventual decision to construct the Dillon Dam to mitigate future disasters. This was a classic case of "let's not repeat that mistake," wrapped in a ribbon of determination and a bit of grit.

With the dam completed in 1963, Dillon Reservoir transformed into a recreational oasis. The lake became a hot spot for fishing, boating, and all sorts of water sports. Families flocked to its shores, where laughter filled the air, and children fished with dreams of catching "the big one." You could practically hear the fish rolling their eyes, thinking, "Here we go again!" Today, the reservoir offers over 26 miles of shoreline, making it a perfect destination for those seeking a bit of adventure or relaxation.

One of the most charming aspects of Dillon Reservoir is the legends that surround it. Among locals, the tale of the "Dillon Sea Monster" is a favorite. According to some, the creature lurks in the depths, waiting to surprise unsuspecting fishermen. Whether or not the monster exists, the stories have certainly added a delightful sense of mystery to the lake, encouraging imaginations to run wild—and probably scaring a few fish in the process!

As with many lakes, Dillon Reservoir faces human impacts that challenge its ecological balance. The introduction of invasive species, such as the infamous zebra mussels, has sparked concern among conservationists and local residents alike. But the community is rallying, with various conservation initiatives in place to protect the lake's delicate ecosystem. From regular clean-up efforts to educational programs aimed at reducing pollution, the people around Dillon Reservoir are committed to preserving the beauty of their cherished lake for future generations.

In recent years, Dillon Reservoir has become an integral part of the local economy, attracting tourists and residents alike. The development of parks and recreational facilities has only enhanced its status as a beloved retreat. Dillon Marina offers boat rentals, fishing supplies, and even a cozy café for those who prefer to sip their coffee while watching the sunrise over the water. Outdoor activities abound, with hiking and biking trails winding through the stunning scenery, providing the perfect backdrop for family outings, picnics, and even romantic sunset strolls.

But let's not forget the unexpected twists that can come with nature! The area is known for its unpredictable weather—sunny one moment, snowstorm the next. The locals have learned to embrace this quirk, often joking that if you don't like the weather, just wait ten minutes! Whether it's a sun-drenched summer day or a winter wonderland, Dillon Reservoir continues to be a place where memories are made, and laughter echoes across the water.

As we reflect on the journey of Dillon Reservoir, we see a story of resilience, community, and the joy that comes from nature. This remarkable body of water is more than just a reservoir; it's a testament to the spirit of those who have worked to protect and preserve it. So whether you're casting a line, paddling out on a kayak, or simply enjoying the breathtaking views, remember that you're part of a vibrant legacy—one that celebrates the beauty of the natural world and the bonds that bring us together.

Dillon Reservoir stands as a symbol of hope, adventure, and a touch of mystery, reminding us all that while life may throw us challenges, we can always find joy and laughter along the way. So grab your fishing rod, put on your sunscreen, and head out to Dillon Reservoir—where every splash of water tells a story and every moment is an opportunity for new adventures!

Grand Lake

In the breathtaking Rocky Mountains of Colorado, Grand Lake is not just a scenic spot; it's a vibrant tapestry of history, adventure, and a sprinkle of mystery. Known as the "Gateway to Rocky Mountain National Park," this magnificent lake boasts a charm that has captivated visitors for centuries. So, grab your fishing pole and let's dive into the delightful history of Grand Lake, where the water sparkles like diamonds and the stories are just as rich.

Grand Lake is located in Grand County, Colorado, and is the largest natural lake in the state, spanning around 500 acres. It was formed by the natural processes of glacial activity, which sculpted the landscape and left behind this stunning body of water. Imagine glaciers like enormous ice sculptors, shaping the mountains while they hummed a catchy tune. The flora and fauna around the lake are just as impressive; you'll find towering pine trees, vibrant wildflowers, and a variety of wildlife that might even consider auditioning for a nature documentary.

Long before the arrival of European settlers, the area surrounding Grand Lake was home to the Ute people, who revered the land and its resources. The lake served as a vital source of fish and fresh water, making it an essential part of their daily lives. The Utes embraced the beauty of their surroundings, creating a culture deeply connected to the land. Their legends, often filled with wisdom and humor, celebrated the natural world, teaching generations the importance of respect and stewardship.

Fast forward to the mid-1800s, when the lure of gold brought settlers to Colorado. The landscape around Grand Lake underwent significant changes as miners and homesteaders arrived, seeking fortune and new beginnings. The population surged, and towns began to sprout up like wildflowers in spring. However, with progress came challenges. Floods in the late 1800s caused significant damage to settlements around the lake, leading to a sobering reminder that nature can be both beautiful and unforgiving. Local residents, however, faced these challenges with resilience and a sense of humor that would make even the grumpiest bear smile.

As settlers established their foothold in the region, Grand Lake became a hub for transportation and trade. The lake's waters facilitated the movement of goods and supplies, while fishing became a vital industry. Picture families casting their lines, with the hopes of catching dinner, only to be outsmarted by wily fish. It's a tale as old as time, proving that fish are, in fact, the ultimate comedians of the aquatic world. With a growing community, recreational activities flourished, allowing people to enjoy the beauty of the lake while fostering connections with each other.

Grand Lake is also steeped in myth and legend. One popular tale involves the "Grand Lake Monster," a creature said to dwell in the depths of the lake. Local lore claims that the monster is as elusive as the perfect fishing spot, and despite numerous attempts to capture it on camera, it remains a mysterious enigma. The stories of the Grand Lake Monster have sparked imaginations and inspired playful banter among locals and visitors alike, adding a layer of excitement to fishing trips and family outings.

With the growth of the community came the introduction of invasive species, which posed significant challenges for the lake's ecosystem. Efforts to combat these unwelcome guests have been met with both determination and creativity. Conservation groups have organized clean-up events and educational programs, encouraging residents and visitors to take an active role in protecting the lake's delicate balance. It's a classic case of "teamwork makes the dream work," proving that when it comes to preserving nature, every little bit helps—like giving a fish a pep talk before releasing it back into the wild.

Over the years, Grand Lake has developed into a premier recreational destination, attracting visitors year-round. From fishing and boating in the summer to snowshoeing and ice fishing in the winter, there's something for everyone. Parks and resorts have popped up along the shores, offering accommodations and activities that enhance the lake experience. Families gather for picnics, couples stroll hand-in-hand along the waterfront, and laughter echoes across the water, creating a vibrant atmosphere filled with joy and connection.

As we explore the history of Grand Lake, we find a community that embraces both its challenges and triumphs with open arms. The lake is more than just a picturesque backdrop; it's a testament to the resilience of those who have come before us. Every splash of water tells a story, and every ripple carries the laughter and memories of those who cherish this beautiful place.

In conclusion, Grand Lake is not just a destination; it's a living history, full of adventure, humor, and the enduring spirit of community. As you cast your line into its depths or simply sit by its shores, take a moment to appreciate the rich tapestry of life that surrounds you. With its blend of natural beauty and captivating stories, Grand Lake is sure to leave an indelible mark on your heart, inviting you to return time and time again. So whether you're hunting for fish or simply soaking in the stunning views, remember that at Grand Lake, every day is a new opportunity for laughter, connection, and a splash of adventure!

Lake Granby

Lake Granby, a gem nestled in the heart of Colorado's Rocky Mountains, is more than just a stunning body of water; it's a vibrant chapter in the state's history, full of adventure, quirky tales, and a dash of humor. Located in Grand County, this lake is a fantastic destination for outdoor enthusiasts, and its story is as rich as the fishing opportunities it provides. So, grab your fishing gear and settle in as we explore the fascinating history of Lake Granby, where every wave tells a tale.

Lake Granby is situated in the western part of Colorado, specifically within the Grand Lake area, making it the largest lake in the state that is entirely within the confines of Colorado. Formed in the early 1950s, this man-made reservoir was created by the construction of the Granby Dam on the Colorado River. Think of it as the lake equivalent of a big "surprise party" for the local ecosystem. It turned out to be quite a bash, hosting various species of fish, birds, and, of course, those ever-elusive water-loving critters that often slip through our fingers—literally!

Before European settlers arrived, the area around Lake Granby was home to the Ute people. This indigenous tribe flourished in the region, utilizing the land's resources for fishing, hunting, and gathering. The Utes regarded the lake as a vital resource, ensuring that their relationship with the land was one of respect and stewardship. They shared stories of the lake's spirit, which, according to local legend, would occasionally make an appearance in the form of a shimmering fish. This mythical fish, much like a good fishing tale, was said to grant good fortune to those who respected the lake and its inhabitants.

The arrival of settlers in the late 19th century brought significant changes to the landscape. With dreams of prosperity and adventure, people flocked to Colorado, eager to carve out a new life. Although the arrival of the settlers often led to challenges for indigenous populations, it also brought a sense of community and development. Towns sprang up, and Lake Granby quickly became a hub for transportation and trade. Imagine horse-drawn wagons bustling along the newly formed paths, all while the lake glimmered invitingly nearby, whispering promises of good fishing and relaxation.

As settlers established their lives around Lake Granby, they began to utilize the lake's resources, leading to a thriving fishing industry. The initial flora and fauna around the lake included abundant wildflowers, towering pines, and a variety of fish species like trout and kokanee salmon. The lake was alive with the sounds of laughter, the splashes of fishing lines, and the occasional exclamations of triumph from anglers reeling in their catch. If fish could giggle, they would have surely rolled on the lake's surface at the sight of eager fishermen.

However, the serenity of Lake Granby was not without its challenges. In the mid-1970s, the area experienced significant flooding, which served as a stark reminder of nature's unpredictability. The floods disrupted local communities and temporarily altered the landscape. Yet, much like the resilient fish that swim against the current, the people of Lake Granby adapted and persevered. They rolled up their sleeves, got to work, and rebuilt their community, emerging stronger than ever.

One fascinating aspect of Lake Granby is its connection to various myths and legends. Locals have often recounted stories of mysterious lights flickering over the water at night or strange sounds echoing through the valleys. Some believe these to be the spirits of the Ute ancestors, keeping a watchful eye over the lake. Others swear they've seen the ghostly figure of a fisherman still searching for the big one. Whether these tales are based in fact or simply serve to entertain is up for debate, but they certainly add an air of intrigue to the lake.

As the years went on, Lake Granby became a popular destination for recreation. Families flocked to its shores, ready for a day filled with fishing, boating, and picnicking. The lake's stunning beauty and abundant recreational opportunities transformed it into a beloved retreat for locals and tourists alike. Resorts and parks developed around the area, offering activities like hiking, camping, and of course, fishing—lots and lots of fishing. In the summer, the shores are alive with laughter, and in the winter, ice fishing becomes a communal sport, complete with hot cocoa and friendly competitions.

Yet, with the influx of visitors and the growth of local communities came challenges. Invasive species began to rear their heads, threatening the delicate ecosystem that had developed around the lake. Conservation efforts have been put in place to combat these unwelcome guests. Local organizations and volunteers regularly engage in clean-up events, striving to protect Lake Granby's beauty for future generations. It's a testament to the community spirit that thrives here; after all, when it comes to protecting this beloved lake, everyone pitches in—like a well-rehearsed fishing crew, ready to reel in the big one together.

The journey of Lake Granby is one of resilience, laughter, and a deep connection to the land. It serves as a reminder of the beauty that can emerge from challenges, as well as the importance of nurturing the relationships we have with nature and each other. Each time you cast a line into its waters or hike along its scenic shores, remember the rich tapestry of history woven into every ripple and wave.

Lake Granby isn't just a place to fish; it's a community filled with stories, legends, and laughter. As the sun sets over the water, painting the sky in hues of orange and pink, you can almost hear the echoes of the past—an invitation to join in the celebration of life, adventure, and the sheer joy of being present in this beautiful place. Whether you're a seasoned angler or a first-time visitor, Lake Granby promises an experience that will leave you with a heart full of memories and a spirit eager to return.

Shadow Mountain Lake

Shadow Mountain Lake, a serene jewel in Colorado's Rocky Mountains, offers a blend of beauty and history that could rival even the most thrilling adventure novel. Located in Grand County, just a stone's throw from the bustling town of Grand Lake, this body of water boasts not only stunning views but also a narrative rich with quirky tales, legends, and a few delightful surprises. So, grab your paddle and your sense of humor as we embark on a journey through the history of Shadow Mountain Lake!

Shadow Mountain Lake is uniquely positioned in the north-central part of Colorado, nestled between the majestic peaks of the Rockies. Formed in the early 20th century, this picturesque lake is actually a man-made reservoir, created to store water from the Colorado River for irrigation and other uses. It was part of a grand plan, quite literally, to harness the natural beauty of the area while also addressing the water needs of local communities. Who knew that a simple reservoir could hold so many stories, dreams, and even a few ghosts?

Before European settlers arrived, the land surrounding Shadow Mountain Lake was inhabited by the Ute people. These indigenous tribes thrived in the region, relying on its resources for fishing, hunting, and gathering. They viewed the lake as a sacred place, filled with spirits and stories.

Legend has it that the Ute ancestors would often gather by the lake to celebrate the changing seasons, dancing and singing under the starlit sky. The lake was not just a body of water; it was a cornerstone of their culture and spirituality.

As settlers arrived in the late 1800s, the landscape began to change dramatically. The promise of gold and opportunity lured many to the region, and soon, bustling towns emerged. While colonization brought new challenges for the indigenous tribes, it also led to a sense of community and development that reshaped the area. Shadow Mountain Lake became a hub for transportation and trade, as it provided a vital waterway for goods and services. Picture a scene from a classic Western movie: horses, wagons, and the sound of laughter as townsfolk gather to share stories of the lake's bounty.

With the increase in settlers came the need for resources, and the initial flora and fauna around Shadow Mountain Lake began to shift. The landscape was dotted with towering pines, vibrant wildflowers, and abundant wildlife. Fish species such as trout made their homes in the clear waters, while eagles and otters brought life and laughter to the shores. However, nature is unpredictable, and it wasn't long before the area faced its first significant challenge: floods. Heavy rains in the early 1900s led to swollen rivers and overflowing banks, threatening both the newly built communities and the beauty of Shadow Mountain Lake itself.

In the face of adversity, the local community banded together, showcasing the resilience that has come to define this area. They repaired roads, rebuilt homes, and adapted to the changing landscape. It was during this time that the lake began to take on a new identity as a recreational haven. As families flocked to its shores, the lake transformed into a popular destination for fishing, boating, and picnicking. The spirit of togetherness thrived as laughter echoed across the water, and the lake became a backdrop for cherished memories.

Now, let's take a moment to indulge in the legends that surround Shadow Mountain Lake. Locals often recount tales of mysterious lights flickering above the water at night or the echoes of laughter that seem to arise from the depths. Some believe these to be the playful spirits of Ute ancestors, keeping watch over their sacred land. Others swear they've seen the ghostly figure of a fisherman, still in search of the biggest catch. Whether these stories hold a grain of truth or are simply a product of imagination, they certainly add an air of mystery and excitement to the lake.

As the years rolled on, Shadow Mountain Lake continued to grow in popularity, but with that growth came challenges. Invasive species began to threaten the delicate balance of the ecosystem, leading to conservation efforts aimed at protecting this beloved body of water. Local organizations and volunteers rallied together, holding clean-up events and educating the community on the importance of maintaining the lake's health. It was a classic case of "it takes a village" –

or in this case, a lakeside community – to preserve the beauty of Shadow Mountain.

Recreation blossomed around the lake, with the development of parks and resorts catering to both locals and visitors. Shadow Mountain Lake became a go-to destination for outdoor enthusiasts, offering opportunities for hiking, fishing, and simply soaking in the breathtaking scenery. Imagine families gathered around campfires, roasting marshmallows and sharing stories under the twinkling stars, all while the lake quietly laps against the shore.

Yet, with all the joys of a thriving recreational area came the reality of managing human impacts. As more people visited the lake, the need for responsible stewardship became apparent. Local governments and conservation groups began implementing policies to protect the environment while allowing for sustainable use of the lake's resources. It was a delicate dance of balancing enjoyment with responsibility, and the community embraced the challenge.

Today, Shadow Mountain Lake stands as a testament to resilience, laughter, and a deep connection to the land. It reminds us of the importance of cherishing our natural resources and the stories they hold. Each time you cast a line into its sparkling waters or stroll along its peaceful shores, remember the rich history that has shaped this place.

As the sun sets behind the mountains, casting a golden glow over the water, it's hard not to feel a sense of wonder.

Shadow Mountain Lake isn't just a body of water; it's a living, breathing story filled with adventure, spirit, and community. Whether you're fishing for the big one or simply enjoying a quiet moment, this lake offers an experience that touches the heart and soul, inviting everyone to be part of its enduring legacy.

Chatfield Reservoir

Chatfield Reservoir, a sparkling gem located in Jefferson County, Colorado, is a delightful mix of history, nature, and community spirit. As someone who lives nearby, I can attest to the magic that unfolds here—whether it's the joy of a sunny day on the water or the thrill of fishing with friends. The reservoir offers more than just recreation; it has a rich story that blends laughter, adventure, and a few bumps along the way.

Chatfield Reservoir, formed in the early 1970s, is a man-made marvel created primarily for flood control and water storage. The construction of the dam was a response to the devastating floods that plagued the area in the late 1960s. As water levels rose and rivers swelled, the community realized that something had to be done. Enter the Army Corps of Engineers, who put on their superhero capes (and hard hats) to construct a solution that would not only manage water but also provide a space for recreation. The result? A lake that has become a beloved destination for families and outdoor enthusiasts alike.

Before the reservoir, the land around Chatfield was home to a vibrant mix of flora and fauna. The original landscape was dotted with cottonwood trees, lush grasses, and wildflowers that danced in the breeze. Deer, rabbits, and a variety of birds flourished in this diverse ecosystem. It was a natural paradise, and one can imagine the wildlife having their own parties before the humans arrived. "Who knew they'd be building a lake right here?" they must have wondered, as they organized their own version of a wildlife block party.

The area was originally inhabited by Indigenous tribes, including the Arapaho and Cheyenne. For these communities, the rivers and lakes provided not just sustenance but also a deep cultural connection to the land. They fished, hunted, and gathered in harmony with nature, celebrating the seasons and the life that flowed through the waterways. When settlers arrived, they brought their dreams of opportunity, forever changing the landscape. But rather than a tragedy, this transformation also opened doors for new communities to form, blending cultures and traditions in a rich tapestry of life.

With colonization came the introduction of agriculture and trade, utilizing the natural resources available. The lake became a vital water source for farming, and the surrounding area saw growth as towns sprouted up, bringing people together. Chatfield Reservoir quickly became a hub of activity, where farmers could gather to exchange goods, stories, and the occasional friendly ribbing. It was like a big potluck, but instead of casseroles, you had fresh produce and fish tales.

Fast forward to the present, and Chatfield Reservoir has established itself as a recreational paradise. With miles of hiking and biking trails, picnic areas, and a beautiful marina, the reservoir attracts visitors from all walks of life. Families come to enjoy sunny days on the water, while anglers seek the thrill of reeling in a trophy fish. On weekends, the air is filled with the sounds of laughter, splashes, and the unmistakable sound of a frisbee being flung across a picnic area—followed inevitably by the yelp of a startled dog.

Of course, every story has its twists and turns, and Chatfield is no exception. Over the years, human impacts have led to challenges, such as the introduction of invasive species. Species like zebra mussels can wreak havoc on local ecosystems, turning peaceful waters into a battleground. But fear not! Local conservation efforts have risen to the occasion, rallying community members to engage in cleanup days and educational programs. It's a collective effort to protect the beauty of the reservoir, ensuring that future generations can continue to enjoy its wonders.

And speaking of future generations, let's not forget the legends that have grown around Chatfield Reservoir. Local folklore is rich with tales of mysterious creatures that lurk beneath the water's surface, waiting for an unsuspecting angler to challenge them. There's even a story about a legendary fish, dubbed "Old Chatty," rumored to be larger than a Volkswagen and twice as slippery! Whether it's true or just a fish story, these legends add a sprinkle of magic to the lake and keep the spirit of adventure alive.

Throughout the years, Chatfield Reservoir has also fostered community development. Parks, resorts, and recreational activities have flourished, creating a vibrant social scene around the lake. Families gather for summer barbecues, while friends take part in paddleboarding, sailing, or simply enjoying the view. Every visit feels like a reunion, where laughter and shared memories flow as freely as the water itself.

As we look to the future, the importance of sustainable practices becomes ever more critical. The reservoir stands as a reminder of the balance we must maintain between enjoyment and responsibility. Conservation efforts will continue to play a pivotal role, ensuring that Chatfield remains a sanctuary for wildlife and a source of joy for all who visit.

Chatfield Reservoir is more than just a lake; it's a beloved part of the community and a testament to resilience, unity, and the spirit of adventure. Whether you're casting a line, exploring the trails, or simply soaking up the sun, there's a sense of magic in the air—a feeling that we're all part of something larger than ourselves.

So next time you find yourself at Chatfield, take a moment to soak it all in. Breathe in the fresh mountain air, listen to the rustling leaves, and remember that this place is a living history, woven together by stories of joy, laughter, and the indomitable spirit of the people who cherish it.

Pueblo Reservoir

Pueblo Reservoir, a sparkling gem in the heart of Colorado, is a delightful blend of history, nature, and community. Situated in Pueblo County, this expansive reservoir has a story that spans centuries, filled with colorful characters, thrilling events, and the promise of outdoor adventure. As someone who finds joy in the serenity of the water and the laughter of families enjoying the sunshine, I can assure you that the history of Pueblo Reservoir is as vibrant as the lake itself.

The reservoir came into existence in the late 1960s, primarily for irrigation and flood control. The construction of the Pueblo Dam was a direct response to the devastating floods that swept through the region in the 1920s and 1930s. These floods not only wreaked havoc on the landscape but also led to a re-evaluation of water management in the area. Thus, the dam was built, creating a stunning body of water that transformed the landscape and provided essential resources to the growing community.

Before the reservoir, the land was a lush haven, teeming with flora and fauna. Native plants like sagebrush and cottonwoods thrived, while diverse wildlife, including deer, coyotes, and a myriad of bird species, made their homes along the banks. The initial ecosystem was one of harmony, where the delicate balance of life played out in a grand theater of nature. You could almost picture the animals holding meetings: "So, how do we keep these humans from moving in?" they must have wondered, plotting their peaceful coexistence.

Indigenous tribes, notably the Pueblo peoples, inhabited the region long before settlers arrived. For these communities, the rivers and lakes held profound significance, not only as a source of sustenance but as integral parts of their cultural heritage. Fishing, hunting, and gathering were woven into the fabric of their lives, fostering a deep connection to the land. When settlers came, they brought their ambitions and dreams, changing the landscape forever. However, these changes were not entirely negative; they led to new opportunities for trade, commerce, and community development.

As the area evolved, Pueblo Reservoir became a vital hub for transportation and trade. The waterway facilitated movement and connection, allowing farmers and traders to transport goods more efficiently. The lake became a gathering place for families, where picnics and fishing trips turned into cherished traditions. In the early years, it was not uncommon to see families wading into the water with fishing poles in hand, hoping to land the catch of the day. "If you catch a fish big enough, we'll even let you tell the story," became a familiar refrain among friends, inspiring tales that grew taller with each retelling.

Fast forward to the present, and Pueblo Reservoir is a bustling center of recreation and joy. With ample opportunities for boating, fishing, hiking, and camping, it attracts visitors from near and far. Families come to enjoy the sun-soaked shores, while anglers compete for the biggest catch. The sounds of laughter, splashes, and the occasional excited shout fill the air, creating a vibrant atmosphere. It's as if the lake itself has become a storyteller, sharing tales of joy and adventure with each wave that laps at the shore.

However, with human activity come challenges. The introduction of invasive species has posed a significant threat to the delicate ecosystem of Pueblo Reservoir. Species like zebra mussels and Eurasian watermilfoil have made their way into the lake, creating a complex web of issues that conservationists strive to address. But fear not! Local organizations and community members have banded together, launching initiatives to combat these invaders and protect the health of the reservoir. Cleanup days and educational programs aim to foster a sense of responsibility among visitors, ensuring that everyone can enjoy the beauty of the lake for years to come.

Legends and myths have also woven themselves into the fabric of Pueblo Reservoir's history. Local folklore speaks of a mysterious creature that resides in the depths of the water, affectionately dubbed "Pueblo Pete." Some say he's a fish of epic proportions, while others insist he's a playful spirit that brings good luck to those who fish. Whether or not you believe in Pete, the stories add a layer of enchantment to the lake, sparking the imagination of children and adults alike.

As we turn our gaze to the future, it's essential to recognize the ongoing efforts to preserve the natural beauty of Pueblo Reservoir. Conservation groups are dedicated to maintaining the ecosystem, promoting sustainable practices, and ensuring the lake remains a haven for wildlife and recreation. The reservoir serves as a reminder of our responsibility to protect the environment while enjoying the great outdoors.

Pueblo Reservoir is more than just a body of water; it's a cherished part of the community, a source of joy and adventure, and a testament to resilience and unity. The stories of families gathering for picnics, anglers sharing their favorite fishing spots, and friends embarking on boating escapades contribute to the rich history of the reservoir. With each passing year, it continues to be a place where memories are made, laughter echoes, and the spirit of adventure thrives.

So, whether you're casting a line, hiking the trails, or simply soaking in the sun, take a moment to appreciate the magic of Pueblo Reservoir. Breathe in the fresh mountain air, listen to the whispers of nature, and remember that you're part of a living history—a story woven together by laughter, joy, and the love of the great outdoors. Here's to the adventures yet to come, and to the timeless spirit of Pueblo Reservoir!

Horsetooth Reservoir

Horsetooth Reservoir, with its distinct name and stunning vistas, is a slice of Colorado paradise that brings together both nature lovers and thrill-seekers. Located just west of Fort Collins in Larimer County, this reservoir was created in the 1950s as part of a water supply project for the city, but its history and character extend far beyond its practical origins. The name "Horsetooth" is said to come from the distinctive shape of the nearby rock formations that resemble a horse's tooth, which, if you squint just right while hiking, could also be mistaken for a giant toothy grin cheering on adventurers.

The early days of the reservoir were marked by ambitious engineering and community spirit. Construction began in the early 1950s, and the waters of the Cache la Poudre River were diverted to fill the lake, transforming the landscape into a recreational haven. As the reservoir filled, locals watched the old ranching fields disappear beneath the water, and they couldn't help but imagine the legends that would form around this new playground. Stories began circulating about the "Horsetooth Monster," a friendly creature who supposedly resided beneath the surface, waiting to play pranks on unsuspecting boaters. "Watch out!" was a common warning among young locals. "He might just tug your kayak!"

With its completion in 1954, the reservoir quickly became a gathering spot for families looking to escape the hustle and bustle of life in Fort Collins. The beauty of the area attracted visitors eager to fish, sail, or simply lounge on the banks, soaking in the sun. By the 1960s, the Horsetooth community had grown, complete with parks, picnic areas, and hiking trails, drawing in not just locals but tourists from all around.

While the reservoir is a recreational gem today, it has faced its share of challenges. In 1983, a major flood event impacted the area, causing water levels to rise dramatically. Stories of boats floating away like wayward ducks became the stuff of local legend, and the community came together to lend a helping hand. Volunteers were seen with makeshift rafts and ropes, trying to save anything that wasn't tied down. It's said that one adventurous soul even tried to rescue a sunbathing inflatable flamingo that had taken a dramatic dive into the depths. "A true hero of the day!" became the rallying cry.

In the years following the flood, Horsetooth Reservoir began to evolve. As the community embraced water sports, the reservoir became a training ground for budding kayakers and paddleboarders. The annual "Horsetooth Regatta," where locals donned their most outrageous costumes while racing across the water, transformed into a cherished tradition. Spectators lined the shores, laughing as competitors dressed as mermaids, pirates, and even the occasional inflatable unicorn splashed their way to victory.

In terms of flora and fauna, the area surrounding the reservoir is a vibrant mix of native vegetation. Wildflowers bloom along the banks, while ospreys and bald eagles glide overhead, making their homes in the surrounding trees. The initial landscape was home to various species, from deer to rabbits, each adapting to their new aquatic neighbor. As the reservoir drew people in, it also attracted wildlife, leading to a balance that enriched the local ecosystem.

For centuries before European settlers arrived, the Ute and Arapaho tribes roamed this region. They relied on the land and water for sustenance, weaving their lives around the natural cycles of the area. While Horsetooth Reservoir was ultimately developed for recreational use, its waters still hold echoes of the past. Local legends often recount the wisdom of these tribes, who understood the land deeply and revered the waters. Modern conservation efforts often reference their respect for nature, inspiring initiatives to maintain the health of the reservoir and its surroundings.

The landscape transformed with colonization, but many positive changes emerged. As communities formed around the reservoir, a thriving environment for fishing, boating, and camping blossomed. People began to hold community events that promoted environmental awareness and stewardship. "If you can't catch a fish, at least pick up some trash!" became a humorous motto during clean-up days, and volunteers would often find themselves laughing and joking while making a difference.

Human impacts on the reservoir haven't all been positive, of course. Invasive species like the zebra mussel made their way into the waters, prompting the need for regular monitoring and control efforts. Local groups sprang into action, educating visitors about the importance of keeping the reservoir clean and free of non-native species. "Don't let the zebra mussels crash our party!" became a cheeky slogan seen on posters around the reservoir, emphasizing the community's commitment to preserving their beloved waterway.

Development efforts at Horsetooth have focused on enhancing recreational opportunities. Parks and picnic areas were created, providing ample space for families to gather and enjoy the outdoors. Hiking trails snake through the surrounding foothills, offering breathtaking views of the reservoir and the majestic Rocky Mountains beyond. Wildlife watching has become popular, as the area attracts not just locals but also tourists hoping to catch a glimpse of ospreys diving for fish or deer wandering near the shore.

One of the most heartwarming aspects of Horsetooth Reservoir is the way it brings people together. Families celebrate birthdays by the water, friends gather for summer barbecues, and community members band together for seasonal festivals that fill the air with laughter. Each event is a testament to the resilience and joy of the human spirit, thriving alongside the natural beauty of the reservoir.

As the sun sets behind the foothills, casting a warm glow over the water, laughter and stories mingle in the air. The reservoir stands as a symbol of community and camaraderie, a place where adventure meets tranquility. Every splash, every smile, and every shared experience weaves a narrative that goes beyond the surface—a reminder that in every corner of this beautiful state, the spirit of connection and joy can be found.

Whether you're out on a paddleboard, fishing from the dock, or simply enjoying a picnic with friends, Horsetooth Reservoir embodies the spirit of Colorado—a land of adventure, laughter, and shared moments that make life a bit sweeter. And who knows? As the breeze rustles through the trees, you might just hear the echoes of the past whispering tales of the "Horsetooth Monster," ensuring that the legends—and the laughter—live on.

Green Mountain Reservoir

Green Mountain Reservoir, a hidden gem nestled in the heart of Colorado, brings together stunning views, a rich history, and a sense of adventure that captures the spirit of the Rockies. Located in Summit County, just west of the charming town of Heeney, this man-made reservoir is as enchanting as its name suggests. The reservoir's moniker originates from the lush, green hills that surround it, providing a picturesque backdrop for countless memories and stories.

The history of Green Mountain Reservoir is not without its dramatic flair. The area, which was once a bustling valley filled with vibrant flora and fauna, underwent significant changes with the construction of the dam in the 1930s. Initially, the reservoir was created to provide water for irrigation and to help manage the waters of the Blue River. However, this transformation came with its share of challenges. The valley that would become the reservoir was home to several small settlements, and when the dam was built, those communities had to be relocated. While it's hard to imagine packing up and moving for a reservoir, those who made the journey ultimately found new opportunities and a fresh start.

As the waters rose, the landscape transformed dramatically. The initial flora and fauna were diverse, with aspens, willows, and an array of wildflowers adorning the valley floor. Deer, elk, and countless bird species thrived in the area, creating a vibrant ecosystem. Yet, when the dam was completed, these inhabitants found themselves in a watery world. Legend has it that some fish, wise beyond their years, developed a knack for swimming in circles, trying to find their way back to their original homes—though they might have just been enjoying the view!

The indigenous tribes, including the Ute and Arapaho, were the original stewards of this land, relying on the rich resources of the area. The riverbanks provided food, water, and a deep connection to the natural world. The Ute people, known for their harmony with nature, were particularly skilled at utilizing the land's offerings, whether it was fishing in the rivers or gathering plants from the valleys. The construction of Green Mountain Reservoir significantly impacted their way of life, but the natural beauty and spiritual significance of the land remained strong, even as the waters rose.

With the arrival of European settlers, the landscape shifted further. Colonization brought new farming practices and trade opportunities, transforming the economy of the region. While the settlers faced their own challenges, including harsh winters and rocky terrain, they also found a wealth of resources in the area. The Blue River became a vital transportation route, facilitating trade and commerce as the community began to grow. In time, Green Mountain

Reservoir emerged as a prime location for fishing, boating, and recreational activities, turning a once-forgotten valley into a lively hub of adventure.

The reservoir soon gained a reputation as a haven for outdoor enthusiasts. Boaters, fishermen, and campers flocked to its shores, eager to explore the scenic landscapes. On summer weekends, the area bustled with families setting up picnic blankets, anglers casting lines, and adventurers kayaking across the shimmering waters. It became a place of connection and joy, where laughter echoed off the surrounding hills.

However, as the human population grew, so too did the challenges facing the reservoir. The introduction of invasive species, such as zebra mussels and various aquatic weeds, threatened to disrupt the delicate ecosystem. These uninvited guests didn't receive the warm welcome they anticipated, leading to increased efforts to monitor and manage their presence. Local conservationists and volunteers joined forces to tackle these issues, determined to protect the integrity of Green Mountain Reservoir for future generations.

Over the years, conservation efforts have made significant strides in preserving the reservoir's natural beauty. Organizations have developed programs to educate the community about responsible recreation, emphasizing the importance of keeping the waters clean and the environment healthy. Clean-up days, community events, and ongoing monitoring of water quality have become essential to maintaining the reservoir's status as a beloved outdoor destination.

The myths and legends surrounding Green Mountain Reservoir add an extra layer of intrigue to its history. Local tales tell of a giant fish named "Greenie" that roams the depths, offering good luck to those fortunate enough to spot it. Some claim that Greenie grants wishes—if only you have a fishing pole in hand and a good story to tell. Whether or not you believe in Greenie, the stories of adventure and camaraderie that emerge from the reservoir are enough to inspire anyone to grab a rod and reel.

As we look toward the future, the potential for development and recreation at Green Mountain Reservoir remains bright. Parks and trails have been established to enhance the visitor experience, offering breathtaking views and opportunities for exploration. Seasonal festivals celebrate the natural beauty of the area, drawing in locals and tourists alike to partake in the festivities. The bond between the community and the reservoir continues to flourish, creating a legacy of connection to this beautiful landscape.

In the end, Green Mountain Reservoir stands as a testament to the resilience of both nature and community. Its waters hold the stories of those who came before, while also inviting new generations to create their own adventures. Whether you're casting a line, hiking a scenic trail, or simply enjoying a peaceful sunset, Green Mountain Reservoir captures the essence of Colorado's natural beauty and the spirit of adventure.

So grab your fishing gear, pack a picnic, and head to the shores of Green Mountain Reservoir. Every ripple in the water tells a story, and every moment spent there adds another chapter to the ever-evolving history of this stunning Colorado treasure. Here's to the memories yet to be made and the adventures that await—let's make a splash at Green Mountain Reservoir!

Twin Lakes Reservoir

Twin Lakes—a place where serenity meets adventure and where the beauty of Colorado shines in perfect harmony. Located in Lake County, just a stone's throw from the charming town of Leadville, Twin Lakes comprises two sparkling bodies of water nestled at the foot of the majestic Collegiate Peaks. The name itself is a straightforward reflection of their geographical arrangement, but don't let that simplicity fool you; these lakes are steeped in rich history and captivating tales that are sure to inspire.

The formation of Twin Lakes is a tale of nature's artistry, sculpted by glacial activity during the last Ice Age. These lakes are the remnants of a time when massive glaciers carved out the landscape, leaving behind deep basins that would fill with water. The result? Two stunning lakes that beckon visitors from near and far, like a beautiful siren calling from the depths of the mountains. As you gaze upon the crystal-clear waters, it's hard not to be overwhelmed by a sense of wonder—though a little voice in your head might whisper, "Just don't fall in; it's colder than your ex's heart!"

Initially, Twin Lakes was surrounded by diverse flora and fauna, from aspen groves swaying gently in the breeze to the iconic Rocky Mountain elk that grazed along the shore. The lakes provided a crucial habitat for many species, making them a vibrant ecosystem. The shimmering surface of the water reflected not only the surrounding peaks but also the diverse life that thrived in this beautiful setting.

For centuries, the indigenous Ute people roamed the lands around Twin Lakes, forging a deep connection with the water and its bounty. To the Utes, the lakes were not merely geographical features; they were sacred places where fishing, hunting, and gathering took place. The lakes provided fish and other resources vital to their way of life. Today, you can still sense the echoes of their laughter and stories in the rustling leaves and the rippling water.

As the landscape began to change with the arrival of European settlers, Twin Lakes became a focal point for community development and trade. The lakes' natural resources attracted miners and adventurers during the Colorado Gold Rush, transforming the region into a bustling hub. Boats were launched on the waters, carrying supplies and goods between burgeoning communities. Picture it: a crowd of miners, decked out in dusty hats and boots, huddled together on the shore, nervously exchanging tales of fortune, while one bold soul offers to paddle them to their dreams—though let's hope they don't tip over!

Of course, like any great adventure, Twin Lakes has had its share of challenges. The area is not immune to the fickle whims of nature. Floods and heavy rains have occasionally wreaked havoc on the landscape, reminding everyone that Mother Nature can be a real diva sometimes. One particularly memorable flood back in 1943 transformed the shores and temporarily altered the lakes' contours, leaving behind a tale to be recounted at every summer picnic.

Amidst these challenges, myths and legends have flourished around Twin Lakes. Locals share stories of a mysterious creature lurking in the depths, lovingly dubbed "Lakey McLakeface" (yes, the name is as ridiculous as it sounds). According to legend, this elusive beast roams the waters, leaving ripples and stirring up stories. Fishermen swearing they saw a fin or two have been known to weave wild tales over a campfire, transforming "just a big fish" into a legendary monster that would put even the Loch Ness Monster to shame!

With human development came the introduction of invasive species, which proved to be the unwelcome guests at this scenic gathering. Just like that friend who overstays their welcome at a party, these invasive species started to disrupt the delicate balance of the lakes' ecosystems. The community rallied, launching conservation efforts to protect the native flora and fauna. These efforts have included regular clean-ups and education programs that emphasize the importance of keeping the lakes pristine.

Today, Twin Lakes serves as a haven for recreation and relaxation. Visitors flock to the area for fishing, kayaking, hiking, and picnicking. The scenery is nothing short of breathtaking, with the towering peaks providing a majestic backdrop to your outdoor adventures. Imagine casting a line into the water while a group of ducks quack in agreement, as if cheering you on for a big catch. Who needs a fishing buddy when you've got an audience of feathered friends?

Parks and campsites have been established around Twin Lakes, creating a friendly environment for families and friends to gather. Seasonal festivals bring the community together, celebrating the rich heritage of the area through music, food, and, of course, plenty of fishing contests. The annual "Twin Lakes Fish-Off" is a highlight, where fishermen compete for bragging rights, with tales of "the one that got away" becoming more exaggerated with each passing year.

Looking to the future, Twin Lakes continues to evolve while holding on to its rich history. Ongoing conservation efforts aim to preserve the ecological balance, ensuring that this enchanting destination remains a paradise for generations to come. The lakes stand as a testament to the power of nature, community, and the human spirit, providing solace and adventure to all who visit.

So, whether you're there to cast a line, paddle a kayak, or simply bask in the beauty of the mountains, Twin Lakes invites you to create your own stories and memories. With each visit, you're not just experiencing a slice of Colorado; you're becoming part of a living history that flows as freely as the waters that grace this extraordinary place. Embrace the laughter, the legends, and the adventure that awaits—because at Twin Lakes, every ripple holds a story just waiting to be told!

Emerald Lake

Located in Rocky Mountain National Park, specifically in Larimer County, this glacial lake is known for its breathtakingly vibrant turquoise waters, a hue that rivals the most extravagant of gemstones. The name "Emerald" is a nod to its stunning color, a jewel among Colorado's many natural wonders.

The lake was formed during the last Ice Age, sculpted by the relentless forces of glacial movement that carved out the landscape, leaving behind this beautiful, sparkling body of water. While it may not be man-made, its creation feels like something from a fairy tale—imagine glaciers sliding down the mountainside with the grace of a ballerina, only to leave behind a stunning lake that dazzles everyone who stumbles upon it. The initial flora and fauna surrounding Emerald Lake created a vibrant ecosystem, filled with wildflowers blooming in every color imaginable and the occasional squirrel who seems to have auditioned for a part in a Disney movie, complete with acrobatics and dramatic flair.

Before settlers arrived, the area was home to indigenous tribes, primarily the Arapaho and Ute peoples. These tribes revered the land, finding sustenance in its bountiful resources. The lake was more than just a pretty spot; it was a source of fish and fresh water, critical for survival. One can imagine gatherings of families around the shores, sharing stories while watching their children skip stones or practice their fishing skills—though it's likely that "practice" meant throwing in a line and promptly getting distracted by a butterfly.

As European explorers ventured into the area, they brought with them the wave of colonization that forever changed the landscape. While the settlers may have disrupted the natural harmony, they also introduced agriculture and trade that positively impacted the local economy. You could say they brought a bit of chaos, but with it came the promise of new beginnings. Emerald Lake, with its breathtaking views, became a favored spot for weary travelers and budding adventurers looking to bask in nature's glory, sip on some mountain air, and, let's face it, take a selfie worthy of a magazine cover.

The lake has seen its share of disasters, too. In the 1980s, heavy rains led to flash floods that altered the surrounding landscape, reminding everyone that nature can be as temperamental as a toddler denied dessert. But don't fret! The resilient flora and fauna quickly bounced back, as if they had taken a deep breath and decided to embrace the chaos with open arms.

Legends and myths swirl around Emerald Lake, adding an enchanting layer to its already rich history. One such tale involves a mystical creature rumored to inhabit the depths, known affectionately as "Emerald Eddie." Local lore suggests that Eddie is a friendly spirit who protects the lake and its visitors, occasionally surfacing to make sure everyone is enjoying their time. If you hear splashes that sound suspiciously like laughter, it's probably Eddie reminding you not to take life too seriously!

Emerald Lake has also faced the challenges of human impact. With the influx of visitors, invasive species have begun to creep into the ecosystem, much like that one friend who brings their chaotic energy to a quiet gathering. Conservation efforts are underway to protect the lake's native species, and the community has rallied around the cause, proving that teamwork can truly make a difference.

The lake is a hotspot for recreation, attracting hikers, fishers, and photographers eager to capture its beauty. With the picturesque mountain backdrop and the vibrant waters, it's no wonder people flock here to enjoy outdoor activities. The trails around the lake provide stunning views that can make even the most camera-shy individual feel compelled to snap a picture—or five—while shouting, "I can't believe this is real!"

Parks and facilities have been developed to accommodate visitors, ensuring that everyone can experience the magic of Emerald Lake. Seasonal events bring the community together for activities like guided hikes, fishing derbies, and even an annual "Emerald Lake Cleanup Day," where families come together to enjoy the great outdoors while protecting it. Imagine the camaraderie as participants share laughter, snacks, and their most ridiculous "almost caught a fish" stories!

As the years roll on, Emerald Lake continues to thrive and evolve. Conservation efforts, coupled with the love and dedication of the local community, aim to preserve its enchanting beauty for future generations. So, whether you're casting a line in hopes of reeling in the "big one," hiking along the picturesque trails, or simply soaking in the stunning views, Emerald Lake invites you to connect with nature, create lasting memories, and perhaps even share a laugh with Emerald Eddie.

In this magical haven, every ripple tells a story, and every visitor leaves with a piece of that history tucked away in their hearts. As you walk along the shores or gaze into the crystalline waters, let the spirit of Emerald Lake inspire you—because sometimes, amidst the adventure, we find ourselves reflecting on life's beauty, much like the shimmering surface of this captivating lake.

Maroon Lake

Maroon Lake is like the enchanted jewel of Colorado, a stunning body of water that has dazzled all who've laid eyes on it. Nestled in the heart of the Elk Mountains, specifically in Pitkin County, this picturesque lake has become an iconic destination for adventurers and nature enthusiasts alike. Its name, "Maroon," is said to derive from the reddish-brown hue of the surrounding Maroon Bells, two towering peaks that appear to have been dipped in a giant pot of sunset. Legend has it that if you gaze long enough at the lake, you might just see the peaks blush back at you!

Maroon Lake was shaped by glacial activity thousands of years ago. As glaciers slowly carved out this stunning landscape, they left behind a pristine lake, sparkling like a diamond in the rough. While not man-made, the lake's natural formation feels like a whimsical accident, as if the mountains decided to drop a beautiful lake right there for the world to enjoy. Initially, the area was alive with diverse flora and fauna—wildflowers danced in the meadows, and the air was filled with the sweet scent of pine. If you were a deer back then, you'd have considered it a five-star buffet!

Long before settlers arrived, the Ute tribes thrived in the region, relying on the land's resources for their survival. Maroon Lake was not just a pretty view; it was a source of life and sustenance. The Ute people utilized the lake for fishing and gathered at its shores for spiritual ceremonies, forging a deep connection to the land that remains to this day. One can imagine them gathering around the lake, telling stories of creation and the spirits of the mountains while the waters glistened under the sun—a true sense of community.

As the waves of colonization rolled in, the landscape began to shift. Settlers brought agriculture and trade, transforming the region while introducing a variety of crops and livestock. It was like a new chapter in a storybook, one where the Ute were joined by newcomers, each contributing to the evolving narrative of the area. Maroon Lake became a respite for weary travelers, a place where they could stop, rest, and appreciate the beauty of nature.

Of course, every fairy tale has its twists. In the early 20th century, a series of heavy rains led to flooding that impacted the surrounding areas. The lake's tranquility was momentarily disrupted, and locals probably exchanged worried glances while wondering if the mountains were having a particularly dramatic mood swing. But as with all things in nature, balance was restored, and Maroon Lake emerged from the chaos, reminding everyone that it could weather any storm—literally and figuratively.

Among the tales that surround Maroon Lake, there's one about a mythical creature known as the "Maroon Mermaid." Legend has it that on moonlit nights, this enchanting being would surface, enticing onlookers with her song. Many adventurers have claimed to hear her melodies echoing across the water, but the real mystery remains whether they were simply listening to the wind or had actually caught a glimpse of her! After all, nature has a way of weaving its own legends, doesn't it?

Despite its ethereal charm, Maroon Lake has not been immune to human impacts. With increasing visitation, invasive species have made their way into the ecosystem, much like uninvited guests at a party. Conservation efforts are actively underway to address these challenges, with local communities banding together to protect the lake's native species. After all, it's hard to enjoy a beautiful day on the lake while worrying about who (or what) is crashing the ecosystem!

Maroon Lake is a hub for recreation, drawing people for activities such as fishing, hiking, and photography. The iconic views of the Maroon Bells reflecting on the lake's surface create postcard-perfect moments, ensuring that visitors leave with more than just memories. Park services have developed trails and facilities to enhance the experience, allowing people to connect with the environment and appreciate its beauty. The annual "Maroon Lake Clean-Up Day" has become a beloved tradition, where families come together to enjoy the outdoors while giving back to the lake that has given them so much.

As we look to the future, Maroon Lake stands as a symbol of resilience and community. Its beauty continues to inspire conservation efforts and sustainable practices, ensuring that generations to come will be able to experience its magic. Local initiatives aimed at educating visitors about the importance of protecting this gem reflect a deep commitment to preserving the delicate balance of nature.

Maroon Lake is not just a body of water; it's a living testament to the power of nature, history, and community. With each ripple and wave, it invites us to reflect on our place in the world and encourages us to cherish the beauty that surrounds us. As the sun sets over the Maroon Bells, casting golden rays across the water, one can't help but feel a sense of awe—reminded that sometimes, the most magical experiences come from simply being present in nature's embrace. So, whether you're casting a line for the catch of the day or capturing the perfect sunset photo, know that Maroon Lake has stories to tell and beauty to share, and it's waiting for you to become part of its enchanting history.

Ruedi Reservoir

Ruedi Reservoir, a shimmering gem in the heart of Colorado, boasts a name that is as intriguing as its history. Named after the nearby Ruedi Creek, which itself is thought to have been named for an early settler, Ruedi became a sanctuary for water enthusiasts and nature lovers alike. The reservoir sits just east of Basalt in Eagle County, surrounded by the stunning backdrop of the Rockies—a postcard perfect scene that makes even the most jaded of Instagrammers pause in awe.

The story of Ruedi Reservoir begins with a stroke of ingenuity and necessity. Created in the late 1960s, this man-made marvel was built primarily for water storage and flood control, as well as to provide irrigation for the surrounding lands. The U.S. Bureau of Reclamation, armed with blueprints and hard hats, constructed this reservoir to tame the wild waters of the Fryingpan River. The result was a scenic lake that, unlike its cousins, was crafted by human hands. But hey, sometimes the best art comes from a little elbow grease!

Before the reservoir, the area was a tapestry of natural beauty, with meadows alive with wildflowers and forests full of deer, elk, and the occasional curious bear (who probably wondered what all the fuss was about). The original flora and fauna flourished until construction began. But the creators of

Ruedi didn't just bulldoze everything in sight; they worked diligently to preserve the spirit of the land. Imagine a team of engineers donning hard hats and singing folk songs as they planted new trees and shrubs, making it a beautiful compromise between nature and progress.

Long before the engineers arrived, the Ute tribe roamed these lands. They thrived on the region's natural resources, and the Fryingpan River was their lifeline. The lake became a symbol of the change that came with colonization, transforming a once-pristine environment into a more cultivated landscape. While some may argue that colonization brought chaos, it also brought opportunity. The Ute people adapted to these changes, engaging in trade and embracing new agricultural practices that emerged in the wake of settlement.

With the establishment of Ruedi Reservoir, the landscape shifted once more. Floods that once threatened the land became a tale of the past, thanks to the carefully engineered dam that regulated water flow. It's almost as if the reservoir took on the role of a responsible adult, reminding the rivers who was boss. The local communities began to flourish, with new homes and businesses sprouting like wildflowers in spring.

However, with great water comes great responsibility, and Ruedi Reservoir has seen its fair share of ups and downs. Over the years, heavy rains and snowmelt have tested the dam's strength, leading to some tense moments where everyone held their breath and crossed their fingers. But don't worry; Ruedi has proven to be a resilient waterway, weathering storms and continuing to provide for those who depend on it.

Ruedi also comes with its own colorful tales and folklore. Among them is the legend of the "Ruedi Monster," a playful twist on the classic lake monster story. Locals claim that on particularly still nights, you might see a strange silhouette gliding through the water, perhaps a bear or just a trick of the light. Kids dare each other to spot the "monster" while parents chuckle, knowing it's all in good fun. Rumor has it that the only thing lurking beneath the surface is an abundance of trout, just waiting for a well-cast fishing line!

Fishing at Ruedi Reservoir has become a rite of passage for many Coloradoans. The lake is teeming with trout, and anglers often find themselves telling tales of "the one that got away." Every year, fishing derbies bring the community together, filled with friendly competition and laughter as families bond over a shared love for the great outdoors. Imagine folks standing shoulder to shoulder, casting lines and trading fishing secrets—everyone knowing full well that the biggest fish stories are half the fun!

Despite its allure, Ruedi Reservoir has faced challenges due to human impact. Invasive species, like the notorious zebra mussel, have made their way into the waters, causing headaches for conservationists. The battle against these uninvited guests is ongoing, and local groups work tirelessly to educate visitors about keeping the reservoir pristine. The motto here? "Take only pictures, leave only footprints!" It's a mantra that resonates, reminding everyone that with beauty comes the responsibility to protect it.

In recent years, Ruedi has transformed into a hub for recreation. The surrounding area has developed parks and trails, making it easy for families to enjoy picnics, hiking, and cycling. The reservoir has also become a popular spot for paddleboarding and kayaking, drawing in adventurers who relish the thrill of exploring the lake's serene waters. Summer weekends bring a flurry of activity, as visitors flock to the reservoir to bask in the sun and enjoy the vibrant community atmosphere.

The local community is deeply invested in preserving Ruedi's charm and natural beauty. Conservation efforts are continually underway, with volunteers hosting clean-up days and educational workshops. It's a heartwarming sight: families and friends coming together, armed with trash bags and enthusiasm, making the reservoir even more beautiful while creating lasting memories.

As we look toward the future, Ruedi Reservoir remains a vibrant oasis amid the Colorado wilderness. It stands as a testament to the human spirit—how we can shape the environment while also nurturing it. Every ripple in the water carries with it the laughter of children, the stories of families, and the hopes for a sustainable future.

So, whether you're casting a line, exploring a trail, or just taking in the breathtaking views, remember that Ruedi Reservoir is not just a body of water; it's a community, a legend, and a cherished part of Colorado's beautiful landscape. And who knows? Perhaps if you listen closely, you might just hear the echoes of the Ruedi Monster splashing playfully in the depths below, reminding us all to embrace the joy and magic of nature.

Eleven Mile Canyon Reservoir

Eleven Mile Canyon Reservoir, with a name that sounds like it was plucked straight out of a quirky Western novel, is a captivating body of water tucked away in the heart of Colorado. Nestled in Park County, this scenic reservoir has a backstory as rich as its surrounding landscapes. It's not just a place for fishing and picnicking; it's a reservoir that carries tales of history, community, and a sprinkle of local folklore.

The name "Eleven Mile" has origins that are as intriguing as they are practical. Early explorers and settlers named the reservoir after the Eleven Mile Creek, which flows into it. This creek itself is believed to have been named because it was eleven miles from a key point along the old South Park Road. It's a perfect example of that wonderful blend of geography and creativity that characterizes much of Colorado's history. It's also a reminder that sometimes, practicality wins over poetry when it comes to naming places!

Eleven Mile Canyon Reservoir was constructed in the late 1950s and officially opened in 1963, thanks to the diligent work of the U.S. Bureau of Reclamation. Designed primarily for irrigation and water supply, the reservoir quickly transformed the region's landscape and economy. While some lakes are the result of natural formations, Eleven Mile Canyon is proudly man-made, standing as a testament to the human spirit of innovation and community development.

Initially, the area surrounding the reservoir was a beautiful tapestry of forests, meadows, and wildlife. The initial flora consisted of aspen and ponderosa pine, with wildflowers adding splashes of color in the warmer months. Fauna included elk, deer, and the occasional adventurous bear—though the bears likely preferred to stay out of the human way, especially when picnics were on the agenda. This vibrant ecosystem provided sustenance for local Indigenous tribes, particularly the Ute, who thrived on the natural resources, using the waterways for fishing and gathering.

Colonization brought significant changes to the landscape, but it wasn't all doom and gloom. Settlers introduced agricultural practices that contributed to the region's economy, enhancing community development. The reservoir soon became a lifeline, providing water for irrigation and creating a haven for both locals and visitors. Imagine families coming together for fishing trips or picnics, forging bonds while casting lines and sharing stories. This sense of community remains a vital part of the reservoir's charm today.

But like every good story, Eleven Mile Canyon Reservoir has had its share of challenges. Over the years, heavy rains and rapid snowmelt have occasionally led to flooding, reminding everyone of nature's unpredictable power. Residents have recounted tales of rushing waters that transformed the peaceful landscape into a roaring spectacle. Those who witnessed it are left with stories that blur the line between excitement and sheer terror—a reminder that, in Colorado, Mother Nature likes to keep us on our toes!

Legends and myths abound in the area, particularly one about a mysterious "water spirit" said to inhabit the reservoir. Locals whisper that if you listen closely on a quiet night, you might hear the faint echoes of laughter or even the splash of a fin—perhaps a playful reminder from the spirit that this reservoir is full of life and stories. It adds a sprinkle of magic to the fishing trips, as kids dare each other to stay out a little longer, hoping for a glimpse of the legendary being.

Fishing has become one of the main attractions at Eleven Mile Canyon Reservoir. The lake is stocked with a variety of fish, including rainbow trout and kokanee salmon. Anglers flock to its shores, casting their lines with hopes of landing "the big one." Fishing tournaments have become a popular summer pastime, with families and friends joining together in friendly competition, sharing laughter and making memories under the Colorado sun.

The reservoir also serves as a vital recreational site. It's not just about fishing; visitors enjoy hiking, biking, and boating along its serene waters. The surrounding landscape features numerous trails, making it a haven for outdoor enthusiasts.

In the winter, the area transforms into a snowy wonderland, attracting cross-country skiers and snowshoers. Picture families bundled up, hot cocoa in hand, marveling at the winter beauty—if that doesn't warm your heart, what will?

However, Eleven Mile Canyon Reservoir hasn't escaped the impacts of human activity entirely. Invasive species, like the infamous zebra mussel, have made their unwelcome appearance, leading to concerns about ecological balance. Local conservation efforts are underway to combat these threats, with passionate volunteers and organizations working diligently to protect the reservoir's natural beauty. The community remains engaged, participating in clean-up days and educational initiatives, all with a shared goal of maintaining the reservoir's integrity.

Efforts to enhance the area surrounding the reservoir have also flourished over the years. Parks have been developed, complete with picnic areas and restrooms, making it more accessible for families. It's a joy to see parents setting up the grill while kids run around, laughter filling the air. Local resorts have popped up nearby, offering cozy lodgings for those who wish to extend their stay and immerse themselves in the beauty of the area.

As we look to the future, Eleven Mile Canyon Reservoir stands as a reminder of the balance between nature and human intervention. It reflects the importance of community, the beauty of recreation, and the need to protect the environment for generations to come. The stories told around its shores and the adventures embarked upon its waters create a rich tapestry that binds the community together.

So, whether you're angling for a trophy trout, hiking the scenic trails, or simply soaking in the stunning views, remember that Eleven Mile Canyon Reservoir is more than just a body of water; it's a living story filled with laughter, love, and a dash of magic. Here's to the reservoir, where every ripple holds a tale, and every visit promises a new adventure waiting to unfold!

Bear Creek Lake

Bear Creek Lake is more than just a picturesque spot in Colorado; it's a treasure trove of history, community, and a splash of wild adventure. Located in Jefferson County, just southwest of Denver, this lake is nestled against the backdrop of the majestic Rocky Mountains, making it a beloved haven for both locals and visitors.

The name "Bear Creek" might conjure images of big, furry friends wandering the shores, but the origin is more about the creek than the creatures. The creek, flowing through the area, was likely named for the bears that roamed the region, leaving an indelible mark on the local lore. Imagine early settlers telling tales around campfires, sharing stories about close encounters with these magnificent animals, each retelling embellished with a little extra excitement!

Bear Creek Lake itself was created in the 1970s, thanks to a little engineering magic that transformed a natural valley into a vibrant recreational spot. Originally, the area was part of a water diversion project aimed at providing water to the growing populations of the Front Range. Although it's man-made, this lake has developed a character all its own, evolving into a community hub where families come to relax, recreate, and reconnect.

In the beginning, before construction, the area was a beautiful blend of aspen groves, wildflowers, and dense shrubs. The initial flora offered a feast for the eyes, with splashes of color adorning the landscape during warmer months. As for fauna, deer and various birds flitted about, creating a lively ecosystem that thrived in the untouched wilderness. Indigenous tribes, particularly the Arapaho and Cheyenne, utilized the area for hunting and gathering, appreciating the resources that the land and waters provided. The creek and its surrounding habitat were essential to their way of life, supporting their communities for generations.

The arrival of European settlers marked a turning point for the area. Colonization brought significant changes, but not all of them were negative. Settlers introduced agricultural practices that improved local economies and paved the way for community development. As Bear Creek Lake emerged, it became a crucial resource for irrigation and water supply, effectively transforming the landscape into a vital lifeline for the growing population. Families could often be found at the lake, casting lines into the water while sharing stories and creating lifelong memories.

Throughout the years, Bear Creek Lake has witnessed its fair share of dramatic events, too. The region has experienced floods that turned calm waters into a raging torrent, reminding everyone of nature's raw power. Locals recount tales of sudden rainstorms that caused the creek to swell, flooding nearby trails and washing away picnic setups. It's said that if you listen closely, you might still hear the echoes of those frantic, splashing footsteps as people dashed to save their sandwiches from being swept away!

Myths and legends about Bear Creek Lake abound as well. One popular tale suggests that on certain quiet nights, you can hear the whispers of those who once called the area home, their stories carried on the breeze. Some claim that if you look closely at the water, you might just see the shimmering figure of a bear watching over the lake, a guardian spirit keeping watch on the vibrant life that flourishes there.

Fishing is one of the lake's main attractions, with anglers flocking to its shores to try their luck at landing bass, trout, and catfish. Tournaments and friendly competitions have become a staple, with families spending weekends honing their skills and exchanging good-natured ribbing over who caught the biggest fish. It's a sight to behold: families gathered on the shore, laughter mixing with the sounds of nature, and the occasional triumphant shout as someone reels in a prize catch.

Recreation opportunities at Bear Creek Lake abound. Hiking trails wind through the surrounding areas, offering breathtaking views and the chance to spot local wildlife. Birdwatchers flock to the region, eager to catch a glimpse of the various species that call this habitat home. In winter, the lake transforms into a snowy paradise, inviting cross-country skiers and snowshoers to explore its frosty beauty.

However, not everything has been smooth sailing. Like many Colorado lakes, Bear Creek has faced challenges from human activity and invasive species. The introduction of non-native plants and fish has posed threats to the local ecosystem, causing concern among conservationists and community members alike. Efforts to combat these issues are underway, with local organizations rallying to protect the natural beauty of the lake and its surroundings.

Conservation initiatives have grown stronger over the years, with volunteers dedicating time to clean up the lake and educate visitors about the importance of maintaining the ecosystem. Regular events, like clean-up days and nature walks, bring the community together, reinforcing the idea that protecting Bear Creek Lake is a shared responsibility. It's heartwarming to see families joining in, teaching their children the value of caring for their environment, ensuring that future generations can enjoy the beauty of the lake.

As for parks and recreational facilities, Bear Creek Lake is home to several well-maintained areas for picnicking, playing, and enjoying the great outdoors. Campgrounds and picnic spots line the shores, allowing visitors to set up for the day or spend the night under the stars. Local resorts have developed nearby, offering cozy lodgings for those wanting to extend their stay and immerse themselves in the beauty of the area.

As we look to the future, Bear Creek Lake continues to stand as a symbol of community, resilience, and the harmony between nature and human development. Each splash of water, every rustle of leaves, and the laughter of children echo the stories that make this place special. So, whether you're casting a line, hiking a trail, or simply enjoying a sunny day by the water, remember that Bear Creek Lake is more than just a reservoir; it's a living tapestry of experiences and adventures waiting to be woven together. Here's to the reservoir where memories are made, and every visit promises a new chapter in the ongoing story of Colorado's Bear Creek Lake!

Stagecoach Reservoir

Stagecoach Reservoir is not just another body of water; it's a storybook waiting to be opened, filled with tales of adventure, community, and the kind of fun that makes you want to grab your fishing pole and hit the water. Located in Routt County, this charming reservoir sits just south of Steamboat Springs, cradled in the embrace of the Rocky Mountains.

The name "Stagecoach" is a nod to the area's storied past as a bustling stop on the stagecoach route in the 1800s. Imagine a dusty trail where horses galloped, delivering mail and passengers through the rugged wilderness. The sounds of creaking wheels and the chatter of travelers filled the air. Today, you might not see the stagecoaches, but you'll surely find a variety of recreational vehicles zooming around, making new memories.

The reservoir itself was formed in the late 1970s, primarily as part of a water storage and irrigation project. This man-made marvel transformed a natural valley into a vibrant playground for outdoor enthusiasts. Although constructed by human hands, Stagecoach Reservoir has developed a personality of its own, becoming a beloved spot for families, fishermen, and wildlife alike.

Before the reservoir was built, the area was a canvas of aspen groves, meadows, and the original waterways that flowed gracefully through the landscape. It was home to diverse flora and fauna, with wildflowers painting the meadows in vibrant hues and animals like deer, elk, and a variety of birds thriving in the lush environment. Indigenous tribes, particularly the Ute, traversed these lands for centuries, relying on the natural resources for sustenance, shelter, and spiritual practices. The waters were not just a source of life; they were central to their cultural identity.

As settlers arrived in the 19th century, they brought significant changes to the landscape. The introduction of agriculture transformed the area, fostering community growth and development. Fields replaced meadows, and the stagecoach routes evolved into vital transportation networks. The establishment of the reservoir turned a once quiet valley into a hub of activity, facilitating irrigation and providing water to the burgeoning agricultural community. Farmers and families found a new resource that enhanced their livelihoods, and Stagecoach Reservoir became an integral part of their lives.

Stagecoach Reservoir has experienced its share of dramatic moments, too. The area is no stranger to storms that roll in with little warning, sometimes leading to sudden changes in the reservoir's water levels. Locals have humorous tales of fishing lines that were nearly yanked out of hands during unexpected gusts of wind, or boats that had to be docked quickly when ominous clouds threatened a downpour. "Hold onto your hats and your fishing poles!" seems to be the unofficial motto during such weather.

Myths surrounding Stagecoach Reservoir add a whimsical touch to its history. One charming legend tells of a "stagecoach ghost" that wanders the shores, searching for lost passengers from days long past. Campers and fishermen have reported mysterious sounds echoing through the trees at night, prompting more than a few wide-eyed discussions around the campfire. If you're lucky, you might just catch a glimpse of the ghostly figure, perhaps still trying to deliver a message or two about the importance of sunscreen and proper fishing techniques!

Fishing at Stagecoach Reservoir is a cherished pastime. Anglers flock to its waters to catch trout, bass, and kokanee salmon, turning quiet mornings into spirited competitions. Tournaments bring excitement, with families and friends gathering to test their skills. Who wouldn't want to catch a fish while surrounded by stunning mountain views and the laughter of loved ones? It's a recipe for cherished memories.

Recreational opportunities abound at Stagecoach Reservoir. The surrounding area features hiking trails that meander through the picturesque landscape, offering breathtaking views and a chance to spot local wildlife. Birdwatchers can revel in the variety of species, making it a perfect spot for some "avian espionage." When winter arrives, the reservoir becomes a playground for ice fishing and snowshoeing, creating a magical winter wonderland.

However, like many natural areas, Stagecoach Reservoir faces challenges. The introduction of invasive species, including non-native fish and aquatic plants, has raised concerns about the delicate ecosystem. Local conservation groups have mobilized to address these issues, organizing clean-up events and educational workshops to inform the public about the importance of protecting this cherished resource.

Efforts to conserve the beauty of Stagecoach Reservoir are ongoing, with volunteers dedicating time to monitor water quality, restore habitats, and promote sustainable practices. Community engagement is key, and events like "Lake Appreciation Days" bring together locals to celebrate the reservoir's significance while working to protect it for future generations.

Parks and recreational facilities surrounding the reservoir have blossomed, offering picnic areas, campgrounds, and boat ramps. Visitors can enjoy a variety of activities, from paddleboarding to picnicking on sunny afternoons. As families gather for barbeques, children splash in the water, and laughter fills the air, the spirit of community thrives.

Looking ahead, Stagecoach Reservoir is poised to continue its legacy as a beloved destination for outdoor enthusiasts. With its rich history and vibrant community, it stands as a testament to the harmony between nature and human activity. Each ripple in the water carries the echoes of laughter, the thrill of a fishing catch, and the stories of those who have come before.

So whether you're casting a line, hiking a trail, or simply soaking in the views, remember that Stagecoach Reservoir is not just a reservoir; it's a living story, a shared experience, and a place where adventure awaits. Here's to the reservoir that brings people together, where every visit adds another page to the ongoing tale of Colorado's Stagecoach Reservoir!

Navajo Lake

Navajo Lake, a sparkling treasure nestled in the San Juan Mountains of Colorado, is not just a reservoir; it's a tapestry woven with history, culture, and a sprinkle of folklore that makes it a unique destination for locals and visitors alike. Located in Archuleta County, this beautiful lake invites adventurers to explore its shores and embrace the stories that have shaped its existence.

The name "Navajo" echoes the legacy of the Indigenous peoples of the region. While the lake itself may not have been directly named after the Navajo tribe, its proximity to their ancestral lands connects it to a broader narrative of Native American history in Colorado. For centuries, these tribes relied on the natural resources of the land for sustenance and spiritual practices, developing a deep respect for the environment. You can almost hear the whispers of ancient stories carried by the mountain winds when you visit.

Navajo Lake was formed in the mid-20th century as a man-made reservoir, primarily constructed for water storage and irrigation. The project aimed to support local agriculture and provide water resources for the growing communities in the area. While this transformation involved considerable engineering efforts, it ultimately enhanced the natural beauty of the region, creating a picturesque lake surrounded by lush forests and stunning mountain vistas.

In the years leading up to its creation, the landscape was a tapestry of rich flora and fauna. Pine and aspen trees adorned the slopes, while wildflowers dotted the meadows in vibrant colors. Animals such as elk, deer, and a multitude of bird species thrived in this biodiverse ecosystem. The lake now serves as a habitat for fish and aquatic creatures, but it also plays host to diverse wildlife that has adapted to the changed environment.

As settlers moved into the area in the late 1800s, they brought significant changes to the landscape. The introduction of agriculture and ranching transformed the surroundings, making it a center of community life. Farmers relied on the rivers and streams that meandered through the valley, using them for irrigation and trade. The construction of Navajo Lake allowed for more stable water sources, enabling agriculture to flourish and communities to thrive.

But with every tale of progress, there are also bumps along the road. Flooding has been a recurring theme in the area's history, with heavy rains causing rivers to overflow and water levels to rise unexpectedly. Local legends tell of fishermen who've experienced the oddity of suddenly finding themselves in deeper water than anticipated, leading to humorous tales of unexpected swims and near-miss adventures. In the spirit of community camaraderie, locals often gather to share these stories around campfires, each trying to outdo the last with their flood-related exploits.

One particularly colorful legend surrounding Navajo Lake involves a mysterious creature said to dwell beneath its surface—a playful "water sprite" that enjoys teasing anglers by stealing their bait and making a splash. Fishermen have claimed that if you leave a small offering of shiny objects by the shore, you might just catch a glimpse of this mischievous sprite darting through the water. Of course, skepticism is abundant, but the fun of the legend keeps the spirit of fishing lively!

Fishing at Navajo Lake is a cherished tradition, attracting anglers eager to reel in trout and bass. The lake's crystal-clear waters make it a popular spot for both seasoned fishermen and families looking to bond over a shared love of the outdoors. The annual fishing tournament brings excitement, as competitors battle for the biggest catch, turning the shores into a buzzing hub of activity and laughter. Who wouldn't want to witness a friendly rivalry while enjoying the stunning backdrop of the Rockies?

Beyond fishing, Navajo Lake has evolved into a recreational haven for outdoor enthusiasts. Hiking trails wind through the surrounding forests, offering breathtaking views and opportunities to spot local wildlife. In the summer, families gather for picnics, while kayakers and paddleboarders glide gracefully across the water. When winter blankets the area with snow, the lake becomes a playground for ice fishing and snowshoeing, adding another layer of adventure to its charm.

As with many natural areas, Navajo Lake faces challenges, particularly from invasive species. Non-native fish and aquatic plants can disrupt the delicate ecosystem, prompting local conservation efforts to protect the lake's health. Community members have rallied together to promote awareness about preserving the environment, organizing clean-up days and educational events to ensure the lake remains a vibrant resource for generations to come.

Efforts to conserve Navajo Lake have garnered attention and support, leading to the development of parks and recreational facilities that enhance the experience for visitors. Campgrounds line the shores, offering families a chance to disconnect from their busy lives and reconnect with nature. Events like "Navajo Lake Day" celebrate the community's love for the area, featuring activities, music, and local food that bring everyone together.

Looking ahead, Navajo Lake is poised to continue its legacy as a treasured destination for adventure seekers and nature lovers alike. Its rich history and the vibrant community surrounding it serve as a reminder of the bond between humans and nature. As visitors cast their lines into the water or hike along the trails, they become part of the ongoing story of Navajo Lake, contributing their own chapters to its history.

So, whether you're sharing laughter over a fishing line or marveling at the stunning views, remember that Navajo Lake is more than just a reservoir. It's a lively narrative filled with excitement, camaraderie, and the spirit of adventure. Here's to the reservoir that brings people together, where every ripple on the surface reflects the joy and beauty of the great outdoors!

Tarryall Reservoir

Tarryall Reservoir, a serene expanse of water nestled in the foothills of the Rockies, offers a unique blend of history, adventure, and humor that can make even the most seasoned angler chuckle. Located in Park County, this picturesque reservoir lies about 20 miles west of the charming town of Jefferson, surrounded by the stunning vistas of the Colorado wilderness. But let's dive deeper into what makes Tarryall not just a body of water, but a living, breathing storybook of Colorado's past.

The name "Tarryall" is said to have originated from a legendary mix-up of local lore. Some tales suggest it comes from the Ute word "Tarryall," meaning "to wander," a fitting name for a place where adventurers roam free. Others claim it's a derivative of "Tarryall River," which flows nearby. Whichever tale you prefer, it's clear that Tarryall has a way of captivating the imagination and inviting people to explore.

Tarryall Reservoir was created in the 1950s as part of a larger effort to manage water resources for agriculture and municipal needs. The construction of the reservoir was no small feat, involving the damming of the Tarryall Creek to create a reliable water supply for the surrounding communities. While it was man-made, the reservoir quickly became a vital part of the local ecosystem, supporting both flora and fauna that thrive in its watery embrace.

Initially, the area surrounding Tarryall was a rich tapestry of life. Towering pines and wildflowers blanketed the landscape, while deer and elk roamed freely, making it a paradise for nature lovers. As settlers moved into the region, they recognized the potential of the land and began to cultivate it, introducing agricultural practices that shaped the landscape in positive ways. The Tarryall area became a hub of community life, with farming and ranching at its heart.

Indigenous tribes, particularly the Ute people, had long inhabited these lands, relying on the rich natural resources for their livelihoods. For them, Tarryall Reservoir represents a connection to the past—an area where fishing and hunting were once abundant. The creation of the reservoir brought new opportunities for recreation, allowing modern-day visitors to enjoy the same bounty that the Utes once did, albeit in a different way.

But with every grand tale comes a sprinkle of chaos. Tarryall has seen its fair share of floods, particularly during the spring melt. Stories circulate of fishermen who were blissfully unaware of the rising water, only to find themselves inadvertently swimming with the fish! Locals often recount tales of spontaneous swimming lessons as unsuspecting boaters find themselves unexpectedly launched into the water, proving that nature has a sense of humor and an ability to surprise even the most experienced outdoor enthusiasts.

One of the most endearing legends tied to Tarryall is that of "Old Man Tarryall," a mythical figure said to guard the waters of the reservoir. Folklore suggests that if you bring an offering of a shiny lure or a handcrafted wooden boat, Old Man Tarryall might just grant you the fishing luck you seek. Anglers have reported catching fish under strange circumstances, leading many to believe that Old Man Tarryall is indeed watching over them. Whether or not you believe in the legend, it certainly adds a whimsical charm to a day on the water.

As time marched on, Tarryall Reservoir became more than just a water source; it transformed into a recreational paradise. The serene waters attract fishermen, kayakers, and paddleboarders from all over. Families flock to the shores for picnics, while hikers explore the stunning trails that wind through the surrounding mountains. The annual "Tarryall Fishing Derby" draws crowds who come to compete for the title of the biggest catch, all while sharing laughter and camaraderie that can only come from a community brought together by a shared love of the outdoors.

However, with the joy of recreation also comes the responsibility of stewardship. Tarryall Reservoir faces challenges, particularly from invasive species that threaten its delicate ecosystem. Species like the zebra mussel have found their way into many Colorado lakes, prompting local conservationists to launch educational campaigns aimed at preventing their spread. Efforts to preserve Tarryall's natural beauty include regular clean-up days and community workshops, where residents learn about the importance of protecting their cherished reservoir.

The establishment of parks and recreation areas around Tarryall has enhanced its allure. Campgrounds dot the shores, offering families the chance to unwind in nature, while trailheads invite hikers to explore the breathtaking landscapes. Events like the "Tarryall Summer Festival" celebrate the community spirit, featuring local crafts, food, and activities that bring everyone together in joyful harmony.

As we look to the future, Tarryall Reservoir remains a beloved destination for adventure seekers, families, and anyone seeking solace in nature. Its history, filled with stories of floods, legends, and community bonding, continues to be woven into the lives of those who visit. Each cast of the fishing line, each paddle across the water, and each moment spent with loved ones creates new memories that will be shared for generations to come.

So, whether you're chasing fish or simply soaking in the mountain air, Tarryall Reservoir invites you to become part of its ongoing narrative. Here's to the laughter, the legends, and the adventures that await at this stunning Colorado treasure—a reservoir that truly captures the heart of the community and the spirit of the great outdoors.

Clear Creek Reservoir

Clear Creek Reservoir, a stunning oasis in the heart of Colorado, offers not just a place to fish or picnic, but a rich tapestry of stories that reflect the spirit of this beautiful state. Located in Clear Creek County, just a short drive from the bustling town of Georgetown, this reservoir has been a beloved destination for locals and visitors alike. But let's dive into the depths of its history, where the water sparkles with laughter and the shores echo with tales of adventure.

The name "Clear Creek" comes from the crystal-clear waters that flow into the reservoir, a fitting moniker that captures the essence of this picturesque spot. Nestled in the Rockies, the reservoir is formed by the damming of Clear Creek, which has been meandering through the mountains for centuries. While it may have been shaped by human hands, its natural beauty is undeniable, making it a favored spot for all who seek solace in the outdoors.

Historically, the area around Clear Creek Reservoir was a bustling hub during the Colorado Gold Rush in the mid-1800s. The lure of gold drew prospectors and settlers into the region, and the surrounding landscape transformed rapidly. The clear waters of the creek became a lifeline for those seeking fortune, with miners setting up camp along its banks. However, the pursuit of gold also led to significant environmental changes, as the landscape was reshaped to accommodate the growing population.

In terms of its natural surroundings, Clear Creek Reservoir boasts a variety of flora and fauna that thrive in its ecosystem. Towering pines, vibrant wildflowers, and the occasional aspen grove paint a beautiful backdrop, while wildlife such as deer, elk, and numerous bird species frolic nearby. However, this idyllic setting hasn't always been tranquil. The area has experienced its fair share of floods, particularly during spring melt when the creek swells. Locals have shared stories of fishermen who found themselves in the unexpected position of rowing against a tide of rushing water, making for unforgettable fishing tales.

Among the myths surrounding Clear Creek Reservoir, one of the most charming involves the "Spirit of the Creek." Local lore suggests that a benevolent spirit watches over the waters, granting good luck to those who approach with respect and kindness. Fishermen often leave small offerings, like colorful lures or hand-tied flies, as a way to appease the spirit, believing it enhances their chances of reeling in the big one. Whether or not the spirit is real, the camaraderie among anglers as they swap stories and share laughter adds a sprinkle of magic to the lake.

The Indigenous peoples, particularly the Ute and Arapaho tribes, were the original stewards of this land. They utilized the rich resources of Clear Creek for fishing and hunting, and the area held cultural significance in their way of life. With the arrival of European settlers, however, the landscape began to change drastically. While colonization brought new opportunities, it also disrupted the natural harmony that had existed for centuries.

With the creation of the reservoir in the 1950s, the landscape transformed yet again. While it was primarily built for water storage and flood control, the reservoir quickly became a recreational hotspot. Boating, fishing, and hiking trails flourished, bringing families together for picnics by the water and weekends filled with adventure. Community events, such as summer fishing tournaments and outdoor movie nights, became staples, creating a sense of unity and joy among residents and visitors.

However, with growth came challenges. As human activities increased, so did the impact on the lake. Invasive species, like the notorious zebra mussel, posed threats to the local ecosystem. Conservation efforts sprang into action, with local organizations leading initiatives to educate the public about responsible boating and fishing practices. Clean-up days became a community tradition, reminding everyone that protecting the reservoir's natural beauty is a shared responsibility.

Despite these challenges, Clear Creek Reservoir continues to thrive as a recreational haven. Parks and picnic areas have been developed along the shore, inviting families to enjoy everything from barbecues to fishing competitions. The scenic hiking trails offer breathtaking views of the surrounding mountains, providing the perfect backdrop for outdoor enthusiasts. In the winter, the area transforms into a winter wonderland, drawing snowshoers and ice fishermen eager to embrace the cold.

As we look to the future, the story of Clear Creek Reservoir remains unwritten, with each visitor adding their own chapter. The laughter of children playing at the water's edge, the thrill of a big catch, and the quiet moments of reflection all contribute to the tapestry of life surrounding this reservoir. It is a place where nature and community come together, where the spirit of adventure thrives, and where stories of the past continue to inspire those who visit.

So, whether you're casting a line, hiking a trail, or simply enjoying the stunning views, Clear Creek Reservoir invites you to become part of its ongoing saga. Here's to the laughter, the legends, and the adventures that await at this remarkable Colorado treasure—a reservoir that truly reflects the heart and spirit of the great outdoors.

Spinney Mountain Reservoir

Spinney Mountain Reservoir, located in the heart of Colorado, is a hidden treasure that many may overlook while planning their next outdoor adventure. Situated in Park County, not far from the quaint town of Hartsel, this reservoir is more than just a body of water; it's a place where history flows as freely as the rivers that feed it. Its name, derived from the nearby Spinney Mountain, evokes a sense of exploration, as if the landscape itself is inviting you to discover the tales that lie within.

The reservoir was created in 1981 by the construction of a dam on the South Platte River, making it a relatively young addition to Colorado's rich tapestry of lakes and reservoirs. Before it was dammed, the area was characterized by meandering streams and lush valleys, home to a variety of flora and fauna. Towering pines and colorful wildflowers dotted the landscape, while deer, elk, and an array of bird species thrived in the region. The transformation from a serene landscape to a vibrant reservoir brought with it new opportunities for recreation and community engagement.

Historically, the land surrounding Spinney Mountain was frequented by the Ute and Arapaho tribes, who valued the area for its natural resources. These Indigenous peoples relied on the rivers for fishing and hunting, and they understood the land's rhythms intimately. They knew where to find the best fishing spots long before it was fashionable for weekend warriors to cast their lines. The creation of the reservoir, while altering the natural landscape, also preserved some of the traditions and stories of those early inhabitants.

The name "Spinney" itself has roots in the area's history. It is believed to be derived from the word "spinney," which refers to a thicket or grove of trees, hinting at the lush vegetation that once thrived in the valley. While this area has evolved dramatically over time, the name serves as a reminder of its verdant past.

As with many places in Colorado, Spinney Mountain Reservoir has faced its share of challenges. Among the most notable events in its relatively short history was the 2014 flood, which tested the resilience of the dam and the surrounding infrastructure. Although the reservoir weathered the storm, the incident served as a wake-up call, emphasizing the importance of proper maintenance and community awareness.

Adding to the local lore are the myths and legends that have sprouted around the reservoir. One particularly charming tale involves the "Spirit of the Reservoir," said to be a guardian of the waters. Fishermen and boaters alike share stories of good fortune bestowed upon those who respect the environment and leave behind no trace of their visit. Some even claim to have seen flickering lights on the water at night, believing them to be the spirit watching over the lake and its visitors.

The transformation brought by colonization was marked by the introduction of new species, some of which proved detrimental to the ecosystem. For instance, invasive fish species began to appear, disrupting the natural balance of the reservoir. Local conservation groups have since rallied together to tackle these challenges, conducting regular monitoring and cleanup efforts to ensure the health of the ecosystem. Education programs have also been implemented to raise awareness about the importance of protecting the natural environment.

Despite these hurdles, Spinney Mountain Reservoir has flourished as a recreational paradise. Its calm waters are a favorite among kayakers, canoeists, and paddleboarders, while its banks attract anglers hoping to hook a trophy trout. The reservoir has earned a reputation for its excellent fishing opportunities, drawing in enthusiasts from across the state and beyond. The sense of camaraderie among fishermen, who share tips and tales of their biggest catches, creates a warm community spirit that echoes throughout the area.

The introduction of parks and picnic areas along the reservoir has made it a popular destination for families looking to enjoy a day in nature. Whether it's a family reunion complete with burgers sizzling on the grill or a quiet afternoon spent reading a book under a shady tree, Spinney Mountain offers a variety of experiences for everyone. The trails around the reservoir provide breathtaking views of the surrounding mountains, enticing hikers to explore the beauty of the Rocky Mountains.

In winter, the reservoir transforms once again, offering a stunning backdrop for snowshoeing and ice fishing. The community gathers to celebrate winter festivities, showcasing the reservoir's versatility as a year-round destination. The laughter of children playing in the snow and the crackle of bonfires create a sense of warmth and togetherness, even in the chill of winter.

As we look toward the future, Spinney Mountain Reservoir stands as a testament to resilience and adaptation. The challenges it has faced have only strengthened the community's commitment to preserving its natural beauty. Local organizations continue to advocate for sustainable practices, ensuring that future generations can enjoy the same breathtaking views and recreational opportunities.

With its rich history, stunning landscapes, and vibrant community, Spinney Mountain Reservoir is more than just a destination—it's a living story, one that invites all who visit to be a part of its ongoing narrative. So grab your fishing rod, pack a picnic, or simply take a moment to bask in the serenity of this special place. Whether you're a first-time visitor or a longtime local, Spinney Mountain is ready to welcome you with open arms and a heart full of adventure.

Lake Isabel

Tucked away in the picturesque Wet Mountains of Colorado, Lake Isabel is a tranquil retreat that embodies the spirit of adventure and the whispers of history. Located in Custer County, this serene alpine lake, named after the daughter of a prominent local family, Isabel Jones, has captivated visitors since its discovery. Unlike many of Colorado's larger reservoirs, Lake Isabel is a hidden treasure, waiting to share its stories with those who wander its shores.

The lake itself is a natural wonder, formed by glacial activity thousands of years ago. The glaciers carved out the basin, creating a stunning landscape dotted with towering pines and vibrant wildflowers. Before human hands altered the land, this area was a flourishing ecosystem, home to deer, elk, and a myriad of bird species. These creatures thrived among the granite outcrops and verdant meadows, weaving a rich tapestry of life that continues to enchant those who visit today.

Indigenous tribes, particularly the Ute people, were the first stewards of this land. They revered the mountains and lakes, understanding their vital role in the ecosystem. Lake Isabel provided fresh water and abundant fish, serving as a critical resource for fishing and gathering. The Utes' deep connection to the land infused the area with legends, such as stories of a great spirit residing in the lake, believed to grant good fortune to those who respected the natural world.

As settlers arrived in the 19th century, the landscape began to change. The area surrounding Lake Isabel was no longer just a natural haven but a canvas for new beginnings. The name "Isabel" was adopted to honor the family that owned the surrounding land, capturing the spirit of community and connection. The lake quickly became a favored spot for locals seeking solace from their daily lives, drawing picnickers and anglers eager to bask in its beauty.

However, as is often the case in the history of land use, change brought challenges. With colonization came the introduction of agriculture and the demand for timber, altering the landscape dramatically. But in the case of Lake Isabel, these changes also led to the creation of a community that cherished the land. The small nearby town of Lake Isabel flourished as visitors flocked to the area for recreation. Fishing became a popular pastime, and the lake's crystal-clear waters were teeming with trout, delighting anglers of all skill levels.

The community that developed around Lake Isabel wasn't just about fishing; it was about connection and shared experiences. Families would gather for weekends filled with laughter, barbecues, and stories shared around campfires. The air was alive with the sounds of children playing, the aroma of grilled burgers, and the gentle lapping of the water against the shore. These gatherings fostered a sense of belonging and a love for the natural world.

Unfortunately, the serenity of Lake Isabel hasn't been without its troubles. The reservoir has faced challenges from human activity and environmental changes. The lake's health became a topic of concern, prompting local organizations to implement conservation efforts aimed at preserving its natural beauty. Clean-up events and educational programs were initiated, encouraging the community to take responsibility for protecting their beloved lake.

These initiatives have proven successful, as the community rallied around Lake Isabel, fostering a deep sense of stewardship. Volunteers worked tirelessly to remove invasive plants and restore the lake's natural habitat. Their dedication has not only preserved the ecosystem but has also brought the community closer together. Today, Lake Isabel stands as a testament to what can be achieved when a community unites for a common cause.

As the seasons change, so does the allure of Lake Isabel. In the summer, it's a haven for hikers, fishermen, and families. The shimmering surface reflects the vibrant colors of wildflowers, while the air buzzes with the joyful sounds of nature. In winter, the lake transforms into a serene landscape blanketed in snow, offering opportunities for snowshoeing and ice fishing. Each season brings its own magic, reminding visitors of nature's endless capacity for beauty and renewal.

Moreover, the lake has become a focal point for local events and activities. The annual Lake Isabel Fishing Derby attracts anglers from all over Colorado, fostering camaraderie and a friendly spirit of competition. These events not only celebrate the lake's recreational opportunities but also highlight the importance of community involvement and conservation.

Looking ahead, Lake Isabel is poised to continue its journey as a cherished destination for generations to come. The local community remains committed to preserving its beauty while welcoming new visitors with open arms. Efforts to educate visitors about the importance of responsible recreation are ongoing, ensuring that the legacy of Lake Isabel endures.

In essence, Lake Isabel is more than just a reservoir; it's a place where history, nature, and community converge. Its tranquil waters hold stories of resilience, connection, and the enduring spirit of adventure. So, whether you're casting a line, taking a leisurely hike, or simply soaking in the views, Lake Isabel invites you to be part of its ongoing narrative—a narrative that celebrates the beauty of nature and the power of community.

Saratoga Lake

In the heart of Colorado's Larimer County, Saratoga Lake emerges as a serene oasis, often overlooked but brimming with history and character. This picturesque lake, nestled near the charming town of Wellington, offers a refreshing escape from the hustle and bustle of daily life. Its name pays homage to the famous Saratoga Springs in New York, evoking images of healing waters and tranquil landscapes. But while Saratoga Lake may not be a bustling spa destination, it certainly has its own tales to tell.

The lake's origins are fascinating; it was formed through natural geological processes long before the arrival of European settlers. Nestled among rolling hills and expansive meadows, the lake became a vital resource for wildlife and local tribes. Initially, it served as a seasonal wetland, drawing in an array of flora and fauna, from vibrant wildflowers to diverse bird species. The wetlands provided a rich habitat, nurturing a vibrant ecosystem that has captivated nature enthusiasts for generations.

Long before the lake gained its current name, the area was inhabited by indigenous tribes, particularly the Arapaho and Cheyenne peoples. These tribes respected the land, recognizing its bounty and the sacred nature of water. Saratoga Lake, with its abundance of fish and game, became a crucial resource for sustenance. Legends abound of spirits dwelling in the lake, believed to protect those who honored the earth. The tribes utilized the surrounding landscape for fishing, hunting, and gathering, forming a deep connection to the land that persists even today.

As settlers arrived in the mid-1800s, the landscape began to change. While colonization often brought disruption, the establishment of Saratoga Lake marked a positive shift for the community. In the late 19th century, the lake was dammed and enlarged to serve as a water supply for nearby agricultural lands. This transformation paved the way for the region's growth, allowing farmers to cultivate the fertile soil and thrive in an otherwise arid environment.

The establishment of Saratoga Lake as a water resource spurred the development of the surrounding area. The local community flourished, with the lake becoming a focal point for recreation. People flocked to the shores for fishing, boating, and picnicking, creating cherished memories amidst the tranquil surroundings. Families would gather for weekends filled with laughter and adventure, forging a sense of belonging that intertwined their lives with the rhythm of the lake.

However, like many natural resources, Saratoga Lake faced its own set of challenges. Human activity, including agricultural runoff and urban development, impacted the lake's health. Conservation efforts were initiated to address these issues, fostering a renewed commitment to preserving the lake's natural beauty. Community organizations and local residents joined forces, organizing clean-up events and educational programs aimed at restoring the ecosystem.

These efforts have borne fruit, as Saratoga Lake has seen a resurgence in its ecological health. Volunteers dedicate their time to monitor water quality and combat invasive species, ensuring that the lake remains a vibrant habitat for wildlife. The community has embraced a culture of stewardship, recognizing that the health of Saratoga Lake is inextricably linked to their own well-being.

Despite its challenges, the lake continues to be a hub of activity and joy. Fishing remains a beloved pastime, with anglers casting their lines in hopes of landing a trophy trout. The lake's clear waters are ideal for kayaking and canoeing, offering a unique perspective on the surrounding landscapes. On warm summer days, families can be seen enjoying leisurely picnics along the shore, while children splash in the shallows, creating lasting memories.

Seasonal festivals have become a staple of life around Saratoga Lake. The annual Saratoga Lake Days celebrate the community's connection to the water, featuring local artists, music, and delicious food. These gatherings not only highlight the lake's recreational opportunities but also serve as a reminder of the importance of preserving this cherished resource for future generations.

As the sun sets over Saratoga Lake, casting a warm glow on the water's surface, the stories of the past echo through the hills. The lake stands as a testament to resilience, adaptation, and the enduring bond between nature and community. Whether you're a fisherman hoping for the catch of the day, a family enjoying a day of adventure, or simply a soul seeking solace, Saratoga Lake welcomes all with open arms.

In essence, Saratoga Lake is more than just a body of water; it's a living narrative, a tapestry woven with threads of history, culture, and community spirit. Its tranquil shores beckon those who seek refuge from the world, inviting them to share in its beauty and embrace the joy of being part of something greater. As visitors cast their lines, paddle their kayaks, or simply breathe in the fresh mountain air, they become part of the legacy of Saratoga Lake—a legacy that will continue to flow for generations to come.

Catamount Reservoir

Tucked away in the breathtaking beauty of Colorado's Rocky Mountains, Catamount Reservoir stands as a testament to nature's artistry and human ingenuity. Located in the heart of Teller County, near the historic town of Woodland Park, this stunning body of water offers a rich tapestry of history, myth, and community spirit.

The name "Catamount" is derived from the early settlers' term for mountain lions, which once prowled the area. These majestic creatures served as a reminder of the wild, untamed spirit of the region. Today, while mountain lions may be less common, the legacy of the land remains vibrant, with the reservoir reflecting the natural grandeur that has captivated visitors for generations.

Catamount Reservoir was formed in the early 20th century as part of a larger water management system designed to supply the growing city of Colorado Springs. Constructed in the 1930s, the reservoir was a critical response to the increasing demand for water in the region, particularly in light of the area's booming population. As water flowed into the reservoir, it transformed the landscape, creating a haven for wildlife and a recreational paradise for locals.

Before the reservoir's creation, the land was inhabited by various indigenous tribes, including the Ute and Arapaho peoples. These tribes held a deep reverence for the land

and water, using the area for hunting, fishing, and gathering. Their legends spoke of the spirits of the mountains, believed to inhabit the waters of what would eventually become Catamount Reservoir. Stories of bravery and respect for nature were passed down through generations, reminding all who ventured into the wilderness of their connection to the earth.

The initial flora and fauna surrounding the reservoir were abundant. Wildflowers danced in the alpine meadows, while pine forests provided shelter for deer, elk, and a myriad of bird species. The reservoir soon became a sanctuary for both wildlife and humans, offering a space for fishing, boating, and picnicking. With the creation of Catamount Reservoir, families flocked to its shores, creating memories of laughter and adventure that would echo through time.

As colonization progressed, the landscape underwent significant changes. While the introduction of agriculture and infrastructure initially disrupted some natural ecosystems, the establishment of Catamount Reservoir represented a positive shift. Farmers and residents benefited from the reliable water supply, leading to increased agricultural production and a thriving community. The reservoir not only supported irrigation but also provided a recreational outlet for the townspeople, further entwining the lake with their daily lives.

Historically, the reservoir served not just as a water source but also as a vital transportation route for logging and mining operations in the region. Boats were once a common sight, ferrying supplies across its surface. However, as the area modernized, the reliance on water transport diminished, giving way to a new era of recreational use. Today, Catamount Reservoir is a beloved destination for outdoor enthusiasts, who flock to its shores to kayak, fish, and hike the scenic trails that weave through the surrounding mountains.

Despite its beauty, Catamount Reservoir has faced its share of challenges. Invasive species, such as the pesky zebra mussel, have been a growing concern for local conservationists. These unwelcome guests threaten the delicate balance of the ecosystem and have prompted concerted efforts to monitor and manage their spread. Community initiatives have sprung up to educate residents and visitors about responsible boating and fishing practices, fostering a culture of stewardship that is vital for the lake's health.

In response to these challenges, conservation efforts have gained momentum over the years. Local organizations and state agencies have partnered to implement measures aimed at preserving the reservoir's natural beauty and ecological integrity. Water quality monitoring, habitat restoration projects, and public outreach campaigns have all played a role in safeguarding Catamount Reservoir for future generations.

The beauty of Catamount Reservoir is further enhanced by the surrounding parks and trails that offer outdoor enthusiasts a chance to explore the landscape. The area is dotted with picnic spots, hiking trails, and scenic viewpoints, all inviting visitors to immerse themselves in nature. The Catamount Trail, in particular, winds its way around the reservoir, providing a picturesque route for walkers and cyclists alike. Seasonal events, such as fishing tournaments and community clean-up days, foster a sense of camaraderie among locals and celebrate the lake's significance.

As the sun sets over Catamount Reservoir, painting the sky in hues of orange and pink, it's easy to feel the magic of the place. The echoes of laughter and joy resonate through the air, a reminder of the countless memories forged on its shores. Whether casting a line into the water, paddling a kayak through its gentle waves, or simply soaking in the stunning vistas, visitors find themselves enchanted by the reservoir's beauty and tranquility.

Ultimately, Catamount Reservoir is more than just a body of water; it's a living history, a place where stories of nature and community intertwine. As visitors come and go, they become part of a legacy that honors the past while looking to the future. The reservoir serves as a reminder that we are all stewards of the earth, connected by our shared experiences and our love for the land.

In the embrace of the Rocky Mountains, Catamount Reservoir continues to thrive, a testament to resilience and the enduring spirit of those who cherish its waters. So, whether you're a local resident, an adventurous tourist, or a curious soul seeking respite, Catamount Reservoir invites you to join its story—a story of laughter, adventure, and the timeless beauty of nature.

Jumbo Reservoir

In the expansive plains of northeastern Colorado, Jumbo Reservoir stands as a large and lively testament to the ingenuity of its creators and the beauty of the land. Nestled in Logan County, near the charming town of Sterling, this artificial lake has a story as rich as its waters are deep.

The name "Jumbo" is a nod to the reservoir's impressive size. Originally called "Jumbo Dam" when it was constructed in the late 1940s, the reservoir was intended to store water for agricultural irrigation and to provide a reliable water supply for the growing communities in the area. Its name became synonymous with the concept of "larger than life," and it has certainly lived up to that reputation, not just in size but in the impact it has had on the region.

The creation of Jumbo Reservoir was a response to a growing need in northeastern Colorado. The post-World War II boom led to increased agricultural production, which in turn demanded a reliable water source. As farmers sought ways to irrigate their fields, the idea of a reservoir took shape. In 1950, construction began, transforming the landscape and paving the way for a vibrant community centered around this massive body of water.

Before Jumbo Reservoir arrived, the land was home to various indigenous tribes, primarily the Arapaho and Cheyenne. These tribes had a profound connection to the land, relying on its resources for hunting, fishing, and gathering. The legends of these peoples often revolved around the spirits of the rivers and lakes, celebrating the life-giving waters that nourished their communities. The reservoir, while a product of colonization, also holds echoes of these rich histories, reminding us of the bond between nature and those who came before.

Jumbo Reservoir itself is not a natural lake but a man-made marvel created by damming the South Platte River. The initial flora and fauna in the area included vibrant grasslands and wetlands teeming with life. The reservoir has since become a sanctuary for diverse wildlife, including migratory birds, deer, and a variety of fish species. The beauty of the lake attracts outdoor enthusiasts who come to fish, boat, and enjoy the stunning vistas.

With its creation, Jumbo Reservoir significantly changed the local landscape. It brought irrigation opportunities to farmers, which helped to establish a thriving agricultural community. This new water source transformed the arid plains into fertile fields, fostering a sense of optimism and growth. Communities flourished as they embraced the opportunities provided by the reservoir, leading to a bustling environment where families could thrive.

While the reservoir primarily serves agricultural purposes, it has also become a popular recreational destination. Anglers flock to its waters, hoping to catch walleye, catfish, and trout. The reservoir's expansive shoreline provides ample opportunities for boating, camping, and picnicking. The Jumbo Reservoir State Wildlife Area, established around the lake, offers trails for hiking and biking, making it a hub for outdoor activities. Events like fishing tournaments and community gatherings often take place, further enhancing its status as a cherished local spot.

However, the reservoir has faced challenges over the years. Like many bodies of water, Jumbo has dealt with invasive species that threaten its delicate ecosystem. Species such as Eurasian watermilfoil have made their way into the reservoir, prompting conservationists and local agencies to take action. Awareness campaigns educate visitors on the importance of responsible boating practices and the need to keep invasive species at bay.

Conservation efforts are crucial in maintaining the health of Jumbo Reservoir. Local organizations work diligently to monitor water quality and manage habitats, ensuring that both wildlife and visitors can continue to enjoy this natural treasure. Collaboration between community members and environmental agencies has fostered a culture of stewardship, encouraging everyone to participate in preserving the beauty and integrity of the reservoir.

One of the most heartwarming aspects of Jumbo Reservoir is its role in bringing people together. Families often gather at its shores for summer barbecues, while friends embark on fishing trips that forge lasting memories. The laughter of children echoes through the air as they splash in the water, their joy a reflection of the spirit of the place. Whether it's a quiet afternoon of reading on the dock or a lively family reunion under the stars, Jumbo Reservoir serves as a backdrop for countless cherished moments.

In recent years, developments around the reservoir have further enhanced its appeal. New parks, picnic areas, and facilities have been established to accommodate the growing number of visitors. These improvements have made it easier for families to connect with nature and each other, enriching the community's bond with the land.

As the sun dips below the horizon, casting a golden glow across Jumbo Reservoir, it's hard not to feel the magic of the place. The shimmering water reflects the vibrant colors of the sky, creating a breathtaking spectacle that captivates all who behold it. Here, under the vast Colorado sky, the stories of the past blend seamlessly with the hopes of the future.

Ultimately, Jumbo Reservoir is more than just a reservoir; it's a living testament to the resilience of nature and the spirit of community. As people come together to enjoy its beauty, they become part of a larger narrative—one that celebrates connection, conservation, and the joy of shared experiences. Jumbo Reservoir invites everyone to create their own stories, leaving behind a legacy of laughter, love, and a profound appreciation for the natural world.

In the heart of Colorado, Jumbo Reservoir continues to thrive, a symbol of human ingenuity and the enduring spirit of the land. Whether you're casting a line, hiking along the shores, or simply soaking in the view, the reservoir beckons you to immerse yourself in its wonders and make memories that will last a lifetime.

Bear Lake

Tucked away in the majestic Rockies of Colorado, Bear Lake is a shimmering treasure that captures the essence of adventure and tranquility. Located in Larimer County, near the charming town of Estes Park, this picturesque lake has a story as layered and vibrant as its surroundings.

Bear Lake gets its name from the area's history, steeped in local lore and the wildlife that once roamed the land. According to local legend, early settlers would often spot black bears meandering through the lush foliage surrounding the lake, searching for food and shelter. The name stuck, evoking images of the wilderness that still enchants visitors today.

The formation of Bear Lake is a story of natural beauty and human ingenuity. While its origins date back to glacial activity during the last Ice Age, the lake has been shaped over the years by various human interventions, especially in the 20th century. Originally, it served as a vital water source for both wildlife and the early settlers in the region, becoming an integral part of the community's livelihood.

Before European settlers arrived, the land was inhabited by the Ute and Arapaho tribes. These indigenous peoples revered the land, using the resources from Bear Lake for fishing, hunting, and gathering. They saw the lake not just as a water source but as a sacred space, rich with spiritual significance. As the tribes moved through the area, they shared stories of the lake and its surrounding mountains, passing down legends that still resonate today.

With colonization came a significant transformation of the landscape. The initial flora and fauna included a thriving ecosystem of coniferous forests, wildflowers, and an array of wildlife, from elk to beavers. The settlers introduced agricultural practices and roads, paving the way for a community to blossom. As farmers utilized the water from Bear Lake to irrigate their crops, the area began to flourish, drawing more settlers who sought to make a life in this beautiful corner of Colorado.

Bear Lake has always played a dual role: providing essential resources while also serving as a site for recreation and community gatherings. In the early 1900s, it became a popular destination for families looking to escape the hustle of city life. People would flock to the lake for fishing, boating, and picnicking, fostering a sense of togetherness that continues to thrive today. The echoes of laughter and joy that fill the air have made Bear Lake a beloved gathering place for generations.

In more recent years, the lake has faced challenges typical of many natural areas, including the introduction of invasive species. Species like the Eurasian watermilfoil threaten the local ecosystem, prompting conservation efforts to maintain the lake's health. Local organizations have implemented educational programs to raise awareness among visitors about the importance of protecting Bear Lake's delicate environment. Boaters are reminded to clean their equipment before launching to minimize the risk of spreading these invaders.

Despite these challenges, the community's commitment to conservation shines through. Various organizations work tirelessly to monitor water quality, restore habitats, and protect wildlife. These efforts have fostered a culture of stewardship among residents and visitors alike, ensuring that Bear Lake remains a vibrant ecosystem for future generations.

Over the years, the infrastructure around Bear Lake has evolved to accommodate the increasing number of visitors while preserving the natural beauty of the area. Parks, trails, and recreational facilities have been developed to enhance the visitor experience. The Bear Lake Trailhead serves as a gateway to numerous hiking trails that weave through the lush forest and offer breathtaking views of the surrounding mountains. Whether you're looking for a leisurely stroll or a challenging hike, the area has something for everyone.

As you approach Bear Lake, the first sight that greets you is the stunning blue water framed by towering peaks. The lake's beauty is especially striking at sunrise, when the morning light dances across the surface, casting a warm glow that invites you to pause and reflect. It's a moment of serenity that feels almost magical, reminding you of the wonders of nature.

Fishing enthusiasts flock to Bear Lake, where the waters are teeming with cutthroat and brook trout. Anglers often share stories of the "big one that got away," turning each fishing trip into an adventure filled with laughter and camaraderie. The lake has become a cherished spot for families to bond over fishing, creating lasting memories as they reel in their catches.

While fishing and hiking are popular, Bear Lake is also a haven for winter sports. In the colder months, the area transforms into a winter wonderland, attracting snowshoers, cross-country skiers, and ice skaters. The laughter of children building snowmen echoes through the crisp air, a delightful reminder that Bear Lake is a year-round destination for adventure.

Community events, such as the annual Bear Lake Fun Run and the summer music series, draw people from near and far. These gatherings celebrate local culture, encouraging friendships and fostering a sense of belonging. As residents and visitors come together to enjoy music, food, and outdoor activities, the spirit of Bear Lake shines brightly, illuminating the deep connections formed around this cherished body of water.

As the day winds down, the sun dips below the horizon, casting hues of orange and pink across the sky. The tranquil waters of Bear Lake reflect this stunning display, a moment that feels like a warm embrace from nature itself. Whether you're lounging by the shore or taking a leisurely paddle in a kayak, the beauty of Bear Lake is a reminder to slow down, appreciate the moment, and connect with the world around you.

In the end, Bear Lake is more than just a picturesque destination; it is a testament to the resilience of nature and the enduring spirit of community. The stories, laughter, and memories created here weave together a rich tapestry that celebrates both the natural beauty of Colorado and the deep connections formed among those who visit. Whether you're a first-time visitor or a longtime local, Bear Lake welcomes you with open arms, inviting you to become part of its story.

Antero Reservoir

Set against the backdrop of the stunning Rocky Mountains, Antero Reservoir sparkles like a hidden treasure in central Colorado. Named after the nearby Antero Mountain, which itself has roots in the Ute language meaning "a place of shelter," this reservoir is more than just a body of water; it's a sanctuary for wildlife, a playground for outdoor enthusiasts, and a canvas for countless memories.

Antero Reservoir is located in Park County, just a stone's throw from the charming town of Jefferson. Originally created in the 1950s as a water storage facility for the Denver metropolitan area, it has evolved into a vibrant hub for recreation and community gatherings. This man-made reservoir was born from the meticulous engineering of the Upper South Platte River, designed to capture runoff and provide water for irrigation and municipal use. But while it serves a practical purpose, the magic of Antero lies in its breathtaking surroundings.

The landscape surrounding the reservoir is a stunning tapestry of wildflowers, towering pines, and rolling hills. When the water levels are high, the beauty of the lake reflects the surrounding peaks, creating a picture-perfect postcard at every turn. This environment was once home to abundant wildlife, including elk, deer, and an array of birds. The indigenous Ute tribes thrived in this area, using the resources provided by the land for hunting and gathering. They held deep spiritual connections to the mountains and waters, viewing them as sacred elements of their existence.

As the 19th century rolled in, settlers began to arrive, drawn by the promise of fertile land and the allure of the Rockies. While their arrival brought change and opportunity, it also transformed the natural landscape. Agriculture blossomed, and the introduction of farming practices altered the ecosystems that had thrived for centuries. Still, the construction of Antero Reservoir marked a positive turning point, bringing water to previously arid lands and enabling communities to flourish. Farmers rejoiced at the prospect of irrigating their fields, creating a tapestry of green amid the golden grasses.

One whimsical legend that locals enjoy recounting involves the "Antero Monster." According to stories passed down through generations, some fishermen claim they've caught glimpses of a mysterious creature lurking beneath the surface of the lake. While some dismiss these tales as mere fabrications, others fervently believe that something extraordinary lives in the depths. The creature's reputation has drawn a curious crowd, each hoping to catch a glimpse of the legendary being while casting their lines into the shimmering waters.

Despite its picturesque charm, Antero Reservoir has faced challenges throughout its history. The reservoir was built to manage the water levels for both the community and the ecosystem, but heavy rainfall in certain years has led to fluctuations in the water levels that can sometimes be dramatic. Flooding has been a concern, causing damage to infrastructure and altering habitats. However, the community has remained resilient, coming together to address these challenges and ensure the reservoir continues to thrive.

Antero Reservoir has long been known as a fisherman's paradise, attracting anglers with its ample supply of trout. From the thrill of reeling in a big catch to the quiet joy of casting a line at dawn, the lake offers something for everyone. Fishing derbies and family-friendly events are frequently held, fostering a spirit of camaraderie among locals and visitors alike. As the sun sets and the water reflects shades of pink and gold, the laughter of families fills the air, creating an atmosphere of joy and connection.

The impacts of human activity on Antero Reservoir have not gone unnoticed. With the influx of visitors has come the challenge of invasive species threatening the delicate ecosystem. Species like the New Zealand mudsnail have made their way into the waters, prompting local conservation efforts to keep the lake healthy and vibrant. Education programs have been implemented to inform boaters and anglers about best practices for preventing the spread of invasive species, ensuring that future generations can enjoy the beauty of the reservoir.

Community involvement has played a pivotal role in the preservation of Antero Reservoir. Local organizations have launched initiatives to restore habitats, clean up shorelines, and promote sustainable fishing practices. The establishment of parks and picnic areas around the reservoir has created a welcoming atmosphere for families, providing a space for gatherings, birthday parties, and leisurely afternoons. The area around the lake has blossomed into a place where nature and community intertwine, reminding everyone of the beauty of the outdoors.

In the winter, Antero Reservoir transforms into a snowy wonderland, drawing visitors for ice fishing, snowshoeing, and simply enjoying the quiet beauty of the season. Families bundle up and venture out to create snowmen, while ice fishermen brave the cold for the thrill of the catch. The laughter and camaraderie experienced in winter reflect the reservoir's role as a year-round destination for joy and adventure.

Antero's charm lies not just in its scenic beauty, but in the connections it fosters. Every fishing trip, every picnic, and every sunset shared along its shores builds a sense of community that stretches beyond the water's edge. Whether it's the newcomer casting a line for the first time or the seasoned angler sharing tales of past catches, Antero Reservoir is a place where stories are born and friendships are formed.

As the sun dips below the horizon, casting a warm glow across the water, the essence of Antero Reservoir shines through. It's a place of laughter, adventure, and connection—a reminder of the beauty that arises when nature and community come together. With its captivating landscape and rich history, Antero Reservoir continues to be a cherished haven for all who seek solace and excitement in the heart of Colorado. Here, at this remarkable reservoir, every ripple tells a story, every breeze carries laughter, and every sunset paints a promise of new adventures to come.

Lake McConaughy

Nestled in the heart of western Nebraska, Lake McConaughy stands as a testament to human ingenuity and the ever-changing landscape of the American West. Named after the former Nebraska Governor, Arthur McConaughy, this expansive reservoir has become a beloved destination for adventure and relaxation. With its shimmering blue waters and surrounding rolling hills, it beckons to visitors seeking both recreation and respite.

The lake was formed in the early 1940s as part of a federal project to manage water resources and prevent flooding. The construction of the Kingsley Dam on the North Platte River created one of Nebraska's largest reservoirs, and with a capacity of over 600,000 acre-feet of water, it was no small feat. Originally envisioned to provide irrigation and flood control, Lake McConaughy has evolved into a vibrant hub for outdoor activities, making it a vital part of the community's lifestyle.

Before the dam, the area was characterized by the natural beauty of the Great Plains, home to a rich array of flora and fauna. The region was populated with native grasses, wildflowers, and shrubs, providing habitat for a diverse wildlife population, including deer, prairie dogs, and numerous bird species. Indigenous tribes, such as the Lakota and Cheyenne, thrived here for centuries, relying on the land for sustenance, hunting, and trade. They wove intricate stories about the rivers and lakes, viewing them as sacred and essential to their way of life.

As settlers moved into the area, the landscape began to change. The introduction of farming and ranching reshaped the land, and while this development brought economic opportunity, it also meant significant alterations to the local ecosystem. With the construction of Lake McConaughy, the area experienced a remarkable transformation. The reservoir became a crucial resource for irrigation, enabling farmers to cultivate crops in an otherwise arid region, creating a flourishing agricultural community. The promise of water turned the High Plains into a tapestry of green fields and vibrant farms.

One of the more whimsical legends surrounding Lake McConaughy involves its "mermaid." According to local folklore, a mysterious figure can sometimes be seen gliding across the lake's surface, captivating the imaginations of those who catch a glimpse. Whether it's the effect of sunlight dancing on the water or the tales of locals weaving a narrative for fun, the mermaid has become a charming part of the lake's lore, inviting laughter and storytelling during summer evenings by the shore.

Throughout its history, Lake McConaughy has faced its share of challenges. While it has provided vital water resources, there have been floods, especially during heavy rain events, leading to temporary overflows and the need for careful management of water levels. The dam's construction itself was a monumental task, requiring thousands of workers and the careful consideration of environmental impacts. Yet, the foresight of planners has generally kept the lake stable, allowing it to thrive as a recreational hotspot.

The lake quickly became known for its excellent fishing opportunities. Anglers from near and far flock to its shores, eager to cast their lines for walleye, catfish, and trout. Many stories are told around campfires about the one that got away, adding to the lake's reputation as a place where great memories are made. In the summer, the bustling activity around the lake reflects the community's deep connection to this body of water, with families enjoying picnics, boat rides, and fishing tournaments.

Human impacts on the lake extend beyond recreational use. As more visitors and residents began to appreciate the natural beauty, conservation efforts emerged to protect the lake and its surrounding habitats. While invasive species, like zebra mussels, have posed threats to the ecosystem, local organizations and state agencies are dedicated to monitoring and mitigating their effects. Education programs have been established to inform visitors about the importance of clean boating practices, ensuring the health of Lake McConaughy for generations to come.

The development of parks and recreational areas around the lake has also evolved over the years. The Lake McConaughy State Recreation Area boasts campsites, hiking trails, and picnic areas, creating a welcoming environment for visitors to connect with nature. The pristine beaches that line the shores offer sandy spots for sunbathing and swimming, making it a popular summer destination for families and friends. With its stunning sunsets and peaceful atmosphere, it's no wonder that many visitors return year after year, forming lifelong bonds with the lake.

In winter, the reservoir transforms, offering a completely different landscape. Ice fishing becomes a popular pastime, and the lake's frozen surface draws adventurers seeking solitude and reflection. The laughter of families can still be heard as they bundle up and explore the snowy surroundings, creating a different kind of magic as they make snowmen and enjoy hot cocoa by the fire.

Lake McConaughy has also played a role in community development. Festivals and events, such as the annual Lake McConaughy Bluegrass Festival, bring together locals and visitors alike to celebrate music, culture, and the great outdoors. These gatherings foster a sense of belonging and community, emphasizing the lake's importance not just as a recreational site but as a cultural touchstone for the region.

As the sun sets over the horizon, painting the sky in hues of orange and pink, the beauty of Lake McConaughy becomes a reminder of nature's splendor and the connections it fosters. Whether it's the laughter of children splashing in the water, the calm of a solitary fisherman casting his line, or the stories shared around a campfire, Lake McConaughy encapsulates the spirit of adventure, community, and the simple joys of life.

In the heart of the High Plains, Lake McConaughy is more than just a body of water; it is a vibrant ecosystem, a community cornerstone, and a sanctuary for all who seek solace and excitement. Its history is a mosaic of resilience, innovation, and laughter, inviting everyone to be part of its ever-evolving story.

Williams Fork Reservoir

Nestled in the breathtaking terrain of Colorado's Rocky Mountains, Williams Fork Reservoir is a hidden treasure that boasts a rich history and a vibrant ecosystem. Located in Grand County, this serene body of water is a man-made reservoir that emerged from the ambitious vision of engineers in the 1950s, designed primarily to store water for the Denver metropolitan area. With a nod to the river that feeds it, the reservoir captures the essence of both nature and human ingenuity.

The name "Williams Fork" derives from the nearby Williams Fork River, which itself was likely named after a local trapper and pioneer who first traversed the area in the 1800s. The river flows through stunning landscapes and lush forests, eventually feeding into the reservoir, creating a picturesque scene that captivates all who visit. As the water glistens under the Colorado sun, it reflects not just the surrounding mountains but the rich tapestry of stories that have unfolded here.

As we dive into the history of Williams Fork Reservoir, it's hard not to chuckle at some of the local legends that have emerged over the years. One popular tale involves a "water spirit" that is said to guard the depths of the reservoir, ensuring the safety of those who fish its waters. Fishermen often joke about the spirit's mood swings, claiming that on particularly foggy mornings, the fishing is fantastic, while on sunny days, the fish seem to vanish into thin air. Whether it's a myth or just a playful superstition, it adds a layer of charm to the reservoir, making every fishing trip an adventure filled with possibility.

The construction of the reservoir was no small feat. Engineers faced numerous challenges, including unexpected weather conditions and rugged terrain. Yet, through determination and teamwork, they completed the project in 1958, creating a reservoir that not only served a critical function for water storage but also became a beloved recreational spot for locals and visitors alike. The lake quickly attracted families, anglers, and outdoor enthusiasts, transforming the landscape into a hub of activity.

Initially, the area surrounding Williams Fork Reservoir was a rich tapestry of flora and fauna, home to diverse wildlife. The initial inhabitants of this land were the Ute tribes, who thrived in the lush environment, using the natural resources for food, shelter, and trade. The reservoir has impacted their descendants as well, as they often gather for fishing and cultural events, weaving the traditions of the past with the activities of today.

With the arrival of settlers in the late 19th century, the landscape began to change dramatically. Ranching and farming introduced new practices, altering the ecosystems that had flourished for centuries. Still, the creation of the reservoir marked a significant positive shift. It provided vital irrigation and supported agriculture, turning arid lands into fertile fields. The new water source brought life to the area and fostered community growth, transforming Williams Fork into a gathering place for families seeking solace and adventure.

Fishing is a beloved pastime at Williams Fork Reservoir, with anglers flocking to its shores to cast their lines for rainbow and brown trout. Every summer, the reservoir hosts fishing derbies, where families and friends compete for the biggest catch while sharing laughs and stories. Kids run along the banks, their excitement palpable as they reel in their first fish, creating memories that will last a lifetime. The sense of community here is palpable, as people gather to share tips, swap fish tales, and enjoy the beauty of nature together.

However, not all stories surrounding Williams Fork Reservoir are lighthearted. In 1982, a major flood changed the landscape dramatically, testing the resilience of the local community. Heavy rains caused the reservoir to overflow, leading to property damage and altering the surrounding ecosystems. Yet, through collaboration and determination, residents came together to rebuild, and the reservoir emerged from this disaster even more cherished and vital than before.

Over the years, Williams Fork Reservoir has faced environmental challenges as well. The introduction of invasive species, particularly invertebrates like the zebra mussel, has posed threats to the local ecosystem. In response, conservation efforts have ramped up, focusing on education and prevention to protect the lake's natural beauty and biodiversity. Local organizations have spearheaded initiatives to raise awareness about the importance of maintaining the reservoir's ecological health, encouraging responsible boating and fishing practices to mitigate the spread of invasive species.

The reservoir is also home to a plethora of recreational activities that keep the community buzzing year-round. In the summer, boating, kayaking, and paddleboarding are popular pursuits, while winter transforms the lake into a haven for ice fishing and snowmobiling. Picnic areas along the shores provide families with the perfect backdrop for barbecues and gatherings, and hiking trails wind through the nearby forests, inviting exploration and adventure. The area around the reservoir is a stunning playground, ensuring that there's always something to do, no matter the season.

Wildlife enthusiasts flock to Williams Fork to witness the diverse array of animals that call this area home. From soaring eagles to playful otters, the reservoir offers glimpses of nature's wonders. Birdwatchers revel in the opportunity to catch sight of migratory birds as they make their way through the region, creating a sense of connection to the natural world.

As the sun sets over Williams Fork Reservoir, painting the sky in hues of orange and pink, the beauty of this remarkable place becomes even more evident. Families gather on the banks, sharing stories and laughter as the stars begin to twinkle above. Each wave that laps against the shore seems to carry with it a whisper of history, a reminder of the resilience of the community and the enduring connection between people and nature.

Williams Fork Reservoir is more than just a reservoir; it's a living testament to the spirit of adventure, community, and the beauty of the Colorado landscape. Whether it's the thrill of the catch, the joy of a family picnic, or the simple pleasure of watching the sunset over the water, this reservoir has something to offer everyone. It's a place where stories are shared, memories are made, and the wonders of nature are celebrated, inviting all who visit to embrace the magic that lies within its waters.

Sloan's Lake

Nestled in the heart of Denver, Colorado, Sloan's Lake is not just a body of water; it's a vibrant tapestry of community, recreation, and rich history. With its stunning views of the Rocky Mountains and the Denver skyline, it serves as a beloved oasis for locals and visitors alike. Named after a prominent Denver businessman, John Sloan, who purchased the land surrounding the lake in the late 1800s, Sloan's Lake has evolved from its agricultural roots into a bustling recreational hub.

The lake's story begins long before it was named after Sloan, with a history steeped in the traditions of the indigenous peoples who called this area home. The Cheyenne and Arapaho tribes frequented the region, drawn by the natural beauty and the resources that the land provided. They used the area for hunting and gathering, thriving in the rich ecosystems that the lake and surrounding plains offered. Legend has it that the spirits of their ancestors still dance across the waters, watching over the lake and its visitors, a fact that lends a sense of magic to every sunset reflected on its surface.

Sloan's Lake was originally a natural body of water, but in the late 1800s, the area underwent significant transformations as settlers arrived. Initially used for irrigation, the lake quickly became a recreational site as the city of

Denver expanded. With the advent of the 1900s, the lake saw increased popularity for fishing, boating, and picnicking. It became a focal point for community gatherings, offering residents a serene escape from urban life.

One particularly memorable event in the lake's history occurred in the summer of 1965, when an unexpected storm swept through Denver, causing flooding that affected not only the lake but also the surrounding neighborhoods. Residents remember the scene vividly: a sudden downpour transformed familiar trails into rushing streams, and the lake's banks overflowed, washing away picnic tables and kayaks alike. Rather than discouraging outdoor fun, the community rallied together, helping each other salvage what they could and organizing clean-up efforts. The sense of camaraderie that emerged from this disaster only strengthened the bond among locals, and today, many share stories of that wild summer as a testament to the resilience of their community.

As the 20th century progressed, Sloan's Lake continued to evolve. The area surrounding it was developed into a park, and more amenities were added, turning it into a bustling destination for families. Joggers, dog walkers, and cyclists flocked to the scenic paths that encircle the lake, while children played on the playgrounds that dot the park. On any given weekend, you can find people barbecuing, playing frisbee, or simply enjoying a lazy afternoon in the sun. The atmosphere is infectious; laughter and joy seem to ripple across the water like the gentle waves.

The flora and fauna of Sloan's Lake are as diverse as its visitors. The lake supports a variety of wildlife, including ducks, geese, and even the occasional heron that graces the shoreline. The surrounding parkland is adorned with trees that provide shade and beauty throughout the seasons. In the spring, cherry blossoms bloom, transforming the area into a pastel paradise. Fall brings a fiery display of colors, as the leaves change and carpet the ground. The lake is a natural haven, and many conservation efforts have been implemented to maintain its ecological health and beauty.

Yet, like many lakes, Sloan's Lake faces challenges. Invasive species, particularly Eurasian watermilfoil, have made their way into the lake, threatening native plant life and disrupting the ecosystem. Local organizations have initiated programs aimed at controlling these invasive plants and educating the community about their impact. The city's Parks and Recreation department works diligently to ensure that Sloan's Lake remains a thriving environment for both wildlife and the people who cherish it.

Despite these challenges, the lake has remained a centerpiece of the community, hosting events that bring people together. The annual Sloan's Lake Summer Festival, for instance, draws crowds from all around, featuring live music, food trucks, and activities for children. Residents gather to celebrate, share their stories, and enjoy the beauty of their beloved lake. The festival is a vibrant reminder of the strong community spirit that has flourished around Sloan's

Lake, turning it into more than just a recreational area, but a source of pride for the city.

Transportation and trade have also played a role in the lake's history. While not a major trade route, Sloan's Lake was once part of the larger network of waterways that helped connect early settlers to resources and markets. Today, the lake continues to facilitate the movement of people, with paddleboarding and kayaking offering unique perspectives on the surrounding cityscape and natural beauty. It's not uncommon to see families out on the water, enjoying a sunny afternoon, or couples paddling along while sharing stories of their adventures.

The impact of Sloan's Lake on the local community cannot be overstated. It serves as a gathering place where friendships are forged, where families create memories, and where nature can be enjoyed in an urban setting. The vibrant culture surrounding the lake is a reflection of the community itself—dynamic, diverse, and resilient. Local artists often showcase their work in the park, and pop-up markets allow small businesses to thrive. The lake has become a canvas for creativity, inviting everyone to participate in its ongoing story.

As the day winds down, Sloan's Lake takes on a magical quality. The sun sets behind the Rocky Mountains, casting a warm glow over the water. People gather on the shores, sharing stories and laughter, and the tranquility of the lake envelops them like a warm embrace. It's a moment of connection—not just to nature, but to one another. As families and friends sit together, watching the sky transform into a tapestry of colors, there's a sense of gratitude for the shared experiences that have unfolded around this cherished reservoir.

In this way, Sloan's Lake is much more than a lake; it is a living testament to the strength and spirit of the community that surrounds it. It's a place where history, nature, and people converge, where every ripple in the water carries with it a story waiting to be told. The laughter of children, the tranquility of early morning joggers, and the beauty of the changing seasons all contribute to the unique mosaic that is Sloan's Lake—a beloved landmark that continues to inspire joy, connection, and a deep appreciation for the natural world.

Hanging Lake

Tucked away in the heart of Glenwood Canyon, Colorado, Hanging Lake is a stunning testament to nature's artistry and resilience. With its crystal-clear turquoise waters cascading into a series of smaller pools, it feels like a hidden treasure waiting to be discovered. The lake's name derives from its remarkable position; perched on the edge of a cliff, it appears to dangle above the valley below, giving visitors the delightful impression that they've stepped into a fairy tale.

This enchanting lake is believed to have formed over thousands of years through a combination of geological processes and natural springs. As rainwater percolated through the limestone cliffs, it created a spectacular waterfall that feeds the lake, resulting in the vibrant hues that captivate the eyes of all who visit. But it's not just the lake itself that enchants; the journey to reach it is an adventure all its own, requiring a hike through lush forests and steep switchbacks, all while being surrounded by the dramatic scenery of the canyon.

Hanging Lake's history is deeply intertwined with the indigenous Ute tribes, who inhabited this beautiful region long before it became a popular destination. The Utes revered the area for its natural beauty and resources, using the surrounding land for hunting and gathering. Legend has it that the lake was considered sacred, a place where spirits danced in the mist of the waterfall. Elders would share stories of the lake, teaching younger generations about the harmony of nature and the importance of respecting sacred sites.

The story of Hanging Lake took a turn in the late 1800s when it began to draw the attention of settlers. The arrival of European Americans led to significant changes in the landscape. The railroad, built nearby to facilitate transport and trade, opened the area to tourism, allowing more people to experience the lake's breathtaking beauty. In 1895, the U.S. Forest Service designated the area as a public site, and in 2013, Hanging Lake became part of the newly established Glenwood Canyon Scenic Area, ensuring its protection for future generations.

One of the more colorful tales associated with Hanging Lake involves the legend of a beautiful maiden who fell in love with a brave warrior. As the story goes, the couple would meet by the lake to share stolen moments of romance. However, when the warrior was called away to battle, he promised to return. Heartbroken, the maiden waited by the water, her tears creating the lake's enchanting beauty. To this day, visitors often feel a sense of love and longing when they gaze into its depths, as if the echoes of the maiden's story linger in the air.

As with many natural wonders, Hanging Lake has faced its share of challenges. In the spring of 2019, a significant rainstorm led to flash floods that caused landslides in the area, damaging the trails and altering the landscape. The local community, however, rallied together, showcasing the spirit of resilience that has come to define the region. Volunteers and local officials worked tirelessly to restore the hiking paths, ensuring that future visitors could experience the lake's magic.

Today, Hanging Lake is a popular destination for hikers and nature lovers, drawing thousands of visitors each year. The hike to the lake, though challenging, is well worth the effort. As adventurers make their way along the winding trail, they are greeted by stunning vistas and lush vegetation. Wildflowers bloom along the path, their colors vibrant against the rocky backdrop, and the sounds of birds fill the air, creating a symphony of nature that enhances the experience.

However, this popularity has not come without its issues. The influx of visitors has introduced concerns about conservation and the potential for ecological damage. Invasive species have been a growing problem, threatening the delicate balance of the local ecosystem. To combat this, conservation efforts have been implemented, focusing on education and sustainable practices. Visitors are now required to secure permits to hike to the lake, a move aimed at limiting foot traffic and preserving the area's natural beauty.

The commitment to conservation has also led to the development of educational programs and initiatives. Local organizations work closely with the Forest Service to raise awareness about the importance of protecting Hanging Lake and its surroundings. Community clean-up events and educational workshops help engage visitors and locals alike, fostering a deeper connection to this natural wonder.

The beauty of Hanging Lake lies not only in its stunning scenery but also in the sense of community it fosters. Families often return to the lake year after year, sharing their stories and creating new memories in this breathtaking environment. Picnics are a common sight at the lake's shores, with laughter and chatter blending harmoniously with the sounds of rushing water. The lake serves as a backdrop for countless life events, from proposals to reunions, and its allure continues to captivate hearts.

As the sun sets behind the towering cliffs, the light dances across the water, casting a shimmering glow that enchants everyone nearby. The tranquility of the scene invites reflection, allowing visitors to pause and appreciate the beauty of nature and the connections formed in this magical place. It's easy to understand why so many are drawn to Hanging Lake, as it serves as a reminder of life's wonders and the importance of preserving the environment for generations to come.

Hanging Lake is more than just a destination; it's a living story, a place where nature, legend, and community intertwine. The lake's journey from a sacred site of the Ute people to a beloved recreational area showcases the profound impact of nature on our lives and the importance of protecting these precious resources. As visitors leave, many take a piece of its magic with them, but only carrying the stories and beauty of Hanging Lake into their own lives, ensuring that the legacy of this enchanting place continues to thrive. Because every stone, every shell, every piece of sand removed can erode this beautiful wonder even further.

Little Red Lake

Little Red Lake is a picturesque spot that draws adventurers and nature lovers alike. The lake, with its vibrant hues and serene atmosphere, has captured the hearts of those fortunate enough to discover its beauty. But what lies behind its catchy name and the tales woven into its history?

The name "Little Red Lake" comes from the unique color of the sediment found in the area. This striking hue is a result of iron-rich minerals that seep into the water, giving it a reddish tint that glimmers under the Colorado sun. The locals affectionately refer to it as "Little Red" to distinguish it from its larger, less colorful counterparts. It's a charming name that evokes images of sunset reflections and playful ripples, but it also carries a deeper significance.

Located in Grand County, just west of Rocky Mountain National Park, Little Red Lake has been a gathering place for centuries. Before European settlers arrived, the Ute and Arapaho tribes frequented the area, using the lake and its surrounding lands for hunting, fishing, and gathering. The lake served as a vital water source for these tribes, and its edges were often the backdrop for communal gatherings and ceremonies.

Legend has it that the Ute people believed the lake to be a portal to the spirit world. On certain nights, when the moon hung high and full, the spirits of their ancestors would dance across the water's surface, casting shimmering reflections that mesmerized those lucky enough to witness the spectacle. These stories were passed down through generations, adding an air of mystique to the already enchanting landscape.

The first European explorers, drawn by tales of abundant resources, arrived in the mid-19th century. Their encounters with the local tribes were a mix of curiosity and trepidation, and the landscape began to shift as settlers moved in, establishing small farms and mining camps. The vibrant flora and fauna that once thrived in the region began to dwindle, but Little Red Lake remained a sanctuary, a sparkling oasis amid the rush of human activity.

Little Red Lake was not man-made; it formed naturally over thousands of years, shaped by glacial movements and sedimentation. The initial flora around the lake included vibrant wildflowers, hearty pines, and aspens that danced in the wind. The fauna, too, was diverse—everything from deer and elk to various bird species made their homes in the lush surroundings. The lake's presence attracted fish as well, becoming a favored spot for anglers hoping to reel in trout and other native species.

As the population grew, so did the demand for recreational opportunities. Little Red Lake transformed into a recreational haven, attracting families, campers, and fishermen. The lake became a hub for outdoor activities, including fishing, kayaking, and picnicking, with locals and tourists alike reveling in its beauty. The surrounding trails offered breathtaking views and opportunities for hiking, making the lake an ideal destination for those seeking adventure.

As the years rolled on, the impact of human activity on Little Red Lake became more pronounced. The increasing popularity led to environmental concerns, including the introduction of invasive species that threatened the delicate ecosystem. The challenge was twofold: maintaining the lake's appeal while ensuring its health. Local organizations stepped in, focusing on education and community involvement to combat these issues.

One memorable summer, a volunteer cleanup event became the talk of the town. The local high school's environmental club spearheaded the initiative, rallying students, families, and nature enthusiasts to come together for a common cause. Armed with gloves, trash bags, and an abundance of enthusiasm, participants combed the shores, removing debris and restoring the natural beauty of the lake.

In the midst of their efforts, stories flowed like the waters of Little Red. An elderly man recounted fishing at the lake as a child, his eyes lighting up with memories of pulling in the biggest trout he had ever seen. A group of young girls giggled as they shared their dreams of becoming environmental scientists, inspired by the very place they were helping to clean. Each story, each laugh, added to the spirit of the event, creating a tapestry of community connection woven together by a shared love for Little Red Lake.

The community's efforts didn't stop there. In recent years, local governments recognized the potential for developing parks and recreational facilities around Little Red Lake. Camping sites, picnic areas, and even small resorts began to pop up, creating a welcoming environment for families and visitors. The lake became a gathering place for seasonal events, such as outdoor concerts and art festivals, further cementing its role in the community.

One summer festival, known as "Red Lake Days," became a cherished tradition. Families set up tents along the shoreline, children played games, and local artisans showcased their crafts. Live music filled the air as residents and visitors alike came together to celebrate their beloved lake. The festival featured guided nature walks, where local naturalists shared the importance of the ecosystem, fostering a sense of stewardship among attendees.

In the midst of festivities, the lake remained a sanctuary, its waters reflecting the laughter and joy of the community. Children splashed in the shallows, their carefree laughter mingling with the gentle lapping of waves. Couples strolled hand in hand along the shore, their hearts full as they watched the sun dip below the horizon, painting the sky in hues of orange and pink.

As the sun sets over Little Red Lake, casting a warm glow across its surface, the beauty of this serene spot is undeniable. Families gather for picnics, children chase each other across the grassy knolls, and the laughter of friends fills the air. With each passing season, Little Red Lake continues to weave its story, connecting people to nature and to one another in ways that are both profound and joyous.

Little Red Lake stands as a reminder of the importance of preserving the environment and honoring the stories of those who came before. As visitors dip their toes in the water or cast their lines into the depths, they become part of a larger narrative—one that celebrates the spirit of community, the beauty of nature, and the indomitable power of love for the great outdoors.

The lake may be small in size, but its impact is monumental. It serves as a testament to the resilience of nature and the bonds of community that thrive in its embrace.

Lake Loveland

Nestled at the foothills of the Rockies, Lake Loveland is a shimmering oasis that invites people to relax, reflect, and recharge. Its story, woven with threads of laughter, community, and a touch of folklore, captures the spirit of Colorado itself. But how did this picturesque lake earn its name, and what tales ripple beneath its serene surface?

The name "Lake Loveland" originates from the nearby city of Loveland, Colorado, established in the late 1800s. The city was named after a railroad official, William A. H. Loveland, but over time, it has grown to embody a sense of warmth and community. It's fitting that the lake reflects this spirit, serving as a centerpiece for recreational activities and a gathering spot for families. With a name that evokes feelings of fondness and connection, Lake Loveland has become a beloved landmark.

Lake Loveland's history is marked by significant events, including its role in the region's water supply. Initially formed as a natural lake, it was later dammed to create a reservoir that would support the burgeoning agricultural and municipal needs of the area. As settlers arrived, they quickly recognized the importance of the water source for irrigation and livestock, leading to its expansion.

However, like many places shaped by nature, the lake has faced its fair share of challenges. In 1976, a devastating flood in the region caused considerable damage, washing away roads and affecting the surrounding community. But in true Colorado fashion, the spirit of resilience shone through. Local residents banded together to rebuild, and the lake emerged from the chaos as a symbol of unity and strength.

Local legends often swirl around bodies of water, and Lake Loveland is no exception. Some say that on quiet nights, you can hear the whispers of the original inhabitants, the Ute and Arapaho tribes, who once roamed these lands. It is said that they revered the lake as a sacred place, believing it to be a portal to the spirit world. Visitors sometimes claim to see shimmering lights dancing on the water's surface at dusk, igniting stories of ancestral spirits guiding the way for those who seek solace.

One particularly charming tale is that of the "Lovers' Rock." According to local folklore, two star-crossed lovers would meet at the lake, finding solace in each other's arms amid the natural beauty. Legend has it that they vowed to return to the lake for eternity, and to this day, couples frequent the spot, hoping to capture a piece of their romance.

Located in Larimer County, Lake Loveland is a man-made reservoir, formed in the early 1900s through the construction of a dam. The initial flora surrounding the lake included cottonwoods, willows, and wildflowers that paint the landscape with vibrant colors each spring. The area is also home to various wildlife species, from ducks and geese to deer that wander near the water's edge.

The lake quickly became a crucial resource for the local tribes and early settlers alike. Fishing and hunting were primary activities, with the lake providing sustenance for families and communities. As settlers established farms, the water from Lake Loveland allowed for the cultivation of crops, transforming the landscape into fertile ground.

With the arrival of the railroad in the late 19th century, the area experienced a surge in population and economic growth. Lake Loveland became a focal point for the community, offering recreational opportunities and drawing visitors from near and far. The lake's popularity skyrocketed as families embraced the great outdoors, enjoying activities like boating, swimming, and fishing. It soon became a favorite summer destination, with people flocking to the shores to bask in the sun and create lasting memories.

However, the increasing popularity brought challenges as well. Invasive species crept into the ecosystem, threatening the delicate balance of flora and fauna that had thrived for centuries. The community responded by establishing conservation efforts aimed at restoring the lake's natural beauty and health. Local organizations spearheaded initiatives to educate the public on responsible practices, emphasizing the importance of maintaining the lake's ecological integrity.

As Lake Loveland evolved, so did the surrounding area. Parks and recreational facilities began to emerge, offering a range of activities for residents and visitors. The Loveland

Recreation Department organized events such as fishing derbies, outdoor movie nights, and nature walks, creating a vibrant community spirit that thrives to this day.

One summer evening, the annual "Lake Loveland Festival" took center stage. Families gathered with picnic baskets, children darting about with laughter, while local musicians filled the air with melodies. As the sun began to set, the lake became a canvas of colors, reflecting the vibrant hues of twilight. Fireworks lit up the night sky, creating a magical atmosphere that enveloped the crowd. It was moments like these that reminded everyone of the lake's ability to bring people together, creating bonds and memories that would last a lifetime.

Today, Lake Loveland continues to be a beloved sanctuary for all who visit. With its scenic views and recreational offerings, it remains a source of joy and tranquility. Fishing enthusiasts still cast their lines, hoping to snag a prized trout, while families paddle across the surface in kayaks, laughter echoing across the water. The trails surrounding the lake are alive with hikers and cyclists, each enjoying the natural beauty that Colorado has to offer.

Efforts to protect the lake's ecosystem persist, with community members actively participating in clean-up initiatives and educational programs. Local schools have adopted the lake for science projects, teaching students about the importance of environmental stewardship. Children now grow up learning to appreciate the lake's beauty, ensuring that the legacy of Lake Loveland will be cherished for generations to come.

As the sun sets over Lake Loveland, casting a warm glow across its surface, the beauty of this serene spot is undeniable. Families gather for picnics, children chase each other across the grassy knolls, and the laughter of friends fills the air. Each wave that laps against the shore tells a story—of resilience, love, and community, all intertwined with the rich history of this cherished place.

In the heart of Colorado, Lake Loveland stands as a testament to the enduring bond between nature and humanity. With every ripple, it reminds us of the joy that comes from sharing our lives with the ones we love, finding peace in nature, and celebrating the vibrant tapestry of history that continues to unfold.

Lake Valley

In the heart of Colorado lies Lake Valley, a sparkling body of water cradled by the majestic Rocky Mountains. This lake, with its serene beauty and captivating surroundings, has a history as rich and varied as the landscape itself. The name "Lake Valley" evokes a sense of tranquility and connection, perfectly encapsulating the essence of the area.

Lake Valley got its name from the very geography that surrounds it. Settlers, wandering through the verdant pastures and rolling hills, found themselves drawn to the natural amphitheater formed by the mountains. As they gazed at the lake nestled within this stunning valley, it was clear that the name fit. The lake serves as a focal point for community gatherings and outdoor activities, drawing people together in celebration of nature's bounty.

Historically, Lake Valley has faced its fair share of natural challenges. In the late 1800s, heavy rains caused significant flooding, transforming the serene waters into a raging torrent. Local residents, many of whom were farmers, watched helplessly as their crops and livelihoods were swept away. Yet, rather than succumbing to despair, the community rallied together. They organized efforts to build levees and drainage systems, showcasing a resilience that has become a hallmark of the region.

Amid the serious moments, there are whimsical legends that add a touch of magic to Lake Valley's history. One such tale is that of the "Wandering Spirits," said to roam the shores on misty mornings. According to local folklore, these spirits are the souls of settlers who loved the land so deeply that they couldn't bear to leave. If you listen closely, some claim you can hear them whispering secrets to the wind, guiding visitors toward the best fishing spots or the most scenic trails.

Lake Valley is situated in Summit County, where the natural splendor is complemented by a vibrant community. Initially formed as a natural lake, it has been shaped over the years by human hands. The original flora consisted of lush grasses, wildflowers, and towering pines, creating a picturesque landscape that attracted both wildlife and settlers alike. The lake became a sanctuary for species such as elk, deer, and a variety of birds, adding to the biodiversity of the area.

The Ute tribe, the original inhabitants of the region, revered the valley for its resources. The lake provided fresh water, abundant fish, and fertile land for crops. Their connection to the land ran deep, with rituals and gatherings held near the water's edge. As settlers arrived in the 19th century, they found a land rich in resources but also faced the challenge of coexisting with the indigenous tribes. While the colonization brought growth and prosperity, it also marked a shift in the landscape and the traditional ways of life for the Ute people.

With the arrival of settlers, the lake became integral to transportation and trade. Canoes and small boats navigated the waters, allowing goods to flow in and out of the valley. Fishing became not just a source of food but a communal activity that brought families together. Stories were shared over the campfire, laughter echoed across the water, and bonds were forged in the spirit of cooperation and joy.

As Lake Valley transformed into a popular destination, recreational activities flourished. Families flocked to the shores for picnics, swimming, and hiking. Campsites dotted the landscape, and cabins sprang up like wildflowers in spring. The lake became a hub of community development, where friendships blossomed amid the beauty of nature. Festivals celebrating the changing seasons brought joy and laughter, creating memories that would last a lifetime.

However, as with many natural areas, human impacts have not come without challenges. Invasive species began to infiltrate the ecosystem, threatening the balance that had existed for generations. The local community recognized the need for conservation efforts to preserve the lake's integrity. Volunteers organized clean-up events, educating visitors about responsible practices and the importance of protecting native species. Schools incorporated environmental education programs, instilling a sense of stewardship in the younger generation.

The beauty of Lake Valley has not gone unnoticed, leading to the development of parks and recreational facilities that embrace its natural charm. Trails wind through the surrounding landscape, offering breathtaking views and a chance to immerse oneself in the great outdoors. Anglers continue to cast their lines into the shimmering waters, hoping to reel in a trophy catch while basking in the peaceful ambiance.

One summer evening, the community gathered for the annual Lake Valley Festival. The air was alive with excitement as families set up picnic blankets, kids raced around playing games, and local musicians strummed cheerful tunes. As the sun began to set, casting golden rays across the water, it felt as if the very essence of the valley was alive, celebrating with them.

The highlight of the evening was the storytelling session, where elders shared tales of the valley's past, of struggles and triumphs, and of the spirits that still roam the shores. Laughter and gasps filled the air as each story unfolded, weaving a rich tapestry of shared experiences that bound the community together.

As twilight deepened, a bonfire crackled to life, illuminating the faces of those gathered. The lake, now reflecting the starry sky, seemed to hold its breath in anticipation. One brave soul stepped forward to share a personal tale of how the lake had been a refuge during a difficult time in their life—a reminder of the healing power of nature and community. The gathering paused, listening intently as vulnerability gave way to connection, laughter erupting once more as stories of silliness and mishaps were shared.

Lake Valley is more than just a body of water; it is a living tapestry of history, laughter, and connection. Each ripple in its surface tells a story of resilience and community, a testament to the enduring bond between people and the land. As families continue to gather, share stories, and create memories by the lakeside, Lake Valley remains a cherished sanctuary—a place where the past meets the present, and the beauty of nature embraces the warmth of the human spirit.

North Catamount Reservoir

In the shadow of the majestic Pikes Peak, North Catamount Reservoir is a picturesque lake that has captured the hearts of many. Named for its location in the Catamount region, the lake has a rich history marked by natural beauty, human endeavor, and the whimsical tales that often accompany such serene landscapes.

The name "North Catamount" derives from the area's early mining history and the surrounding peaks, particularly Catamount Peak. In the late 19th century, as gold and silver drew adventurers and settlers to Colorado, the mountain's name was bestowed upon the lake to signify both its geographical position and the fierce spirit of those early pioneers who sought fortune in the Rockies. While they may not have struck gold in every venture, many found their true wealth in the breathtaking vistas and the community that grew around this stunning reservoir.

The reservoir itself was created in the mid-20th century, primarily as a water storage facility for the city of Colorado Springs. Unlike some other lakes in the area, North Catamount is entirely man-made, engineered to harness the melting snow from the surrounding mountains and ensure a steady water supply. This construction altered the landscape significantly, transforming what was once a wild, untouched area into a beautifully managed space for both water conservation and recreation.

From the outset, the flora and fauna that thrived around North Catamount Reservoir were diverse and vibrant. The area was home to lush coniferous forests, wildflowers that burst into color each spring, and a variety of wildlife including elk, deer, and an array of birds. The lake provided an oasis for these creatures, ensuring a rich ecosystem where life flourished.

Long before settlers arrived, the Ute people roamed this land, using its natural resources wisely and sustainably. The reservoir, with its abundant fresh water and fertile surroundings, would have been a vital resource for fishing and gathering. As colonization took hold, the landscape transformed, but many aspects of indigenous stewardship were preserved through the values instilled in the community, such as respect for nature and an understanding of the delicate balance within ecosystems.

As the area developed, North Catamount Reservoir became a hub for recreation and community engagement. In its early days, the lake served not just as a water supply but also as a local fishing spot. Fishermen would gather, casting their lines in hopes of catching trout and enjoying the camaraderie that blossomed on its shores. Children learned to fish here, their laughter echoing across the water as they tugged at their lines, bringing a sense of joy that reverberated through the generations.

Over time, the reservoir expanded its role, becoming a cherished recreational destination. Hiking trails began to wind around the lake, inviting locals and tourists alike to explore the breathtaking views. With Pikes Peak looming majestically in the background, the trails offered both challenging hikes and gentle strolls, allowing everyone to connect with nature at their own pace. The popularity of these trails led to increased community involvement, with groups organizing clean-ups and conservation efforts to preserve the beauty of the area.

North Catamount Reservoir has faced challenges over the years, particularly concerning human impacts on the ecosystem. The introduction of invasive species has become a pressing issue. Aquatic plants and fish that do not belong in the reservoir threaten the delicate balance that has existed for decades. Conservation groups sprang into action, launching campaigns to educate the public about the importance of maintaining the lake's natural state. Community members participated in workshops and volunteer days, working together to remove invasive species and promote healthy habitats.

Despite these challenges, the community surrounding North Catamount remains resilient and hopeful. Conservation efforts are ongoing, and initiatives to restore and protect the native flora and fauna have gained momentum. The local schools even incorporate environmental education into their curricula, teaching young students the importance of stewardship and inspiring a new generation to care for their natural surroundings.

The reservoir has also become a site for various events and activities that foster community spirit. The annual "Catamount Days" celebration draws people from far and wide to enjoy local crafts, food, and music. Families gather to partake in fishing contests, nature walks, and educational talks, all celebrating the beauty and significance of the reservoir. Laughter and joy fill the air as the community comes together, sharing stories and building connections amidst the stunning scenery.

One particularly memorable Catamount Day featured a story-telling session where local elders shared humorous and heartfelt tales of their experiences at the reservoir. One elderly fisherman, with a twinkle in his eye, recounted the time he claimed to have caught a fish so large it could have pulled him in if he hadn't been wearing his trusty life jacket. The crowd erupted in laughter as he mimicked the fish's dramatic leaps, creating a moment of pure joy that showcased the deep bond between the lake and its visitors.

As the sun sets over North Catamount Reservoir, casting a golden glow across the water, it becomes clear that this place is more than just a reservoir; it's a tapestry of stories, memories, and connections. From its origins as a water supply to its transformation into a beloved community space,

North Catamount Reservoir embodies the spirit of collaboration, resilience, and love for the natural world. It is a reminder that while challenges may arise, the community's dedication to protecting and celebrating their environment ensures that the beauty of this lake will endure for generations to come.

South Catamount Reservoir

In the picturesque Rocky Mountains, South Catamount Reservoir is a hidden treasure that tells a story of resilience, community, and natural beauty. Located in Colorado Springs, in El Paso County, this reservoir is part of the broader Pikes Peak region, renowned for its breathtaking landscapes and outdoor recreational opportunities. The lake, named in harmony with its northern counterpart, North Catamount Reservoir, captures the essence of the area's rich history and cultural significance.

The name "South Catamount" reflects not only its geographical position but also the spirit of the land. Local lore suggests that early settlers named it after the Catamount Peak, a striking mountain that overlooks the area. The word "catamount" itself is derived from an old term for wildcats, symbolizing the untamed nature of the region. As settlers arrived in the late 19th century, they were drawn not only by the prospect of mining but also by the stunning natural surroundings that promised adventure and opportunity.

Unlike many other lakes that evolved over centuries, South Catamount was created in the mid-20th century primarily for water supply purposes. Built by the Colorado Springs Utilities, this man-made reservoir was designed to capture and store runoff from the surrounding mountains. It quickly became a crucial part of the water management system, helping to ensure a steady supply of fresh water for the growing city.

As with any major construction project, the creation of South Catamount Reservoir transformed the landscape. Prior to its formation, the area was characterized by dense forests of ponderosa pine and aspen, interspersed with wildflowers and rich wildlife habitats. The reservoir not only flooded the valleys but also created a beautiful new landscape, transforming what was once rugged terrain into a shimmering body of water that would soon attract visitors.

Long before the arrival of European settlers, the Ute people roamed these lands, living in harmony with nature and utilizing its resources wisely. They hunted, fished, and gathered, relying on the natural bounty of the area. The establishment of South Catamount Reservoir altered the dynamics of this ecosystem, but it also opened new opportunities for recreation and community engagement, allowing for a different relationship with the land.

As the reservoir developed, fishing became one of its most popular activities. Anglers flocked to South Catamount, casting their lines in hopes of catching trout and other species that thrived in the clean waters. Families spent weekends picnicking along the shore, sharing stories and laughter as they bonded over their love for the outdoors. Children learned to fish here, their faces lighting up with joy at every tug on the line, creating cherished memories that would last a lifetime.

The surrounding landscape also offered a plethora of hiking and biking trails, making South Catamount a favored spot for outdoor enthusiasts. Trails meandered through the forests, leading adventurers to stunning viewpoints that showcased the majesty of the Rockies. The area became a sanctuary for those seeking respite from the hustle and bustle of city life, a place where they could connect with nature and recharge their spirits.

However, South Catamount Reservoir has not been without its challenges. As the popularity of the lake grew, so did the human impact on the ecosystem. The introduction of invasive species became a pressing concern, threatening the delicate balance of the aquatic environment. Community members and conservation organizations sprang into action, working diligently to educate the public about the importance of preserving native species and protecting the reservoir's ecosystem.

One particularly memorable initiative involved local schools organizing a "Save the Lake" day, where students learned about the invasive species threatening South Catamount. Armed with nets and determination, they set out to remove invasive plants while sharing knowledge with their peers about the importance of conservation. Laughter and camaraderie filled the air as they transformed a day of learning into a fun-filled adventure.

The community surrounding South Catamount Reservoir has always prioritized environmental stewardship, recognizing the importance of maintaining the lake's beauty for future generations. Conservation efforts include regular clean-up events, habitat restoration projects, and ongoing monitoring of the water quality and wildlife. The commitment to protecting the reservoir's health has fostered a sense of pride among residents, who often come together to celebrate their collective achievements.

In addition to conservation efforts, South Catamount has become a hub for community events and activities. The annual "Catamount Festival" brings together locals and visitors for a day of fun, featuring food trucks, craft vendors, and live music. Families set up picnic blankets by the water, enjoying the festivities while children splash in the shallows and build sandcastles. The festival not only showcases local talent but also strengthens community bonds, reminding everyone of the shared love for this beautiful reservoir.

As the sun sets over South Catamount Reservoir, casting a warm golden hue across the water, it becomes clear that this lake is more than just a source of water; it's a source of joy, connection, and inspiration. It embodies the spirit of resilience and collaboration, reminding all who visit of the importance of caring for the natural world. With its rich history, vibrant community, and stunning landscapes, South

Catamount Reservoir stands as a testament to the enduring love for nature and the commitment to preserving it for generations to come. Each ripple on its surface tells a story—a story of laughter, adventure, and the beauty of life intertwined with the land.

Crater Lake

Crater Lake in Colorado, a sparkling blue oasis nestled in the heart of the Rocky Mountains, is a site of both natural beauty and rich history. Located in the quaint town of Lake City, in Hinsdale County, this lake is a testament to the geological wonders that shaped Colorado's landscape. Its name, "Crater Lake," may conjure images of a dormant volcano, but the story is quite different. This lake was formed by a unique combination of glacial activity and natural runoff, resulting in a stunning alpine body of water that captivates all who visit.

The lake sits at an elevation of over 9,800 feet, surrounded by towering peaks and lush forests. The vibrant blue of its waters, enhanced by the surrounding greenery, creates a breathtaking contrast that feels like stepping into a postcard. Crater Lake was officially named in the late 19th century, inspired by its round, crater-like shape, which adds to its mystique. Early settlers, attracted by the area's natural beauty and promise of gold, quickly made it a landmark destination, sparking stories that would become part of local lore.

As the area developed, the history of Crater Lake began to intertwine with the stories of those who lived nearby. Among these were the Ute tribes, who inhabited the region long before European settlers arrived. The Utes viewed the land as sacred, with Crater Lake serving as a vital resource for fishing and gathering. They would often hold gatherings and ceremonies by its shores, celebrating the abundant life that the lake provided. The deep connection the Ute people had with this landscape influenced the cultural fabric of the region, fostering a sense of stewardship toward the environment that resonates even today.

With the arrival of miners in the mid-1800s, the landscape began to change. The promise of riches in the surrounding hills led to an influx of settlers, and while this brought growth and development, it also disrupted the delicate ecosystems that thrived around Crater Lake. However, this wave of colonization also led to a greater appreciation for the lake's beauty, turning it into a recreational hotspot. Soon, fishing, hiking, and camping became popular activities, allowing visitors to experience the wonder of this hidden treasure.

Crater Lake's serene waters offered a perfect haven for fishing enthusiasts. Tales of anglers casting their lines and reeling in the occasional trout soon became part of the local lore. On weekends, families packed their picnic baskets and made the journey to the lake, eager to enjoy the beauty of nature together. Laughter echoed across the water as children chased each other, their joy infectious. It was during these moments that bonds were formed, not just among families but also within the wider community.

However, Crater Lake was not immune to the challenges of human impact. The introduction of invasive species, such as the notorious zebra mussel, posed a significant threat to the lake's ecosystem. These little critters can wreak havoc on native species and disrupt the delicate balance of the aquatic environment. Recognizing the potential consequences, local conservationists mobilized to raise awareness and implement measures to protect the lake. Community clean-up days became a regular event, uniting residents and visitors alike in the fight to preserve Crater Lake's natural beauty.

One summer, a particularly enthusiastic group of local children decided to launch a "Save Crater Lake" campaign. Armed with colorful posters and homemade lemonade stands, they raised money to fund educational programs about the importance of conservation. Their creativity and passion inspired adults, creating a ripple effect that brought the community together in ways no one had anticipated. With a mix of laughter and determination, they rallied around a cause that was close to their hearts.

As awareness grew, so did efforts to create a sustainable recreational environment. The establishment of hiking trails and campgrounds allowed for safe and enjoyable access to the lake, promoting eco-friendly tourism that emphasized the importance of preserving the natural landscape. Families visiting the area could now engage in activities that fostered a love for nature while ensuring its protection. The community embraced these changes, often hosting events that celebrated the beauty of Crater Lake and encouraged everyone to be mindful of their impact on the environment.

Despite the challenges, Crater Lake remained a beacon of hope and joy for the residents of Lake City. The annual "Crater Lake Festival" became a cherished tradition, drawing people from all over Colorado to celebrate the lake's beauty. With food stalls, local crafts, and live music, the festival highlighted the vibrant culture of the area while promoting conservation efforts. Children played games, couples strolled hand-in-hand along the water's edge, and old friends reconnected over shared memories.

As the sun set behind the peaks, painting the sky in hues of orange and pink, it became clear that Crater Lake was more than just a body of water; it was a symbol of community resilience and connection to nature. The stories shared around the campfire, the laughter of families, and the whispers of the wind through the trees all wove together to create a tapestry of life that would continue for generations. With every visit, the lake reminded all who came of the importance of preserving the beauty that surrounded them.

In the end, Crater Lake stands as a testament to the harmonious relationship between nature and community. It embodies the joy of shared experiences, the lessons of stewardship, and the enduring spirit of those who call it home. As the seasons change and the years pass, the lake remains a constant, a source of inspiration and a reminder that the most precious treasures often lie within the embrace of the natural world.

Mount Princeton Hot Springs

Mount Princeton Hot Springs, nestled in the heart of Colorado's Rocky Mountains, is a true oasis that draws visitors from near and far to soak in its warm, mineral-rich waters. Located in Chaffee County, just a stone's throw from the picturesque town of Buena Vista, these hot springs have a history as rich and varied as the waters themselves. The name "Mount Princeton" pays homage to the nearby mountain peak, which was named after Princeton University in the late 1800s. The springs themselves, however, have a story that predates any university, steeped in the legends and lifeways of the indigenous Ute people who cherished these natural thermal baths long before they became a destination for settlers.

The hot springs were created through a combination of geological activity and the natural flow of groundwater heated by the Earth's core. This remarkable process resulted in a series of pools that vary in temperature, perfect for relaxing after a long hike or a day of skiing. Surrounded by towering peaks and lush forests, the springs provide a serene escape, blending harmoniously with nature. Local flora, including fragrant wildflowers and resilient evergreens, flourishes in this alpine environment, while fauna like deer and various bird species often grace the area, making it a delight for nature lovers.

As settlers began to arrive in the mid-1800s, the hot springs quickly gained a reputation for their healing properties. Prospectors and miners, weary from their labors, would often seek refuge in the warm waters, believing that they could soothe both their aching muscles and their souls. Stories of miraculous recoveries and newfound energy began to circulate, transforming Mount Princeton into a healing haven. However, this growth also came with challenges. The rush of newcomers led to increased environmental pressures, as the delicate ecosystem surrounding the springs was altered to accommodate the demands of tourism and industry.

One particularly memorable event in the history of Mount Princeton Hot Springs occurred in 1860 when a massive flood swept through the area. Heavy rainfall combined with snowmelt caused the Arkansas River to overflow its banks, inundating nearby mining camps and the fledgling settlement of Buena Vista. While the hot springs remained intact, the flood served as a reminder of nature's power and the need for sustainable development in the face of progress. It also sparked a renewed appreciation for the tranquil waters, as many sought solace at the springs during the recovery efforts.

Local legends abound about the springs, including tales of a mystical creature said to inhabit the waters—a benevolent spirit who ensures the continued flow of the healing springs.

Visitors who take the time to listen often claim to hear whispers in the wind or feel a warm embrace when they immerse themselves in the hot springs. These stories enrich the experience for those who come to enjoy the therapeutic benefits, adding an air of magic and connection to the land.

The Ute people, the original inhabitants of the area, have a profound relationship with Mount Princeton Hot Springs. They viewed the springs as sacred, a gift from the Earth that provided not just physical healing but also spiritual renewal. Their respect for the land influenced their lifestyle, with traditional practices that honored nature's resources. The Utes would often gather near the hot springs for ceremonial purposes, celebrating the land's bounty and sharing stories that have been passed down through generations.

With the influx of settlers and miners, the landscape began to shift. However, this period also saw the birth of community. The hot springs served as a meeting point where people from diverse backgrounds would come together, share stories, and create lasting friendships. Mount Princeton became a hub for social gatherings, where laughter and camaraderie echoed off the surrounding mountains, providing a sense of belonging in a rapidly changing world.

As the decades rolled on, Mount Princeton Hot Springs evolved into a full-fledged resort destination, welcoming families eager to reconnect with nature and each other. Cabins were built, and amenities expanded, transforming the area into a popular retreat. The warm waters became a focal point for relaxation and recreation, with visitors enjoying not only the soothing baths but also hiking, fishing, and exploring the stunning wilderness that surrounds the springs. The spirit of community continued to flourish, as families returned year after year to create new memories.

While the resort has thrived, it has not been without its challenges. Invasive species, such as certain fish and plant varieties, have threatened the delicate balance of the local ecosystem. Recognizing the importance of preserving this unique environment, conservation efforts have been initiated to protect both the flora and fauna of the area. Community members, alongside environmental organizations, have worked tirelessly to monitor and manage the effects of human activity on the springs, ensuring that future generations can enjoy the beauty and benefits of Mount Princeton.

Today, visitors to Mount Princeton Hot Springs find themselves surrounded by the splendor of nature and the echoes of history. The hot springs continue to offer a peaceful retreat, where laughter and relaxation blend seamlessly with the beauty of the landscape. Whether it's families playing in the pools, couples enjoying a quiet moment together, or solo travelers finding peace in solitude, the springs hold a special place in the hearts of many.

The annual "Hot Springs Festival" has become a cherished tradition, celebrating the community spirit and natural beauty of the area. Local artisans showcase their crafts, while food vendors offer delicious fare, creating a lively atmosphere that draws people from all over Colorado. As the sun sets behind the mountains, families gather around bonfires, sharing stories and laughter under a starlit sky, reaffirming the bonds that have been formed at this magical place.

In a world that often feels disconnected, Mount Princeton Hot Springs remains a sanctuary—a reminder of the importance of community, nature, and the simple joys of life. The laughter of children, the warmth of the waters, and the beauty of the mountains create an experience that resonates deep within the soul. With each visit, the hot springs invite all who come to embrace the moment, celebrate the past, and look forward to the future, making it a true treasure in the heart of Colorado.

Lake Alva

Lake Alva, located in Colorado's Gunnison County, is a charming destination that captures the essence of the Rocky Mountains. Named after Alva Adams, a prominent figure in Colorado's political history and a two-time governor, the lake's name pays tribute to a man who played a significant role in shaping the state during the late 19th and early 20th centuries. While the lake may not boast a tumultuous history, its calm waters and breathtaking scenery have made it a beloved spot for both locals and visitors alike.

This serene body of water is a natural lake formed by glacial activity thousands of years ago. The surrounding landscape is a canvas painted with coniferous forests, wildflowers, and dramatic mountain peaks. Initial flora includes aspens, pines, and a variety of colorful alpine plants, creating a vibrant habitat for the diverse wildlife that calls the area home. Deer, elk, and a myriad of bird species thrive in this rich ecosystem, offering nature enthusiasts ample opportunities for observation and photography.

For generations, the Ute tribes inhabited this land, drawing upon its resources for sustenance and spiritual connection. The Utes revered the natural beauty of the area, believing the mountains and lakes were imbued with sacred energy. The lake served not just as a source of food and water but also as a gathering place for community events and rituals.

These traditions established a deep bond between the indigenous people and the land, a relationship that remains an integral part of the region's identity.

As settlers arrived in the late 1800s, the landscape began to change. The influx of miners, ranchers, and other adventurers led to the establishment of communities that embraced the region's natural resources. Lake Alva became a vital part of this development, serving as a source of irrigation for nearby farms and a popular fishing spot for locals. The lake's calm waters teemed with fish, and families often spent weekends casting lines and sharing laughter, creating memories that would last a lifetime.

While the lake's history is not marked by disasters, it has seen its fair share of challenges. One particularly significant event occurred in the early 20th century when a severe drought struck the region, impacting water levels in Lake Alva and threatening the livelihoods of those who relied on it for irrigation. This led to innovative conservation efforts, with local farmers and ranchers collaborating to find sustainable solutions. Their resilience not only helped restore the lake's health but also fostered a sense of community that persists to this day.

Legends and folklore surrounding Lake Alva abound, enriching the experience for those who visit. One popular tale speaks of a mysterious creature said to inhabit the depths of the lake—a playful spirit that occasionally reveals itself to those who venture near the water's edge. Fishermen share stories of inexplicable catches or unusual encounters that leave them pondering the lake's secrets long after they've gone home. These narratives add a sense of magic to the location, inviting visitors to embrace the unknown while enjoying their time in this natural paradise.

In the latter half of the 20th century, Lake Alva underwent a transformation. The establishment of parks and recreational facilities encouraged outdoor activities, making the lake a hub for summer fun. Families flocked to the area for picnics, swimming, and kayaking, while hikers took to the trails that wind through the surrounding mountains. The park's development not only provided a space for relaxation and recreation but also reinforced a strong sense of community as residents came together to celebrate local events and festivals.

Human impact on the lake, however, is a double-edged sword. While increased tourism and recreational activities have boosted the local economy, they have also introduced challenges. Invasive species, such as certain plant and fish varieties, have found their way into Lake Alva, threatening the delicate balance of the ecosystem. Local conservation groups have mobilized efforts to monitor and manage these species, employing strategies that emphasize education and community involvement. Initiatives like "Clean-Up Days" bring together residents and visitors, all eager to protect the beauty of Lake Alva and its surrounding landscape.

Today, Lake Alva stands as a testament to the harmonious relationship between nature and community. The lake's waters continue to glisten under the Colorado sun, drawing people for swimming, fishing, and simply soaking in the stunning views. Families come to create new traditions, just as their ancestors did, while laughter and joy fill the air.

The annual "Lake Alva Celebration" has become a highlight of the community calendar, where local artisans showcase their crafts and families gather for games, food, and live music. As the sun sets behind the mountains, the flickering lights of bonfires illuminate smiling faces, and stories are exchanged under a blanket of stars. It's a reminder that while the landscape may change, the spirit of the community remains strong.

In a world that often feels disconnected, Lake Alva offers a refuge—a place where the natural beauty of the surroundings inspires connection, reflection, and joy. Whether it's a quiet moment spent by the shore or an adventurous day exploring the trails, every visit to this enchanting lake invites all who come to celebrate life and the wonders of nature. The memories made here echo through generations, reminding us of the simple joys found in laughter, love, and the beauty of the great outdoors.

Grizzly Lake

Clear Lake, located in Colorado's Gilpin County, is a stunning natural oasis that offers visitors a blend of breathtaking scenery and rich history. The name "Clear Lake" aptly reflects the lake's pristine waters, which sparkle under the sun like a thousand tiny diamonds. The lake was formed during the last Ice Age, thanks to the retreat of glaciers that carved out this picturesque basin. As nature intended, it has remained a natural wonder, untouched by human hands in terms of artificial modifications.

The area around Clear Lake has been home to various indigenous tribes, primarily the Ute people, for thousands of years. They recognized the lake not just as a vital water source but as a sacred space, integral to their spiritual beliefs and cultural practices. The Utes thrived on the abundant flora and fauna surrounding the lake, from the towering pine trees to the diverse wildlife. They would often gather at the lake for ceremonies and to share stories, fostering a deep connection to the land that continues to resonate today.

With the arrival of European settlers in the mid-1800s, the landscape began to transform. Miners seeking gold rushed into the area, leading to a series of small communities popping up along the nearby rivers and creeks. Although Clear Lake itself wasn't a gold mine, it became a key resource for the burgeoning towns. Settlers utilized the lake for fishing and as a water supply, while its picturesque beauty attracted visitors seeking respite from the rigors of frontier life. Families would travel for miles to spend weekends by the lake, sharing laughter and making memories that would last for generations.

In 1936, a devastating flood swept through the region, forever altering the course of Clear Lake's history. Heavy rains combined with snowmelt caused the nearby rivers to swell, and the lake overflowed its banks, leading to significant damage to the surrounding infrastructure. Yet, amid the destruction, the community rallied together, showcasing their resilience and unity. It was during the rebuilding process that a greater appreciation for Clear Lake emerged. Local leaders began to recognize the importance of protecting this beautiful natural resource, leading to the establishment of conservation efforts that aimed to preserve the area for future generations.

Legends surrounding Clear Lake abound, adding a layer of intrigue to its serene beauty. One popular tale tells of a mysterious creature said to inhabit the depths of the lake—often described as a playful spirit that appears during full moons. Those who claim to have seen it speak of shimmering lights dancing across the water's surface, sparking imaginations and encouraging visitors to keep an eye out for the lake's elusive resident. This story, while whimsical, has only served to enhance the lake's charm, drawing in adventurous souls eager to experience the magic for themselves.

As the years rolled on, Clear Lake evolved into a hub for recreation. The 1960s marked a significant turning point when the area was developed into a state park, attracting outdoor enthusiasts from all over. With the establishment of campgrounds, picnic areas, and hiking trails, families flocked to the lake for summer getaways. Canoeing and kayaking became popular activities, allowing visitors to glide across the water while soaking in the surrounding mountain vistas.

Yet, this newfound popularity brought challenges. The increase in human activity led to concerns about the impact on the lake's delicate ecosystem. Invasive species, including certain fish and aquatic plants, began to encroach upon the native species, disrupting the natural balance. Local conservationists sprang into action, organizing volunteer events to remove invasive plants and educate the public about responsible recreational practices. The community came together, fostering a spirit of stewardship that continues to thrive today.

As Clear Lake became more developed, it also served as a backdrop for community events and gatherings. The annual Clear Lake Festival, featuring local artisans, food vendors, and live music, has become a cherished tradition. This celebration highlights the importance of preserving the natural beauty of the lake while promoting community bonds.

It's an opportunity for families to come together, share stories, and enjoy the simple pleasures of life amidst nature.

In recent years, conservation efforts have focused on maintaining the lake's health while enhancing recreational opportunities. Wildlife watchers and photographers find joy in the vibrant habitats surrounding the lake, where bald eagles soar above and elk graze in the meadows. Educational programs have been established to engage visitors of all ages, teaching them about the unique ecology of the area and the importance of preserving it.

Clear Lake stands as a testament to the resilience of nature and the strength of community. Its waters continue to beckon adventurers, while its legends inspire awe. Whether you're casting a line for trout, hiking the scenic trails, or simply soaking in the beauty of a sunset over the lake, Clear Lake offers a refuge from the hustle and bustle of everyday life.

As families gather for picnics on the shores, laughter and joy fill the air. Children skip stones while adults reminisce about the history of the lake, sharing stories that echo through the years. Each visit adds a new chapter to the lake's story, reinforcing the connection between people and nature.

Ultimately, Clear Lake is more than just a body of water; it's a living testament to the power of community, resilience, and the unbreakable bond between humanity and the natural world. In a world that often feels chaotic, Clear Lake offers a sense of peace and belonging, reminding us all of the beauty that surrounds us and the joy that can be found in the simplest of moments.

Silver Lake

Silver Lake, cradled in the heart of Colorado's Rocky Mountains, is a stunning expanse of water that sparkles like a silver dollar under the bright sun. Located in Boulder County, just a short drive from the bustling city of Boulder, this picturesque lake has captivated the hearts of locals and tourists alike. The lake's name reflects not only its brilliant waters but also the shimmering beauty of the surrounding landscape, often draped in a blanket of wildflowers that bloom vibrantly in the summer.

The origins of Silver Lake trace back to the last Ice Age when glaciers carved out this stunning basin, creating a natural wonder that would later become a vital resource for both nature and humanity. It's an entirely natural lake, fed by the waters from the surrounding mountains, which provides a refreshing retreat for those looking to escape the heat during Colorado's warm summer months.

Before the arrival of European settlers, the area was home to the Ute people, who revered the land and its resources. They recognized the importance of Silver Lake as a water source and a fertile fishing ground. The Utes lived in harmony with the environment, utilizing the lake's bounty while preserving its beauty for generations to come. Their rich cultural traditions included stories of the spirits that inhabited the waters, believed to protect the land and its inhabitants. These legends added a layer of mystique to the lake, making it a place of spiritual significance as well as a source of sustenance.

With the mid-1800s gold rush, the landscape around Silver Lake began to change dramatically. Prospectors flooded into the region, hoping to strike it rich in the nearby mountains. While Silver Lake itself wasn't a gold mine, the nearby areas saw a surge in development. Small towns sprang up to support the miners, and the lake quickly became a social hub for those seeking recreation after a long week of labor. It was common to see families picnicking by the shores, laughter mingling with the sounds of splashing water as children fished for trout or tried to skip stones across the lake's surface.

In 1920, Silver Lake experienced a significant flood that dramatically reshaped the surrounding area. Heavy rains, combined with the rapid thaw of winter snow, caused water levels to rise dangerously high. While the flood resulted in property damage, it also revealed the resilience of the community. Residents came together to support one another, rebuilding homes and repairing the damage. In the aftermath, the local government recognized the need to protect the lake's watershed, leading to the establishment of conservation efforts that aimed to preserve the delicate ecosystem.

As time passed, Silver Lake transitioned from a mining hub to a recreational paradise. The 1960s saw an increase in outdoor enthusiasts who flocked to the area for hiking, fishing, and camping. Trails winding around the lake offered breathtaking views of the surrounding mountains, and the crystal-clear waters became a favorite spot for fishing aficionados. It was during this time that local organizations began advocating for the lake's protection, ensuring that its beauty would be preserved for future generations.

Despite its idyllic setting, Silver Lake faced challenges from invasive species that threatened its ecological balance. Non-native plants and fish began to infiltrate the lake, disrupting the delicate ecosystem that had thrived for centuries. Local conservationists rallied to combat these invasive species, organizing cleanup days and educational programs to inform the public about the importance of maintaining the lake's health. Their dedication has resulted in ongoing efforts to restore the lake's natural habitats, which has been crucial in supporting native wildlife.

Myths surrounding Silver Lake continue to entice visitors. Locals often share stories of a "lake monster," affectionately dubbed "Silver Shadow," said to inhabit the depths of the water. Tales describe how on certain moonlit nights, shimmering shapes can be seen just beneath the surface, sparking the imaginations of those gathered around campfires. These legends have only added to the lake's allure, drawing in thrill-seekers and families eager to experience the magic for themselves.

Today, Silver Lake thrives as a community destination. The surrounding area has been developed into a state park, providing ample opportunities for outdoor activities. Trails have been meticulously maintained, and picnic areas are plentiful, inviting families to gather and create lasting memories. The annual Silver Lake Festival brings together locals and tourists to celebrate the lake's natural beauty with music, food, and activities, reinforcing the sense of community that has flourished around the lake.

For wildlife enthusiasts, Silver Lake is a haven. Birdwatchers often find themselves enchanted by the sight of bald eagles soaring overhead or the sounds of migratory birds nesting along the shore. The surrounding forests provide a habitat for deer, foxes, and other wildlife, making it a perfect spot for nature lovers to explore. The commitment to conservation has ensured that the natural beauty of the lake remains intact, creating an environment where both humans and wildlife can coexist harmoniously.

Each visit to Silver Lake is an opportunity for connection—between people, nature, and history. Families gather for summer picnics, children learn to fish, and friends embark on hiking adventures, all while sharing stories and laughter against the backdrop of stunning mountain vistas. As the sun sets over the lake, casting a golden glow across the water, it's easy to see why Silver Lake holds a special place in the hearts of those who visit.

Ultimately, Silver Lake is more than just a body of water; it is a living testament to the power of community, resilience, and the bond between humanity and nature. In a world that often feels chaotic, this serene lake offers a sanctuary for all who seek solace in its beauty. It serves as a reminder that through connection and conservation, we can protect the wonders of our natural world for generations to come.

Crystal Lake

Crystal Lake, a stunning body of water located in the heart of Colorado's Routt National Forest, is renowned for its pristine clarity and breathtaking scenery. Just a stone's throw from the charming town of Steamboat Springs, this picturesque lake has earned its name not just from its crystalline waters, but also from the way the sunlight dances across its surface, creating a shimmering effect that leaves visitors in awe.

The origins of Crystal Lake date back to the last Ice Age when glaciers carved out this enchanting basin. Formed naturally, it's surrounded by towering peaks and lush forests, providing a haven for local wildlife and a serene escape for nature lovers. The lake itself serves as an important water source for the region, sustaining the flora and fauna that call this area home.

Before the arrival of settlers, the Ute people inhabited these lands, living in harmony with the natural environment. They utilized the resources of the land, including the fish and game surrounding Crystal Lake, creating a deep connection to the area that resonates to this day. The Ute believed that the lake was a sacred space, a place of healing and reflection. Stories were passed down through generations, including tales of the spirits that resided in the waters, believed to bring good fortune and protection to those who approached with respect.

As settlers moved into the region during the mid-1800s, drawn by the promise of gold and new beginnings, the landscape around Crystal Lake began to change dramatically. The lake itself became a vital resource for the burgeoning community. Families would gather by its shores to fish and picnic, using the lake as a backdrop for their everyday lives. The settlers quickly recognized the beauty of the area, transforming it from a land of survival to a place of recreation.

In the late 1800s, Crystal Lake became a popular destination for those seeking respite from the hustle and bustle of city life. With the establishment of a nearby logging industry, the area around the lake began to flourish. Logs floated down from the mountains, often stopping at the lake to rest before being transported downstream. It wasn't long before the lake attracted tourists, who would come to fish, hike, and enjoy the stunning surroundings. They marveled at the reflections of the mountains on the water, snapping photos that would later be shared back home, spreading the word about this hidden treasure in the Colorado wilderness.

Despite its idyllic charm, Crystal Lake has seen its share of natural disasters. In the 1980s, heavy rains led to significant flooding that impacted the area surrounding the lake. The waters rose dangerously high, causing damage to nearby roads and trails. Yet, much like the community that surrounds it, Crystal Lake proved resilient. Local residents banded together to repair the damage, and conservation efforts were initiated to protect the lake's watershed, ensuring that such devastation would be less likely in the future.

Myths and legends have grown around Crystal Lake over the years. Many locals share stories of a mysterious creature said to inhabit the depths of the lake. Known affectionately as "Crystal," this creature is often described as a gentle giant, making appearances during full moons to frolic in the moonlit waters. While many chuckle at these tales, they serve to create a sense of wonder and intrigue that draws visitors to the lake, eager to catch a glimpse of the fabled beast.

With the increased popularity of Crystal Lake, the surrounding landscape has been developed to support the influx of visitors. Hiking trails have been established, winding through the forests and leading to stunning viewpoints that overlook the lake. Campgrounds have popped up, providing families with a place to stay while they explore the natural beauty of the area. The annual Crystal Lake Festival has become a beloved tradition, celebrating the lake with music, food, and outdoor activities that unite the community and visitors alike.

The ecological balance of Crystal Lake has not been without challenges. Invasive species have made their way into the waters, threatening the delicate ecosystem that has thrived for centuries. Local conservation groups have worked diligently to combat these intruders, organizing cleanup days and educational programs to raise awareness about the importance of protecting the lake's health. Their efforts have been met with success, as more and more residents have taken it upon themselves to participate in the preservation of this natural treasure.

One of the most beloved aspects of Crystal Lake is its ability to foster community spirit. Whether it's a family fishing expedition, a group of friends hiking along the trails, or neighbors gathering for a summer barbecue by the lake, it serves as a hub for connection. People come together to share stories, laughter, and sometimes even the occasional ghost story about Crystal lurking beneath the water's surface.

As the sun sets over the lake, painting the sky in hues of orange and pink, visitors find themselves transfixed by the serene beauty that surrounds them. The reflections in the water create a picture-perfect scene that feels almost magical. It's moments like these that remind us of the importance of preserving such natural wonders. Crystal Lake is more than just a pretty spot on a map; it's a testament to the enduring spirit of community, the power of nature, and the legends that enrich our lives.

In every ripple and wave, there lies a history that connects people to the land, a history marked by joy, resilience, and a shared commitment to protect the beauty of Crystal Lake for future generations. It's a place where laughter echoes off the mountains, where friendships are forged around campfires, and where the spirit of adventure thrives. Crystal Lake is not just a destination; it's an experience, a celebration of life, and an everlasting reminder of the magic that can be found in nature.

Guanella Pass Lakes

Guanella Pass Lakes, a breathtaking duo of shimmering bodies of water, resides in the Rocky Mountains of Colorado, just a few miles from the historic town of Georgetown in Clear Creek County. Named after the Guanella Pass itself, which was named for the man who played a significant role in its development, this area is rich in history, beauty, and the kind of magic that seems to spring from the very rocks and trees.

The lakes, Upper and Lower Guanella, were formed through a combination of glacial activity and the slow, deliberate carving of the landscape over thousands of years. As the glaciers retreated, they left behind depressions that filled with snowmelt and rainwater, resulting in the sparkling lakes we see today. These natural wonders are not man-made, but rather products of nature's artistry, surrounded by towering peaks and lush forests.

The name "Guanella" comes from the pass that leads travelers to this scenic spot. It was named after George Guanella, a key figure in the construction of the Georgetown to Leadville Railroad in the late 1800s. His efforts in connecting communities not only facilitated trade but also opened the door to tourism, allowing visitors to experience the stunning landscapes and recreational opportunities that Guanella Pass Lakes offer.

Before the arrival of settlers, the area was inhabited by the Ute people, who revered the land and its resources. They fished in the lakes, hunted game in the surrounding forests, and gathered plants that grew abundantly. The Utes believed that the lakes were places of healing, where the spirits of nature would guide and protect those who showed respect. Local legends tell of shimmering beings seen flitting across the surface of the water during the full moon, enchanting those who dared to gaze upon them.

With the influx of settlers in the late 1800s, the landscape began to change. The lakes became essential resources for the burgeoning communities around them. Miners and loggers relied on the clean water for their camps and operations, while families used the lakes for fishing and recreation. This burgeoning relationship with the lakes led to the establishment of trails and campsites, encouraging a spirit of community and connection to the natural world.

However, this period of growth wasn't without its challenges. In the 1930s, a series of heavy storms led to significant flooding in the region. The banks of Lower Guanella Lake overflowed, causing damage to roads and infrastructure. The local community rallied together, working tirelessly to repair the damages and restore access to the beloved lakes. This resilience reflected the deep-rooted bond that the residents had with the land, as they understood the importance of protecting their natural treasures.

As the decades passed, the lakes continued to draw visitors, becoming a popular destination for hiking, fishing, and camping. The lush surroundings were a paradise for outdoor enthusiasts, and the peaceful ambiance provided a much-needed escape from the busyness of life. Families would gather for picnics along the shores, while adventurers would set out on trails that wound through the forests and led to stunning vistas.

Despite the influx of visitors, the lakes managed to retain their charm and natural beauty. However, the introduction of invasive species began to pose a threat. Species such as the Eurasian watermilfoil found their way into the waters, threatening the delicate balance of the ecosystem. Local conservation groups mobilized, organizing clean-up efforts and educational programs to raise awareness about the importance of preserving the lakes' natural habitats. They worked closely with state parks and wildlife agencies to monitor the lakes and implement measures to mitigate the impacts of invasive species.

In recent years, Guanella Pass Lakes has seen the development of additional recreational facilities. Improved trails, camping areas, and fishing spots have been established, ensuring that the lakes remain accessible for future generations. The area also hosts events such as guided nature walks, where locals and visitors can learn about the ecology of the lakes and the history of the Ute people who once roamed these lands. These programs not only promote environmental awareness but also foster a sense of community and shared stewardship.

The surrounding landscape has changed as well, with a renewed focus on sustainable practices. Efforts to restore native flora and fauna have gained momentum, resulting in a vibrant ecosystem that supports a variety of wildlife. Birdwatchers flock to the area to catch glimpses of the migratory species that stop by the lakes, while anglers enjoy the thrill of casting their lines in search of brook trout and rainbow trout.

As the sun sets over Guanella Pass Lakes, casting a warm golden glow on the water's surface, visitors often find themselves reflecting on the beauty and serenity that this place offers. The laughter of children playing, the soft rustle of leaves in the breeze, and the distant calls of birds create a symphony of nature that brings a sense of peace to all who visit.

Crystal-clear waters mirror the towering peaks above, reminding everyone of the connection between the land and the people who cherish it. It's a place where legends come alive, where stories of the past intermingle with the present, and where the spirit of the community shines brightly.

In every ripple of the water, in every rustle of the trees, there exists a reminder of the resilience and beauty of this landscape. Guanella Pass Lakes is not just a destination; it is a living testament to the harmony between nature and humanity, a cherished treasure in Colorado's vast wilderness. Each visitor leaves with a piece of its magic in their hearts, knowing that they are part of a story that will continue to unfold for generations to come.

Fossil Creek Reservoir

Fossil Creek Reservoir, located in the foothills of the Rocky Mountains in Larimer County, Colorado, has a rich history that's as captivating as the landscape surrounding it. This beautiful reservoir is not just a spot for fishing and picnicking; it's a place steeped in stories and character, named for the fossils that have been discovered in the area, hinting at a time when dinosaurs roamed this very land.

The name "Fossil Creek" hints at the geological wonders beneath the surface. While the reservoir itself is man-made, completed in 1997 to provide water for agricultural and municipal use, the surrounding area has been a significant site for paleontological discoveries. When settlers first arrived, they stumbled upon remnants of ancient life—fossils that included everything from marine creatures to dinosaurs. This discovery ignited the imaginations of many and added a layer of intrigue to the lake's identity.

The history of Fossil Creek Reservoir is intertwined with the Ute tribes who inhabited this region long before European settlers arrived. The Utes lived in harmony with the land, relying on its resources for fishing, hunting, and gathering. They respected the natural world, often holding ceremonies to honor the spirits of the land and water. Legends passed down through generations tell of great spirits residing in the nearby mountains, watching over the lakes and rivers, and guiding the tribes in their daily lives.

As settlers moved in during the 19th century, the landscape began to change dramatically. The gold rush attracted a flood of hopeful prospectors, and the area saw an influx of people eager to claim their fortunes. As towns grew, so did the need for water, leading to the construction of Fossil Creek Reservoir. The reservoir quickly became a vital resource for irrigation and recreation, allowing the surrounding communities to thrive.

The initial construction of the reservoir wasn't without its challenges. Heavy rains and unpredictable weather led to delays and difficulties, with construction crews often working through mud and inclement conditions. The locals rallied together, sharing their own stories of resilience, and encouraging the workers to push through. When the reservoir was finally completed, there was a collective sigh of relief, as well as celebration—local families gathered for a grand opening, complete with barbecues and fireworks lighting up the sky.

Over the years, Fossil Creek Reservoir has become a beloved spot for outdoor enthusiasts. Families flock to the shores to fish for trout and catfish, while hikers and birdwatchers explore the surrounding trails. The beauty of the landscape is stunning, with sweeping views of the mountains framing the calm waters. On weekends, laughter and cheer fill the air as children run along the banks, chasing after butterflies and skipping stones.

But with growth came challenges. Invasive species began to threaten the delicate balance of the ecosystem. Species like zebra mussels and Eurasian watermilfoil made their way into the reservoir, causing concerns among conservationists. Local organizations stepped up, initiating programs to educate the community about responsible boating and fishing practices. They organized clean-up events and monitoring efforts, working tirelessly to preserve the natural beauty of Fossil Creek.

In addition to conservation efforts, the area around Fossil Creek Reservoir has seen developments that enhance the community's connection to the water. Parks and picnic areas have been established, providing spaces for families to gather and enjoy the great outdoors. Interpretive signs along the trails educate visitors about the flora and fauna of the region, as well as the rich history of the Ute tribes and the settlers who came after them.

Fishing derbies, community gatherings, and seasonal events keep the spirit of the reservoir alive, bringing together locals and visitors alike. Children's laughter echoes through the air during summer festivals, while cozy fall evenings see families gathered around campfires, sharing stories and marshmallows. The sense of community that surrounds

Fossil Creek Reservoir is palpable, as neighbors come together to celebrate their shared love for the outdoors.

As dusk falls, the sun casts a golden hue across the water, creating a scene that feels almost magical. The calm surface reflects the sky's vibrant colors, and families pause to take in the beauty around them. For many, it's a moment of gratitude—a reminder of the joys of nature and the connections forged by the shared experience of exploring this special place.

Fossil Creek Reservoir has also played a significant role in education and recreation. Schools take field trips to the area, allowing students to engage with the environment and learn about local ecosystems. Programs that focus on fishing, wildlife observation, and environmental stewardship have become staples in the community. These initiatives foster a sense of responsibility among the younger generation, instilling a love for the land that will hopefully last a lifetime.

In recent years, as climate change and environmental concerns have taken center stage, efforts to protect Fossil Creek Reservoir have only intensified. The community has come together, advocating for sustainable practices and the importance of maintaining the reservoir's health. Initiatives aimed at improving water quality and restoring native vegetation have gained traction, drawing in volunteers eager to make a difference.

Through it all, Fossil Creek Reservoir remains a testament to the power of community and the resilience of nature. The stories of the land, the people, and the water intertwine, creating a tapestry of history that is both uplifting and inspiring. Each visit to the reservoir offers a new adventure, a new memory waiting to be made, and a reminder of the importance of protecting the precious resources we have.

As night falls, the stars begin to twinkle overhead, and the gentle lapping of water against the shore provides a soothing soundtrack. Whether it's fishing at dawn, picnicking at noon, or stargazing in the evening, Fossil Creek Reservoir continues to be a beloved haven for all who seek solace and joy in the great outdoors. Each ripple of the water tells a story—a story of history, community, and the everlasting connection between people and the land.

Lake Clara

Lake Clara, a sparkling body of water located in the heart of Colorado's Rocky Mountain National Park, is a place that encapsulates both beauty and history. Named after Clara Smith, the beloved daughter of one of the early settlers in the area, the lake has become a cherished destination for those seeking adventure and serenity in nature. Clara's family arrived in the late 1800s, and the lake was named in her honor after she frequently explored its shores, often daydreaming about what lay beneath the surface.

Situated in Larimer County, Lake Clara is surrounded by breathtaking mountain vistas and dense forests of pine and aspen. Its formation is a tale of natural artistry. The lake was carved by glaciers thousands of years ago, creating a stunning alpine setting that draws visitors from near and far. Unlike many of Colorado's man-made reservoirs, Lake Clara's clear waters and pristine shoreline showcase the area's geological history and provide a glimpse into the ancient forces that shaped this land.

Before settlers arrived, the area around Lake Clara was inhabited by the Ute tribes, who held a deep reverence for the land and water. They believed the lake was a portal to the spirit world, often visiting to pay homage to the natural beauty surrounding them. Stories circulated among the tribe of a benevolent water spirit that guarded the lake, ensuring its purity and abundance. These legends connected the people to the land, creating a profound respect for its resources and beauty.

As European settlers began to move into the area in the mid-19th century, they brought with them a different relationship with nature. They transformed the landscape for agriculture and settlement, but also sought to preserve its beauty. The early settlers were drawn to Lake Clara's stunning vistas and abundant wildlife. The lake became a popular fishing spot, and tales of anglers catching hefty trout were shared around campfires, bonding families and friends over their love of the outdoors.

Lake Clara saw its fair share of natural disasters, most notably the floods of 1982 that dramatically reshaped parts of the surrounding landscape. A sudden and intense storm caused the lake to swell, overflowing its banks and altering the nearby trails. Local residents and park rangers banded together to clean up the aftermath, showcasing the resilience of the community and their love for the land. This disaster led to a greater focus on conservation efforts, as park authorities sought to protect the lake's natural beauty from future flooding.

Over the years, the lake has transformed into a hub of recreation. Families flock to its shores for picnics, while hikers explore the nearby trails, eager to take in the stunning views and the rich diversity of flora and fauna. The landscape is alive with the sounds of nature—chirping birds, rustling leaves, and the gentle lapping of water against the shore. In spring, wildflowers blanket the area, creating a vibrant tapestry of color that draws photographers and nature enthusiasts alike.

However, with increased popularity came challenges. Invasive species began to infiltrate the lake's ecosystem, posing a threat to its delicate balance. Species like the Eurasian watermilfoil began to spread, and local conservation groups mobilized to tackle the issue. Education campaigns were launched to inform visitors about responsible practices, encouraging them to clean their boats and gear before entering the water.

The community's commitment to conservation has been remarkable. Volunteer days were organized to remove invasive plants and restore native habitats. The Lake Clara Conservation Society formed, bringing together passionate individuals dedicated to preserving the lake's natural beauty for generations to come. These efforts not only protect the ecosystem but also foster a deeper connection between visitors and the land.

Today, Lake Clara stands as a testament to the power of community and the enduring connection between people and nature. New developments around the lake include interpretive trails that highlight the area's history and ecology. Signs educate visitors about the indigenous tribes that once inhabited the land and the importance of respecting the natural environment. Seasonal events, such as guided nature walks and fishing derbies, bring the community together, celebrating the joy of the outdoors.

As summer fades into autumn, the lake transforms into a canvas of warm colors, with golden aspens reflecting on its surface. Families return to their favorite spots, some with generations of memories tied to the water. Campfires crackle as stories are shared, laughter echoing into the crisp evening air. It's in these moments that the legacy of Lake Clara is truly felt—a space where the past and present come together, nurturing a love for nature that transcends time.

As the first snows of winter blanket the landscape, Lake Clara takes on a serene stillness. The icy surface creates a magical setting for winter sports enthusiasts, who come to ice fish and skate on the frozen lake. The area becomes a winter wonderland, attracting adventurers eager to explore the snowy trails and enjoy the peaceful solitude that the cold months bring.

Through the changing seasons, Lake Clara remains a constant—a place of inspiration, reflection, and connection. The stories of Clara Smith and the Ute tribes linger in the air, woven into the fabric of the landscape. It's a reminder that while the world evolves, the essence of nature continues to bind us together, enriching our lives and igniting our imaginations.

The lake invites all who visit to immerse themselves in its beauty, to forge new memories, and to carry forth the legacy of stewardship and love for the natural world. In the heart of

Colorado, Lake Clara is not just a destination; it is a vibrant chapter in the story of the land and its people, a place where history, community, and nature intertwine beautifully.

Lake Fork

Lake Fork, a stunning alpine lake in Colorado, offers a glimpse into both the natural beauty and rich history of the area. Tucked away in the San Juan Mountains of Hinsdale County, the lake draws its name from the nearby Lake Fork River, which meanders through the stunning landscape, providing both life and livelihood to those who call this place home. It's said that early settlers, observing the river's splits and turns, were inspired to name the lake after its winding counterpart, capturing the spirit of the land.

The history of Lake Fork is not without its drama. In the late 1800s, the region was a hub for mining, as eager prospectors flocked to the area in search of gold and silver. The lake became a gathering point for those hoping to strike it rich, with stories of fortune and misfortune echoing through the surrounding hills. Legends arose about the shimmering waters concealing hidden treasures, leading to the creation of local myths that were passed down through generations. Children grew up listening to tales of ghostly miners who would appear on misty nights, hoping to share their secrets with the living.

The lake's beauty can be deceiving, and its tranquility was often interrupted by natural disasters. In 1975, a significant flood struck the region, causing the Lake Fork River to overflow its banks. The rushing waters changed the landscape dramatically, eroding the banks and reshaping the surrounding terrain. The community came together, working hand in hand to restore the damage, showing a remarkable resilience that highlighted their deep connection to the land. This disaster ultimately fostered a sense of stewardship among the locals, leading to an increased emphasis on conservation.

The area surrounding Lake Fork is a vibrant ecosystem filled with diverse flora and fauna. Initially, the region was dominated by lush coniferous forests, with towering ponderosa pines and quaking aspens lining the shores of the lake. Wildflowers painted the landscape in brilliant hues during spring, attracting butterflies and bees, while the clear waters provided habitat for trout and other aquatic life. It was a paradise for wildlife, where elk and deer roamed freely, and the air was filled with the sounds of birdsong.

Before the arrival of settlers, the land was inhabited by the Ute tribes, who viewed Lake Fork as sacred. They believed the lake was a source of spiritual healing, and it played an essential role in their seasonal migrations. Fishing was a vital part of their culture, with the lake providing sustenance for families. The Ute people had a profound respect for the environment, understanding the delicate balance that existed between their lives and the land. Their presence shaped the ecosystem long before it was altered by colonization.

As settlers arrived, the landscape began to change dramatically. While many sought to harness the land for agricultural purposes, there was also a desire to preserve its beauty. The lake soon became a popular destination for recreational activities, drawing visitors for fishing, hiking, and camping. The creation of trails allowed families to explore the area, fostering a sense of community as they gathered to enjoy the great outdoors.

Transportation and trade were vital for the local economy, with the lake serving as a natural resource for both water and fish. The surrounding areas became bustling with activity as goods were transported to and from the lake, helping to build a sense of community among residents. Local fishing tournaments became a highlight of the summer, where families and friends would compete for bragging rights and share stories around the campfire.

However, with increased human activity came challenges. Invasive species, particularly the introduction of non-native fish, began to threaten the delicate balance of the lake's ecosystem. Conservation efforts were mobilized to address these concerns, with local organizations spearheading initiatives to educate the community about responsible fishing practices and habitat preservation. Workshops were held to teach sustainable practices, encouraging residents and visitors alike to protect the lake's natural resources.

Today, Lake Fork stands as a shining example of community resilience and dedication to conservation. The creation of the Lake Fork State Park has further solidified the area's reputation as a recreational paradise. Campgrounds have been developed, offering families a place to connect with nature and each other. The park also features educational programs designed to foster a love for the environment, ensuring that future generations appreciate the beauty of Lake Fork and its surroundings.

As seasons change, the lake transforms, offering a new experience with each visit. In summer, vibrant green surrounds the sparkling waters, drawing families to picnic on its shores. Fall brings a symphony of colors as the aspens turn golden, while winter blankets the landscape in pristine snow, providing opportunities for ice fishing and cross-country skiing. Spring bursts forth with new life, as the flora awakens and wildlife returns, bringing joy to those who venture to explore.

The community continues to host events celebrating the lake's rich history, such as annual fishing derbies and nature walks that share the stories of the Ute people and the early settlers. These gatherings are filled with laughter, shared memories, and a renewed commitment to protecting the land that has given them so much. The spirit of camaraderie that has emerged from these traditions binds the community together, fostering a shared sense of purpose.

Lake Fork is more than just a beautiful body of water; it is a testament to the history, culture, and resilience of the people who have come to cherish it. The laughter of children playing along the shores, the stories of fishermen casting their lines, and the quiet moments of reflection are all woven into the tapestry of this remarkable place. As the sun sets behind the mountains, casting a warm glow on the lake's surface, it's a reminder that nature's beauty endures, echoing the joy and connection that Lake Fork continues to inspire in all who visit.

Loch Vale

Loch Vale, a serene lake tucked away in the Rocky Mountain National Park, has a rich history that intertwines nature, culture, and community. The name "Loch Vale" draws inspiration from the Scottish word "loch," meaning lake, and "vale," referring to a valley. This name evokes images of rugged highlands and tranquil waters, mirroring the breathtaking landscapes found here. Surrounded by majestic peaks, including the towering Mount Hallett and the ever-popular Longs Peak, Loch Vale is a true treasure of Colorado.

The lake's formation dates back to the last Ice Age, when glaciers sculpted the landscape, carving out this stunning valley. The remnants of these ancient glaciers can still be seen today, lending the area a dramatic beauty that feels almost timeless. The lake itself is natural, fed by snowmelt and rainwater, providing a pristine environment that supports a diverse array of wildlife.

Loch Vale's history is not just geological; it also carries tales of the indigenous Arapaho and Ute tribes who inhabited the area long before settlers arrived. These tribes revered the land for its natural bounty. They relied on the lake for fishing and as a gathering place for community activities, making it an essential resource in their seasonal migrations. The shimmering waters were often seen as a sacred place, a spiritual connection to the earth and sky. The Ute people, in particular, believed the lake was a source of healing, and their stories and traditions regarding Loch Vale reflect a deep respect for nature.

With the arrival of European settlers in the 19th century, the landscape began to change. The promise of gold and silver brought prospectors to the region, and the surrounding mountains echoed with the clatter of pickaxes and the laughter of hopeful miners. Loch Vale, despite its tranquil appearance, became part of the hustle and bustle of this mining boom. Legend has it that some miners claimed the lake's depths held secrets of lost treasure and hidden riches, prompting more than a few daring souls to brave its chilly waters in search of fortune.

But nature has a way of reminding us of its power. In the early 20th century, a heavy storm caused significant flooding in the area, resulting in the erosion of trails and the altering of Loch Vale's shoreline. This event galvanized the community into action. The local residents, alongside conservationists, recognized the need for sustainable practices to protect their beloved landscape. Efforts to restore and preserve the area flourished, laying the groundwork for what would become Rocky Mountain National Park in 1915.

The transition into national park status was a pivotal moment for Loch Vale and its surroundings. The park brought about increased visitation, inviting families to enjoy the breathtaking views and outdoor activities. Hiking trails were established, allowing access to the lake and surrounding peaks. The area became known for its stunning wildflower displays in summer, which transformed the landscape into a painter's palette of colors. Families would flock to Loch Vale, setting up picnics by the water, sharing laughter and stories, and creating memories that would last a lifetime.

Flora and fauna thrived in this protected environment. Vibrant wildflowers burst into bloom in the spring, while towering conifers stood watch over the lake, providing shelter to an array of wildlife. Visitors often spotted elk grazing in the meadows and the occasional bear wandering near the water's edge. The lake itself became a haven for fish, particularly brook trout, attracting anglers eager for a catch. The local ecosystem flourished, demonstrating the resilience of nature when given the opportunity to thrive.

However, as with many natural treasures, human impact has not been without its challenges. Invasive species, such as non-native fish, began to threaten the balance of Loch Vale's ecosystem. Conservation efforts ramped up, with park rangers and local organizations working tirelessly to educate visitors about responsible fishing and the importance of preserving the delicate environment. Programs were introduced to monitor and manage these invasive species, aiming to restore the lake's original balance and ensure its health for future generations.

Loch Vale has also become a focal point for community events, celebrating the rich history and natural beauty of the area. Local organizations host annual hikes, educational programs, and clean-up days, fostering a sense of stewardship among visitors and residents alike. These gatherings often culminate in a community potluck, where stories are shared over homemade dishes, reinforcing the connections forged through shared experiences in nature.

In winter, Loch Vale transforms into a serene wonderland, attracting snowshoers and cross-country skiers who traverse the peaceful trails. The crunch of snow underfoot is accompanied by the crisp mountain air, creating a sense of tranquility that washes over all who visit. Families return year after year, building traditions around this beloved lake, from summer camping trips to winter adventures, each visit deepening their connection to the land.

As the sun sets behind the mountains, casting a golden glow on the surface of the water, Loch Vale exudes a sense of magic. The reflections of the peaks in the lake create a picturesque scene that has inspired countless photographers and artists. The harmony of nature here evokes a feeling of peace, reminding everyone who visits that this land is more than just a destination; it is a living tapestry woven from history, culture, and the unbreakable bond between people and the earth.

Loch Vale stands as a testament to the resilience of nature and the importance of community. It encapsulates the laughter, stories, and memories of generations who have found joy in its embrace. With every visit, new tales are born, each one adding to the rich narrative of this extraordinary place. As the seasons change and the years roll on, Loch Vale will continue to thrive, a shining example of how the love for nature can unite us all in pursuit of a brighter, more harmonious future.

Naylor Reservoir

Naylor Reservoir, a vibrant body of water located in the scenic plains of northeastern Colorado, tells a story woven with history, community, and a dash of adventure. Named after the Naylor family, early settlers who made significant contributions to the local agricultural landscape, the reservoir was built to support irrigation in the region. The Naylor family, known for their hard work and determination, helped transform the dry, arid land into a flourishing agricultural hub. Their legacy is a fitting tribute to the life-giving waters of the reservoir.

Formed in the early 20th century, Naylor Reservoir is a man-made wonder created through the construction of a dam on the Cache la Poudre River. This ambitious project was designed to harness the river's waters for irrigation, benefiting the farming community in the surrounding areas. Before the reservoir's creation, the region faced challenges with water scarcity, making agricultural success a tricky endeavor. The arrival of the reservoir changed everything, allowing crops to thrive where once there was only dust and despair.

The reservoir itself is surrounded by lush vegetation, thanks to the carefully managed ecosystem that flourished as a result of its creation. The initial flora included a mix of willows and cottonwoods, which provided shade and habitat for birds and small animals. As the years went by, the area around Naylor Reservoir became home to a diverse array of wildlife, including migratory birds that flock to the waters each season. Fishermen and nature lovers alike find joy in observing the vibrant life that springs forth from this essential resource.

Before settlers arrived, the land was inhabited by various Indigenous tribes, including the Arapaho and Cheyenne. These tribes relied heavily on the natural resources of the area, using the Cache la Poudre River for fishing and gathering. The river was not just a source of sustenance; it was a crucial part of their way of life, guiding their seasonal migrations and providing a spiritual connection to the land. The arrival of European settlers brought significant changes to the landscape, but the impact was not entirely negative. The construction of the reservoir allowed for improved agricultural practices, leading to a more stable food supply and the growth of local communities.

As settlers transformed the landscape, stories began to emerge about the "mysteries" of Naylor Reservoir. Local folklore spoke of hidden treasures beneath the surface, remnants of the early settlers' belongings that had been lost during the construction of the dam. Tales of submerged homesteads and long-forgotten fishing spots captivated the imaginations of children and adults alike, leading to countless afternoons spent fishing and exploring the shores. Some even claimed that on quiet evenings, you could hear the whispers of long-gone settlers carried by the wind across the water.

With the establishment of the reservoir, recreational opportunities flourished. Families flocked to Naylor Reservoir for fishing, picnicking, and boating. The tranquil waters became a hub of activity, drawing people from the surrounding communities who sought respite from their daily routines. Each summer, the banks of the reservoir would fill with laughter and joy as children splashed in the shallows and parents grilled burgers while keeping a watchful eye on their little ones.

Fishing became a central attraction, with anglers casting lines for trout and catfish. The thrill of reeling in a big catch turned lazy afternoons into exhilarating memories. It wasn't uncommon for fishing tournaments to take place, bringing friendly competition and camaraderie among local residents. The reservoir fostered a sense of community, where neighbors became friends and traditions were born.

However, the impacts of human activity also took their toll. Invasive species, such as zebra mussels, began to infiltrate the reservoir, threatening the delicate balance of its ecosystem. These tiny but voracious mollusks multiplied rapidly, causing concerns among conservationists and local authorities. Efforts to control their spread included educational campaigns about the importance of cleaning boats and equipment before entering the reservoir. The community rallied together, recognizing the significance of preserving their cherished waters.

In response to the challenges posed by invasive species and the need for conservation, dedicated groups emerged to advocate for Naylor Reservoir. Volunteers organized clean-up days, restoring the natural habitat and promoting awareness about responsible recreation. Educational programs aimed at local schools helped instill a sense of stewardship in the next generation, ensuring that the reservoir would remain a vital resource for years to come.

As Naylor Reservoir continued to grow in popularity, facilities were developed to enhance visitor experiences. Picnic areas, walking trails, and campgrounds were established, making it easier for families to enjoy the outdoors. The reservoir became a gathering place for events, from community barbecues to outdoor movie nights, creating a sense of belonging among residents. The laughter of children echoed across the water as families made new memories in the shadow of the stunning Colorado sky.

With each passing year, Naylor Reservoir remains a symbol of resilience and community spirit. Its waters are more than just a source of irrigation; they are a gathering place, a playground, and a sanctuary for wildlife. The reservoir has witnessed generations of families coming together, forging bonds through shared experiences and laughter.

As the sun sets behind the horizon, casting a golden hue over the water, Naylor Reservoir becomes a canvas painted with the hopes and dreams of those who cherish it. The shimmering surface reflects not just the beauty of the land but the enduring spirit of the people who have called this place home. Every wave that laps against the shore carries stories of joy, challenges, and triumphs, weaving a rich tapestry of life that continues to inspire and uplift.

In this beloved corner of Colorado, the legacy of Naylor Reservoir thrives, serving as a reminder of the power of nature and community. With laughter echoing across the waters and the warmth of friendship binding people together, Naylor Reservoir is not merely a reservoir; it is a celebration of life itself.

Morrow Point Reservoir

Morrow Point Reservoir, a stunning body of water tucked into the heart of Colorado's breathtaking Gunnison National Forest, has a history as rich and vibrant as its surroundings. The reservoir is named after the Morrow family, early settlers who played a vital role in the area's agricultural development. Their efforts to harness the land's potential laid the groundwork for what would become a remarkable feat of engineering.

Constructed as part of the Aspinall Unit Project in the 1960s, Morrow Point Reservoir was created by damming the Gunnison River. The project aimed to provide irrigation, hydroelectric power, and flood control to the region, transforming the landscape forever. Before the reservoir's creation, the river meandered freely through the rugged terrain, carving out deep canyons and nurturing a rich ecosystem. As the dam was constructed, the waters of the Gunnison were harnessed, creating a reservoir that would soon become a cherished recreational destination.

The reservoir itself is a man-made marvel, but the beauty it encompasses feels timeless. Towering cliffs surround the water, offering a striking contrast to the deep blue hues of the lake. Initially, the flora around Morrow Point included wildflowers and dense shrubs, providing habitat for various wildlife. The area was home to deer, elk, and a plethora of birds, creating a symphony of life that thrived before the dam's construction. Today, the reservoir supports a diverse range of plant and animal life, with its waters serving as a crucial resource for the surrounding ecosystem.

Before settlers arrived, the land was inhabited by the Ute people, who revered the landscape for its natural beauty and resources. The Ute utilized the Gunnison River for fishing and gathering, relying on its bounty for sustenance. As European settlers moved in, the relationship with the land shifted dramatically. The establishment of Morrow Point Reservoir marked a new chapter, allowing for more extensive agriculture and facilitating trade routes that had previously been limited by the rugged terrain.

With the creation of the reservoir, stories began to circulate about the "mysteries" of the lake. Local folklore spoke of hidden treasures beneath the surface, remnants of the original landscape and perhaps artifacts from the Ute people. Rumors abounded of ghostly figures wandering the shores, echoing the lives of those who once thrived in the valley. These tales sparked a sense of adventure and curiosity, drawing visitors to explore the shores and imagine the stories trapped beneath the water.

Morrow Point Reservoir quickly became a hub of recreation and community activity. Families flocked to its shores for picnics, fishing, and boating. The reservoir's clear waters invited swimmers to take a refreshing dip on hot summer days. Anglers cast their lines, hoping to reel in trout, while kayakers navigated the lake's serene surface. The sounds of laughter and excitement filled the air as visitors enjoyed everything from paddleboarding to leisurely hikes along the scenic trails that wound through the surrounding forest.

The reservoir also played a significant role in community development. As more people discovered Morrow Point's beauty, nearby towns flourished. Businesses catering to tourists sprang up, offering everything from fishing gear to cozy lodgings. The economic boost helped strengthen the local community, bringing together people from diverse backgrounds who shared a love for the outdoors.

However, human activity also brought challenges to the reservoir. Invasive species, including aquatic plants that thrived in the warm, nutrient-rich waters, began to take hold. Efforts were initiated to control their spread, with local conservation groups rallying to protect the delicate balance of the ecosystem. Educational programs emerged to teach residents and visitors about the importance of preserving the natural beauty of the area, fostering a sense of responsibility and stewardship.

Recognizing the value of Morrow Point Reservoir as a recreational destination, park services began developing facilities to accommodate visitors. Campgrounds, picnic areas, and boat ramps were established, making it easier for families to enjoy the great outdoors. The reservoir became a backdrop for community events, from summer festivals to fishing competitions, fostering a sense of belonging and camaraderie among those who shared a love for the water.

Morrow Point Reservoir is not merely a body of water; it is a living testament to the harmony between nature and human innovation. Each ripple on its surface tells a story of resilience and community spirit. As visitors gather to witness the sunset painting the cliffs in shades of orange and purple, they become part of a legacy that honors both the past and the future.

The laughter of children echoes across the water as families make memories that will last a lifetime. Friends come together to share stories of their fishing adventures, while couples stroll hand in hand along the shore, captivated by the beauty that surrounds them. Morrow Point Reservoir remains a sanctuary for wildlife, a refuge for weary travelers, and a source of inspiration for those who seek solace in nature.

With each season, the reservoir evolves, adapting to the changing weather and the cycles of life. In winter, the surface may freeze, transforming into a wonderland of snow and ice, while spring breathes life back into the landscape, ushering in vibrant blooms and returning wildlife. Summer invites laughter and joy, and autumn paints the surrounding trees in a riot of colors, creating a breathtaking backdrop for visitors.

Morrow Point Reservoir is more than a destination; it is a celebration of life itself. It is a place where people connect with nature, with one another, and with the stories that have shaped the land. As the sun dips below the horizon, casting a warm glow over the water, the reservoir stands as a reminder of the power of nature and the enduring spirit of community. In this corner of Colorado, Morrow Point Reservoir continues to inspire, heal, and bring joy to all who venture to its shores.

Vallecito Reservoir

Vallecito Reservoir, a picturesque expanse of water in southwestern Colorado, is a delightful blend of natural beauty and human ingenuity. Its name, Vallecito, translates to "little valley" in Spanish, a fitting tribute to the lush, green landscapes that surround this stunning body of water. The reservoir is located just a few miles from the charming town of Bayfield, in La Plata County, and has become a cherished destination for outdoor enthusiasts and families alike.

Constructed in the early 1960s as part of a larger water management project, Vallecito Reservoir was designed primarily to provide irrigation and municipal water supplies for the region. The damming of the Vallecito Creek created this expansive reservoir, which serves as a crucial resource for the communities that depend on it. Though man-made, the reservoir seamlessly integrates with the surrounding environment, creating a haven for wildlife and recreational activities.

Before the reservoir's creation, the Vallecito area was rich with flora and fauna. Towering ponderosa pines, aspens, and wildflowers painted the landscape, while the crystal-clear waters of Vallecito Creek attracted diverse wildlife. Mule deer roamed the hillsides, and an array of birds, from eagles to hummingbirds, filled the air with their songs. The lush environment was not only a beautiful backdrop but also a vital resource for the indigenous Ute people, who had inhabited these lands for centuries. They relied on the river and its tributaries for fishing, gathering, and hunting, forming a deep connection to the natural world around them.

As settlers arrived in the late 19th century, the landscape began to change dramatically. The arrival of new communities brought agriculture, mining, and infrastructure development, leading to both opportunities and challenges. The construction of Vallecito Reservoir represented a significant shift, allowing for the expansion of farming and ranching operations in the area. This project turned what was once a wild landscape into a cultivated paradise, fostering economic growth and community development.

Yet with progress often comes myth. Local legends grew around the reservoir, some humorous, some more mysterious. One story spoke of a "Vallecito Monster" lurking beneath the water's surface, a playful nod to the lake's depth and the imagination of the locals. Campers would gather around campfires to share tales of ghostly fishermen and lost treasures submerged in the reservoir. These stories, whether born of truth or fiction, added a sense of adventure and camaraderie among those who frequented the area.

As the years passed, Vallecito Reservoir evolved into a beloved recreational destination. The clear waters became a playground for fishing, boating, and swimming. Families flocked to its shores for picnics, eager to soak up the sun and create lasting memories. Fishing enthusiasts cast their lines in hopes of catching rainbow and brown trout, while paddleboarders glided across the surface, enjoying the serenity of their surroundings. Laughter and shouts of joy filled the air, mixing with the gentle rustle of the wind through the trees.

With the influx of visitors, the community surrounding the reservoir flourished. Local businesses sprang up to meet the needs of outdoor lovers, from tackle shops to cozy cabins. Festivals celebrating the natural beauty of the area brought people together, fostering a sense of belonging and pride among residents. The reservoir became a centerpiece for community gatherings, creating bonds that would last a lifetime.

However, with increased human activity came challenges. Invasive species began to infiltrate the reservoir, threatening the delicate balance of the ecosystem. Aquatic plants that flourished in the warm waters started to spread, prompting conservation efforts aimed at preserving the lake's natural beauty. Local organizations and volunteers banded together to raise awareness about responsible recreation and the importance of protecting the environment. Education programs were established, teaching visitors about the native species and the impact of their actions on the ecosystem.

Conservation initiatives also focused on habitat restoration, ensuring that the reservoir would continue to support diverse wildlife. Efforts included planting native vegetation along the shores to provide shelter for birds and other animals. The community rallied around these projects, understanding that the health of the reservoir was essential not only for recreation but also for preserving the unique environment that had long sustained them.

Vallecito Reservoir also inspired the development of parks and recreational facilities. Campgrounds and picnic areas were established to accommodate visitors, while trails for hiking and biking meandered through the surrounding forest. The area transformed into a vibrant hub for outdoor activities, attracting adventurers year-round. Winter brought a different kind of magic as snow blanketed the landscape, inviting cross-country skiers and snowshoe enthusiasts to explore the serene beauty of the frozen reservoir.

As the sun sets over Vallecito Reservoir, the sky bursts into hues of orange and pink, casting a warm glow over the water. Families gather around bonfires, sharing stories and laughter while roasting marshmallows for s'mores. Children splash in the shallows, their giggles ringing through the air, and couples stroll hand in hand along the shore, captivated by the enchanting scenery. In these moments, the reservoir serves as more than just a body of water; it becomes a cherished backdrop for life's simplest joys.

Vallecito Reservoir stands as a testament to the harmony that can be achieved between human innovation and the beauty of nature. It is a place where stories are made, where the past intertwines with the present, and where the spirit of the community thrives. Each visit reveals something new, whether it's a secret fishing spot, a breathtaking vista, or a chance encounter with wildlife.

The reservoir will continue to evolve, adapting to the changing seasons and the needs of the community. As visitors come and go, they become part of the tapestry that is Vallecito Reservoir—each thread adding depth and richness to the story of this remarkable place. Whether you come for the fishing, the hiking, or simply to relax by the water, you will leave with a piece of its magic in your heart, eagerly anticipating your next return to the little valley that has captured the spirit of so many.

Huntington Lake

Huntington Lake, a captivating jewel tucked away in the heart of Colorado, is a place where nature's beauty meets human history in a delightful dance. Located in the stunning San Isabel National Forest, in Lake County, this reservoir provides a glimpse into a world where the mountains kiss the sky and the water reflects the laughter of those who visit. Named after the prominent Huntington family, who were early settlers in the area, the lake is steeped in stories that span generations, blending humor, adventure, and the spirit of the outdoors.

The lake itself was created in the 1900s as part of a larger water management project, designed to support irrigation and municipal water supply. Originally a natural basin, it was transformed into the expansive reservoir we see today through the construction of a dam on the river feeding into it. While this was a feat of engineering, the lake retains an air of natural wonder, surrounded by lush forests and towering peaks that create a breathtaking backdrop. It's easy to see why this place has inspired such affection and legend.

Before the arrival of settlers, the region was a thriving habitat for diverse wildlife and a sanctuary for the Ute people. They lived harmoniously with the land, fishing in the lake and hunting in the forests. Their connection to the area was profound, rich with tradition and spirituality. Stories passed down through generations spoke of spirits that inhabited the waters, protecting the lake and its bounty. These legends inspired reverence among the Ute, who saw the landscape as a living entity rather than a mere resource.

As the settlers arrived, the dynamics of the landscape began to shift dramatically. The Huntington family played a significant role in this transformation, establishing homesteads and bringing agriculture to the area. The lake became a vital resource for irrigation, supporting crops and livestock, and transforming the once-wild landscape into a tapestry of farms and orchards. The settlers held lively community gatherings, where tales were exchanged, laughter echoed, and friendships were forged, all while the shimmering waters of Huntington Lake served as the perfect backdrop.

Despite the positive changes, not all stories associated with the lake are lighthearted. One infamous tale involves the Great Flood of 1935, a natural disaster that caught many by surprise. A sudden snowmelt combined with heavy spring rains led to an unexpected rise in water levels. The lake overflowed, and the rushing waters caused chaos in the nearby settlements. One particularly humorous anecdote recounts a group of fishermen who had been having a particularly slow day. Just as they began to pack up their gear, they found themselves wading through water where their truck had been parked only hours before. They joked that the fish had finally come to them, albeit in a rather unconventional way!

In the wake of the flood, the community rallied together to rebuild and adapt. This resilience solidified bonds and led to the establishment of a more organized approach to managing the lake and its surrounding environment. The 1930s also saw the emergence of local legends, such as the "Huntington Lake Monster." This creature, often described as a cross between a giant fish and a playful otter, became a favorite topic around campfires. Children would dare each other to spend the night by the lake, hoping to catch a glimpse of the elusive beast. This playful myth added an extra layer of excitement to family outings, as parents would weave tales of the creature's antics while roasting marshmallows.

Over the decades, Huntington Lake became a beloved destination for recreation. Boating, fishing, and hiking all flourished as families began to flock to its shores. The initial flora and fauna of the area flourished under this new wave of activity. Visitors reveled in the abundance of wildflowers and the fresh scent of pine, while anglers enjoyed the thrill of catching rainbow and brook trout. The lake's serene waters became a gathering spot for families seeking solace in nature, and the laughter of children splashing in the shallows filled the air.

Yet, with the joys of recreation came the challenges of human impact. Invasive species began to appear, threatening the delicate ecosystem that had thrived for centuries. Efforts to combat these invaders became a community priority. Volunteers organized cleanup days, working together to preserve the natural beauty of the lake. Educational programs were introduced, teaching visitors about the importance of protecting the environment and the responsibilities of being a steward of the land.

In response to the increasing popularity of the area, parks and recreational facilities were developed. Campgrounds were established, complete with fire pits and picnic tables, making it easy for families to spend time together. Hiking trails wound through the surrounding forests, offering breathtaking views and opportunities for adventure. The local community embraced these changes, recognizing the potential for Huntington Lake to become a vibrant hub for outdoor activities and family fun.

Events such as the annual Fishing Derby brought locals and visitors together, fostering a sense of community. Families would compete for prizes, sharing tips and tales of the one that got away, while children learned the joy of casting their first line. As the sun set over the lake, the colors danced on the water, and laughter echoed through the trees, a reminder of the connections that bind people to both nature and each other.

The beauty of Huntington Lake lies not just in its landscape but in its ability to bring people together. It is a place where stories are written—whether they are about the monster that lurks in the depths or the fisherman who finally caught the biggest trout of the season. It holds the echoes of laughter, the whispers of legends, and the promise of adventure for generations to come.

With every visit, families leave with a piece of Huntington Lake in their hearts, eager to return to its shores. The reservoir will continue to evolve, adapting to the changing seasons and the needs of the community. Each new chapter in its history will be filled with the warmth of shared experiences, the thrill of exploration, and the enduring connection to the land that has nurtured so many. Huntington Lake is more than just a destination; it is a canvas for life's most cherished moments, a place where the past and present coexist in joyful harmony.

Lake Emma

Lake Emma, a serene oasis tucked away in Colorado's breathtaking Elk Mountains, boasts a history filled with charm, intrigue, and a few cheeky legends. Located within the boundaries of the White River National Forest in Pitkin County, this picturesque lake is named after Emma Crawford, the spirited daughter of a local pioneer family. Her adventurous spirit and infectious laughter left an indelible mark on the area, inspiring the name that has become synonymous with joy and relaxation.

The lake itself is a natural wonder, formed by glacial activity thousands of years ago, resulting in a stunning alpine basin surrounded by towering peaks and lush forests. The water glimmers like liquid crystal, reflecting the grandeur of the sky. Visitors often marvel at the wildflowers that bloom along the shore, their vibrant colors dancing in the breeze, making the area feel like a scene out of a storybook.

Before Emma's family and other settlers arrived, the Ute people called this region home. They revered the land, including Lake Emma, as sacred, often visiting the shores for fishing and gathering. Their deep connection to the area infused the landscape with legends, one of which tells of a great spirit residing in the waters, offering protection and bountiful fish to those who respected the land. The Ute's way of life harmonized beautifully with nature, fostering a balance that allowed both people and wildlife to thrive.

As settlers moved in during the late 1800s, the landscape began to change. Emma's family, among others, established homesteads, cultivating the land and introducing new agricultural practices. The lake soon became a crucial resource for irrigation, helping crops flourish in the challenging alpine environment. Communities grew, and the area transformed into a lively hub of activity. Children played along the shores, and neighbors shared stories over campfires, with Lake Emma as their ever-watchful companion.

One particular story that still brings a chuckle involves a group of early settlers attempting to catch fish for a grand community feast. Equipped with nets and buckets, they gathered at the lake with high hopes. As the sun set, they realized their nets were empty, while a family of ducks quacked gleefully nearby, seemingly mocking their efforts. Undeterred, the settlers made a game of it, challenging each other to "catch" the ducks instead, resulting in a hilariously futile pursuit. That evening ended in laughter, with the community deciding to feast on whatever they had brought instead, and Lake Emma became a symbol of both hope and humor.

Over the years, however, nature had its own plans. In 1934, a sudden storm brought heavy rainfall that led to significant flooding around Lake Emma. The water rose rapidly, forcing local residents to scramble and evacuate. Yet, amid the chaos, the community banded together, helping one another and sharing stories of resilience and laughter as they weathered the storm. It was said that even the lake, in its wild splendor, seemed to calm, as if acknowledging the strength of the people who lived beside it.

As the years rolled on, the lake became a beloved destination for recreation. Hikers would flock to its shores, drawn by the promise of adventure and tranquility. The initial flora and fauna thrived, providing homes for various wildlife, from playful marmots to majestic elk that roamed the nearby mountains. Anglers found joy in casting their lines into the clear waters, catching trout while swapping stories with fellow fishing enthusiasts. Families set up picnics along the banks, children splashing in the shallows, their laughter mingling with the gentle rustling of the trees.

However, with increased human activity came challenges. Invasive species began to make their presence known, posing a threat to the delicate ecosystem. The local community rallied, organizing cleanup events and educational programs to promote awareness about preserving the natural beauty of Lake Emma. Conservation efforts gained momentum, with volunteers planting native vegetation and monitoring the lake's health, ensuring that future generations would inherit a vibrant and thriving environment.

Development in the area also flourished, with the establishment of parks and recreational facilities. Campgrounds sprang up, complete with fire pits and picnic areas, encouraging families to immerse themselves in the great outdoors. Trails meandered around the lake, offering breathtaking views and opportunities for exploration. Events such as the annual Lake Emma Family Day brought the community together for a day of fun, games, and camaraderie, fostering a sense of unity that echoed the spirit of Emma herself.

As time marched on, tales of Lake Emma continued to evolve. New legends emerged, including the "Lake Emma Light," an unexplained phenomenon that some claimed was a sign from the spirit of Emma, watching over her namesake lake. This light, often described as a soft glow dancing on the water's surface, captivated the imaginations of visitors and locals alike. It became a tradition for families to camp by the lake, waiting eagerly for the mysterious light to appear, sharing ghost stories and s'mores as night fell.

Through laughter, challenges, and the enduring spirit of community, Lake Emma has remained a beacon of joy and beauty in Colorado's landscape. It is more than just a reservoir; it is a canvas where memories are painted and connections are forged. Each visit brings with it the echoes of past laughter, the warmth of shared stories, and the promise of adventures yet to come.

As the sun sets over Lake Emma, casting a golden hue across the water, families pack their belongings, leaving behind footprints in the sand and hearts full of cherished moments. With every wave lapping against the shore, the lake whispers tales of resilience and joy, ensuring that its legacy will continue to thrive for generations.

Lake San Cristobal

Lake San Cristobal, with its shimmering waters and breathtaking mountain backdrop, is a treasure in the heart of Colorado's San Juan Mountains. Located in Hinsdale County, near the historic town of Lake City, the lake is not only a natural wonder but also a reservoir of stories, laughter, and a sprinkle of mystery.

The name "San Cristobal" pays homage to Saint Christopher, the patron saint of travelers. Legend has it that a group of explorers passed through the area and, enchanted by its beauty, decided to name the lake after the saint, hoping for safe journeys on their future travels. This connection to adventure resonates in the air, as locals often joke that if you're not careful, you might find yourself lost in the beauty of the landscape for days—or at least until the sun sets!

The lake is a natural formation, created by glacial activity thousands of years ago. Surrounded by towering peaks and lush forests, it serves as a reminder of the earth's ancient artistry. The pristine waters host a variety of aquatic life, while the surrounding land is alive with wildflowers, aspens, and the occasional curious deer peeking through the trees. The flora and fauna create a vibrant ecosystem that welcomes both wildlife and humans alike, fostering a sense of connection to nature.

Long before settlers arrived, the Ute people called this area home. They revered Lake San Cristobal, seeing it as a sacred site that provided not just sustenance but a deep spiritual connection to the land. They fished its waters and gathered around its shores for ceremonies, weaving stories into the fabric of the landscape. One popular myth among the Ute involves a mysterious creature said to dwell in the lake, protecting the area from harm. They would tell tales of how this creature, known affectionately as "Cris," would appear in times of trouble, offering assistance to those who respected the land.

As the late 1800s ushered in waves of settlers seeking fortune and adventure, the landscape began to change. The discovery of gold and silver nearby transformed the area into a bustling hub. Lake San Cristobal soon became a vital resource for the new communities springing up around it. The settlers utilized the lake for irrigation, ensuring their crops thrived in the rugged mountain terrain. With the introduction of agriculture, the land flourished, and families began to build their lives along the shores, forming close-knit communities.

One particularly amusing anecdote from this time involves a local fishing contest that took place during the summer of 1895. Determined to catch the biggest trout, the townsfolk gathered, armed with rods and stories of their past "great catches." The event turned into a comedic spectacle, as one fisherman, who had boasted about his prowess, ended up tangled in his own line and tripping over his tackle box, landing right in the lake. While he emerged drenched, laughter erupted around the shore, and he became an unexpected hero of the day, earning the nickname "Lake Cristobal" as the townspeople cheered him on.

As the years went by, however, nature had its own surprises. In 1970, a devastating flood swept through the area after heavy rains, leading to significant changes in the landscape surrounding Lake San Cristobal. The lake swelled dangerously, threatening the homes and businesses that had grown so fond of its shores. Yet, in true community spirit, residents banded together, sharing resources and rebuilding their lives. The flood, while destructive, brought people closer, creating a bond forged in resilience and hope.

Recreationally, Lake San Cristobal blossomed as a popular destination for hiking, fishing, and boating. Visitors from near and far flocked to its shores, eager to explore the natural beauty that had become a hallmark of the region. The lake quickly gained a reputation for its excellent fishing, and the annual Fishing Festival drew crowds who came to compete for prizes while enjoying the camaraderie of fellow anglers.

However, increased human activity brought challenges. Invasive species, such as zebra mussels, began to make their presence felt, prompting conservation efforts from both locals and environmental organizations. Community meetings were held, where passionate discussions took place about protecting the lake's delicate ecosystem. Volunteers organized clean-up days, removing debris and educating visitors about how to prevent the spread of invasive species. The commitment to preserving Lake San Cristobal became a rallying point for the community, reinforcing their love for the land.

Parks and recreational facilities developed around the lake, enhancing its status as a prime location for outdoor activities. Campgrounds, picnic areas, and scenic trails were established, inviting families to explore and create memories together. The Lake San Cristobal Nature Center opened, offering educational programs about the local environment, wildlife, and conservation efforts. The center quickly became a hub of activity, drawing in both locals and tourists eager to learn about the natural wonders that surrounded them.

As Lake San Cristobal continues to thrive, its stories evolve. New legends emerge, like the "San Cristobal Light," a mysterious glow that some say appears at twilight on certain summer nights. Campers gather around fires, sharing tales of their own encounters with this ethereal phenomenon. The lake's enchanting beauty, combined with its intriguing history, captivates visitors who find themselves drawn to its shores time and again.

In the embrace of the San Juan Mountains, Lake San Cristobal stands as a testament to resilience, community, and the power of nature. As families pack their gear and leave behind laughter echoing in the air, they know they have become part of a legacy woven through time. Each sunset paints a new story across the water, ensuring that the lake remains a beloved destination for generations to come. The spirit of adventure, humor, and connection thrives here, inviting all who visit to discover their own place in the ever-unfolding tale of Lake San Cristobal.

Lake of the Clouds

The Lake of the Clouds, a name that evokes images of serenity and mystery, sits high in the Colorado Rockies, cradled within the stunning landscapes of the Sawatch Range. This picturesque lake, located in Lake County, has a history as rich as the tapestry of colors that dance across its surface during sunrise. The name itself is said to have originated from the way the fog rolls over the water, creating a whimsical illusion that the lake is indeed floating among the clouds. Local lore has it that a passing explorer, captivated by the sight, shouted out, "It's a lake among the clouds!" and the name stuck, much to the delight of future visitors who are often just as awestruck.

Lake of the Clouds is a natural lake, formed by the melting glaciers of eons past. Its pristine waters have long been a magnet for outdoor enthusiasts and a cherished sanctuary for wildlife. The flora surrounding the lake is diverse, with wildflowers in a riot of colors in the summer and aspen groves whispering in the gentle mountain breeze. The initial fauna included everything from small fish darting through the water to deer and elk roaming the nearby meadows. The lake serves as a vital water source, creating a thriving ecosystem that showcases the wonders of nature.

Before the area drew the attention of settlers, it was home to the Ute people, who held the land sacred. The Ute tribes regarded the lake as a source of life and a place of spiritual significance. They fished its waters and hunted nearby, weaving their stories and culture into the fabric of the landscape. Myths abounded, with tales of spirits watching over the lake, protecting it from harm. One story tells of a wise old woman who would appear during storms, guiding lost travelers to safety with her glowing presence, reminding everyone of the lake's protective spirit.

With the arrival of European settlers in the mid-1800s, the landscape began to change. The promise of gold lured many to the area, and Lake of the Clouds quickly became a resource for those hoping to strike it rich. The settlers used the lake for fishing and as a water source for their burgeoning communities, with the first settlements springing up in the nearby valleys. The lake, once a secluded sanctuary, transformed into a vital hub for the new arrivals.

However, the newfound excitement brought challenges. In 1896, a particularly harsh winter led to heavy snowfall, and the resulting spring melt caused flooding that threatened the surrounding communities. Roads washed out, and panic ensued as the lake swelled, covering the meadows in a dramatic display of nature's power. In the face of adversity, the community came together, helping each other rebuild homes and businesses. The flooding became a shared story, a tale of resilience that continues to echo through the generations.

As the years rolled on, Lake of the Clouds became a beloved destination for recreation. Hikers flocked to the area, drawn by its scenic beauty, while families spent summers picnicking along the shores. Fishing became a favorite pastime, with anglers hoping to catch the elusive trout that call the lake home. Local businesses thrived, offering boat rentals and guided tours. In fact, there's a humorous story about a local fishing guide who once tried to impress a group of tourists with his fishing prowess, only to trip and tumble into the lake, much to the amusement of his clients. He emerged soaked but laughing, claiming he had "just made the fish nervous."

The environmental impact of human activity did not go unnoticed, however. Invasive species began to threaten the delicate balance of the lake's ecosystem. The arrival of non-native fish species prompted alarm among local conservationists, who feared the native trout would be outcompeted. To combat this, community-led initiatives sprang into action. Volunteers organized clean-up days, pulling invasive plants and working to restore native vegetation. Conservation groups collaborated with local parks to implement educational programs, teaching visitors about the importance of protecting the lake and its inhabitants.

The community's commitment to preservation paid off. Parks and recreational facilities were developed, enhancing access to the lake while ensuring that its beauty remained intact. Trails were established, allowing hikers to explore the surrounding mountains and view the lake from various vantage points. The Lake of the Clouds Nature Center opened its doors, providing programs that engage visitors in understanding the area's ecology and history. Families often gather there to attend workshops or simply enjoy storytelling sessions, where laughter fills the air, echoing the tales of the lake's past.

The enchantment of Lake of the Clouds continues to inspire those who visit. Campers tell stories around evening fires, sharing legends of the lake and their own humorous mishaps while trying to fish or hike. Each sunset paints the water in shades of gold and purple, offering a moment of reflection and appreciation for the beauty of nature. The lake's charm extends beyond its picturesque views; it serves as a reminder of the resilience of both the land and its people.

The future of Lake of the Clouds looks bright as ongoing conservation efforts flourish. Regular monitoring of water quality ensures that the lake remains a healthy habitat for wildlife. Local schools incorporate environmental education into their curriculums, instilling a love for nature in the next generation. Seasonal festivals celebrate the lake's beauty, from photography contests to fishing derbies, fostering community spirit and involvement.

As families pack up their cars to leave after a weekend of adventure, they carry with them the laughter and memories created at Lake of the Clouds. The stories, myths, and humorous moments become part of the lake's rich narrative, a tapestry woven with threads of joy, resilience, and connection. Each visit contributes to the legacy of the lake, inviting all who come to find their place in the unfolding story of this magical Colorado treasure.

Cameron Lake

Cameron Lake, tucked away in the heart of Colorado's San Juan Mountains, is a hidden treasure with a history that is as vibrant as its turquoise waters. Named after the early 20th-century prospector, John Cameron, who dreamed of striking gold in these rugged mountains, the lake is now a serene reminder of the area's rich mining heritage. It's said that Cameron believed he'd found a fortune hidden in the hills, but all he left behind was a name and a well-worn tale that has been passed down through generations.

The lake itself is a natural wonder, formed during the last ice age by the grinding force of glaciers that carved out the valley. Its deep blue depths are a welcome contrast to the surrounding aspen groves and the wildflower-filled meadows that spring to life each summer. Initially home to a variety of fish, birds, and small mammals, the landscape is a biodiversity hotspot. It's not uncommon to see elk grazing on the banks or hear the cheerful songs of wrens and sparrows as they flit between the branches.

Before the arrival of settlers, the area around Cameron Lake was a vital part of the territory for the Ute tribes. They held the land sacred, using it for hunting, gathering, and fishing. The lake provided sustenance and water for the tribes, and they shared stories of the spirits that watched over it. One popular legend among the Ute speaks of a shimmering fish that granted wishes to those pure of heart. Children would often gather by the shore, hoping to catch a glimpse of the magical creature and whisper their dreams into the water, believing that the fish would carry their wishes to the heavens.

When settlers began to pour into the region in the late 1800s, the landscape shifted dramatically. The promise of gold and silver lured many adventurous souls into the mountains, and Cameron Lake soon became a part of their stories. Roads were constructed to transport miners and their supplies, and the surrounding area saw the development of small communities. The lake became a resource for fishing and recreation, with families spending summers picnicking along its shores, enjoying the bounty of nature while recounting the tales of the Ute people and their mystical fish.

Despite the excitement, not all stories from the lake's history are lighthearted. In 1921, a sudden snowmelt coupled with heavy spring rains caused a catastrophic flood that impacted the region. The water levels of Cameron Lake rose perilously, sending torrents cascading down the mountainsides and washing away parts of the roads that had just been built. Local residents banded together to help each other, forming impromptu rescue teams and clearing debris. It was a challenging time, but it also fostered a sense of community spirit that still resonates today.

Through the decades, the lake became a popular destination for recreation, with fishing enthusiasts flocking to catch native trout. The lake's waters were soon teeming with life, and local guides became well-known for their fishing skills, often boasting about the "big one that got away." One charming tale involves a guide named Hank, who proudly recounted his legendary catch of the "mystical trout," a fish so large it could only be seen from the shore. Every time someone asked to see the catch, Hank would chuckle and say it was "just too slippery to hold."

In recent years, however, Cameron Lake faced challenges from invasive species that threatened to upset the delicate ecosystem. Efforts to combat these intruders became a community effort, with volunteers organizing clean-up days and education programs to raise awareness about the importance of preserving the lake's natural beauty. Local schools got involved, with students learning about ecology while participating in lake clean-ups, all while donning T-shirts that proudly proclaimed, "Save our Lake!" There was even a humorous incident where a group of enthusiastic children mistakenly thought they were supposed to catch the invasive fish and "release them into the wild," leading to a comical but educational day filled with laughter and learning.

Conservation efforts in the area have paid off, with local organizations working diligently to protect the ecosystem. Programs aimed at restoring native vegetation have brought life back to the shoreline, while initiatives to monitor water quality ensure that the lake remains a thriving habitat for fish and other wildlife. Parks have been developed around Cameron Lake, complete with trails for hiking and spots for camping. Families can often be found enjoying summer days filled with fishing, kayaking, or simply lounging by the water, recounting stories of their own adventures.

The enchantment of Cameron Lake extends beyond its natural beauty. Seasonal festivals celebrate local culture and traditions, from fishing derbies that bring out the competitive spirit to storytelling nights where locals share legends of the lake, often with a humorous twist. It's a gathering of generations, where the young listen wide-eyed to the tales of their elders, and laughter fills the air, echoing off the mountains.

As families pack their gear for a weekend of fun, they carry with them not just fishing rods and picnic baskets but also a sense of belonging and connection to a history that is still being written. The legends of the Ute, the stories of the early prospectors, and the humorous misadventures of anglers blend into a shared narrative that grows with each passing year.

Cameron Lake continues to be a place of adventure, camaraderie, and laughter. It serves as a reminder of the importance of community, resilience, and the bond between people and nature. With every sunrise casting its golden glow upon the water, the lake invites all who visit to be part of its ongoing story, to contribute to the legacy of laughter, love, and life that has thrived in this majestic corner of Colorado.

Upper Bear Creek Lake

Upper Bear Creek Lake, a shimmering blue jewel in Colorado's Rocky Mountain foothills, is as rich in history as it is in natural beauty. Located in Jefferson County, this picturesque lake lies at an elevation of about 9,300 feet, surrounded by rugged peaks and lush forests. The name "Upper Bear Creek" pays homage to the nearby Bear Creek, which was likely named for the bears that once roamed these hills. Local folklore suggests that early settlers frequently encountered these magnificent creatures, often having to make a hasty retreat from curious bears that mistook their picnic baskets for an all-you-can-eat buffet.

The lake was formed in the early 1900s when a dam was constructed to help manage water flow for local agriculture and irrigation. Prior to this, the area was characterized by pristine wetlands and meandering streams, a tranquil home for the flora and fauna that thrived in its embrace. Initially, the landscape supported a wealth of life, with willows lining the banks and wildflowers dotting the meadows. Birdwatchers often reported spotting a variety of species, from the striking mountain bluebird to the elusive American dipper, diving into the clear waters to catch their lunch.

Before the arrival of European settlers, the land was inhabited by the Arapaho and Cheyenne tribes, who revered the area for its abundant resources. They relied on the natural bounty for fishing, hunting, and gathering. The lake and surrounding mountains served as sacred spaces, rich in spirituality and history. It's said that certain rock formations around the lake were once considered sacred meeting spots where tribes would gather to share stories and celebrate their culture.

With the influx of settlers in the late 19th century, the landscape began to change dramatically. The charm of Upper Bear Creek Lake became entwined with the growing mining and logging industries, which sought to tap into the area's natural resources. While colonization brought about significant development, it also paved the way for new recreational opportunities. The lake quickly became a hotspot for fishing and picnicking, where families would spend weekends casting lines for trout and sharing hearty lunches amid the beauty of nature. It was not uncommon for a child to reel in a "whopper" while the adults shared a laugh, swapping stories of their biggest catches—or the ones that got away.

However, the area was not without its challenges. In 1965, a significant storm brought torrential rains that caused a flash flood, impacting the lake and the surrounding community. The floodwaters rushed down Bear Creek, overflowing banks and inundating homes. It was a trying time for residents, but they came together, helping one another with recovery efforts. This disaster led to improvements in local infrastructure, ensuring better management of water flow and flood control. The incident is often recounted at community gatherings, humorously referred to as the "Great Wet Adventure," as the locals reminisce about the chaos and camaraderie that ensued during the recovery process.

Legends surrounding Upper Bear Creek Lake abound, with one particularly charming tale about a mischievous spirit named "Ol' Splashy." According to local lore, Ol' Splashy is said to be the ghost of a fisherman who never quite got the hang of casting his line. The story goes that he haunts the lake, helping—or hindering—anglers by either granting them miraculous catches or leading them into snags. Locals often joke that Ol' Splashy has a personal vendetta against anyone who tries to fish during a full moon, insisting that it's best to leave the rods at home during those nights.

As outdoor recreation flourished, Upper Bear Creek Lake became a beloved destination for locals and visitors alike. The area around the lake was transformed into a park, complete with hiking trails and camping spots, allowing families to immerse themselves in the great outdoors. The sight of children darting about, shrieking with joy as they chased after butterflies, is a common one during the summer months. The park hosts various events throughout the year, including fishing tournaments, nature walks, and even local art fairs, showcasing the community's vibrant spirit.

In recent years, concerns about the ecological health of Upper Bear Creek Lake have come to the forefront. Invasive species have made their way into the lake, challenging the delicate balance of the ecosystem. Local environmental groups sprang into action, organizing volunteer days for clean-up efforts and educational workshops to raise awareness about the importance of biodiversity. Children and adults alike have taken part, armed with nets and determination, all while sharing laughter and stories as they work to protect their beloved lake.

These conservation efforts have yielded positive results, and the lake is gradually returning to its former glory. New measures to monitor water quality and restore native vegetation have been implemented, and local residents take pride in their stewardship of the area. As one local put it, "If we want our kids to enjoy this place as much as we have, we need to roll up our sleeves and get to work!"

As the sun begins to set over Upper Bear Creek Lake, casting a golden glow across the water, the laughter of families echoes through the trees. The lake remains a cherished spot where traditions are passed down, and memories are made. Each visit brings with it the promise of adventure and connection, a reminder of the enduring bond between people and nature.

In the end, Upper Bear Creek Lake is more than just a beautiful body of water. It is a canvas painted with stories, laughter, and a sense of community that stretches back generations. Whether you're fishing for trout, hiking along the shore, or simply enjoying a quiet moment of reflection, this lake invites all who visit to be part of its ongoing narrative, weaving together the past, present, and future in a tapestry of joy and connection.

Lower Bear Creek Lake

Lower Bear Creek Lake, a serene expanse of water framed by the stunning foothills of the Rocky Mountains, holds stories as deep as its waters. Located just outside of Morrison in Jefferson County, this picturesque lake gets its name from the nearby Bear Creek, which meanders through the landscape like a ribbon of blue. The origins of the name likely hark back to the days when the area was home to bears aplenty, who would wander down to the creek for a refreshing drink, occasionally startling early settlers who were more interested in picnics than bear encounters.

This reservoir was created in the early 1900s when a dam was built to manage water for irrigation and municipal use. Originally a series of meandering streams and wetlands, the area flourished with diverse flora and fauna. Willows and aspens lined the shores, providing shelter for various wildlife, while the air was filled with the songs of meadowlarks and the rustling of leaves. The lake's initial inhabitants were the Arapaho and Cheyenne tribes, who utilized the area for fishing and gathering. The indigenous people viewed the land as sacred, weaving stories of creation and connection that echo through the ages.

Colonization brought significant changes to the landscape. As settlers arrived, they transformed the natural beauty of Lower Bear Creek Lake, but they also introduced new opportunities for community development. Families gathered at the lake for fishing expeditions, with stories often exaggerating the size of the "one that got away." The laughter of children echoed across the waters as they splashed around, trying to catch frogs, while the smell of grilled burgers wafted through the air on summer afternoons. It became a local tradition to celebrate the Fourth of July with fireworks lighting up the sky, reflecting off the water like stars fallen to earth.

However, not all of the lake's history has been tranquil. In 1936, a devastating flood swept through the area, causing widespread damage to the dam and the surrounding communities. The waters rose dramatically, eroding the banks and uprooting trees. Fortunately, the community came together, rallying to support one another through the aftermath. The flood was often referred to as "the great washout," and locals still tell stories of the chaos that ensued, complete with anecdotes of floaties repurposed as rescue devices and neighbors fishing from rooftops.

Legends have sprouted around Lower Bear Creek Lake over the years, with one particularly amusing tale featuring a playful water sprite named "Bubbling Bob." According to local lore, Bubbling Bob delights in tricking unsuspecting fishermen. He's known to create ripples and splashes, luring anglers to believe they've hooked a big one, only to reveal a sneaky old boot instead. Some fishermen have even claimed that Bob will sometimes jump in their boats to join them for a spell, adding an unexpected splash of humor to their day. Residents chuckle at these stories, often teasing their friends about needing to be on the lookout for the slippery sprite.

The lake became a hub for recreation, with trails developed around its perimeter for hikers and bikers alike. Family picnics became a staple, as locals flocked to the park area, drawn by the promise of sunny afternoons by the water. The community took pride in organizing annual fishing tournaments, where the camaraderie among participants was often more valuable than the fish themselves. Whether one reeled in a trophy trout or a humble perch, the laughter and stories shared over a picnic table were the true catch of the day.

However, as the years rolled on, concerns began to arise about the ecological health of Lower Bear Creek Lake. Invasive species began to infiltrate the waters, disrupting the delicate balance of the ecosystem. Local environmental organizations sprang into action, holding cleanup events and educational workshops aimed at raising awareness about protecting the lake's natural beauty. Schoolchildren, armed with nets and buckets, joined in these efforts, laughing as they collected litter and learned about the importance of preserving their playground. "Look, I found a can! Maybe Bubbling Bob will return it!" one child exclaimed, evoking giggles from their friends.

In response to these challenges, community members rallied around conservation initiatives. They worked with state agencies to monitor water quality, restore native plants, and develop best practices for recreation to mitigate human impact. These efforts fostered a sense of stewardship, where locals felt a deep responsibility to protect their beloved lake for future generations. The sentiment became a part of the community's identity, with annual events focusing on ecological education becoming a highlight on the local calendar.

As the sun sets behind the Rocky Mountains, casting a warm glow over Lower Bear Creek Lake, families gather to enjoy the breathtaking view. Children skip stones while parents relax, sharing stories that echo the laughter of those who came before them. With the lake's rich history intertwining with the joys of the present, it continues to be a cherished destination, where memories are made and stories are written anew.

Each visit to Lower Bear Creek Lake offers a reminder of the importance of community, the power of resilience, and the joy found in the simple pleasures of nature. Whether it's a quiet moment of reflection by the water's edge or the exhilaration of reeling in a fish, this lake remains a beloved part of the landscape—a testament to the enduring bond between people and their environment. As the stars twinkle overhead, one can almost imagine Bubbling Bob laughing along, delighted by the stories unfolding at his watery playground.

Boulder Reservoir

Boulder Reservoir, with its shimmering waters and panoramic views of the Flatirons, offers more than just a scenic backdrop; it's a tapestry woven from the threads of history, community, and a dash of humor. Located in Boulder County, Colorado, this reservoir came to life in the late 1950s, when it was constructed as part of a water storage system to support the growing city of Boulder. The reservoir takes its name from the city itself, which, according to local lore, was either named after the "boulders" that littered the nearby hills or the Native American term for "the place of rocks." Either way, it seems the rocks were just too proud to let Boulder go unrecognized.

The early days of Boulder Reservoir saw it primarily as a utilitarian space—after all, a body of water built for water supply isn't often associated with leisure. However, as the years rolled on, it quickly morphed into a beloved recreational hotspot. But with change comes a few hiccups. In 1965, a particularly rainy season caused significant flooding, leading to a temporary shutdown of the reservoir. Stories of frantic park rangers chasing wayward picnic tables and floating barbecues still circulate among locals, often recounted with a hearty laugh. "Remember the year we almost lost the grill to the great flood?" is a common icebreaker among regular visitors.

As the community grew, so did the legends surrounding the reservoir. One humorous myth involves a supposed lake monster affectionately dubbed "Boulder Bob." According to enthusiastic storytellers, Bob was a giant fish that had somehow developed a taste for diving boards, and would lurk beneath the surface waiting to snatch unsuspecting swimmers. Children, wide-eyed and giggling, would warn each other to stay close to the shore, lest they encounter Bob's hungry gaze. Though many dismissed the tale, others insisted they saw ripples in the water that were "definitely" caused by something far more than a fish.

The creation of Boulder Reservoir transformed the local landscape significantly, leading to the establishment of parks and recreational facilities. As people flocked to enjoy picnics, fishing, and boating, the area flourished with new flora and fauna. Initially populated by native grasses and wildflowers, the shores became lined with families grilling hotdogs and kids building sandcastles, turning the once-quiet environment into a vibrant community gathering space. Birds like pelicans and blue herons found their place along the shoreline, often swooping down to partake in the fish abundance, occasionally provoking the ire of local anglers. "Hey, that's my catch!" became a familiar cry, often met with laughter and shared stories of the one that got away.

Before long, the reservoir became a hub for recreational activities, playing host to sailing regattas, paddleboard races, and even a few friendly kite-flying competitions. Local businesses capitalized on this newfound popularity, offering rentals for kayaks and paddleboards, which led to the humorous sight of novice paddlers wobbling and splashing their way across the water. "If you don't get wet, you're not trying hard enough!" became the unofficial motto of Boulder Reservoir, much to the delight of onlookers.

Despite its recreational charm, Boulder Reservoir faced challenges, particularly with invasive species making their way into the waters. Zebra mussels, known for their tenacious nature, posed a threat to the local ecosystem, leading to concerns about water quality and the health of native species. Community members rallied together, organizing cleanup days and awareness campaigns to educate visitors about preventing the spread of invasives. Kids were seen sporting bright T-shirts that read, "Save Our Reservoir!" while proudly participating in trash collection efforts. "Boulder Bob would be proud!" they'd shout, reinforcing the lighthearted nature of the conservation initiatives.

The local government recognized the need for ongoing conservation efforts and began partnering with organizations dedicated to preserving the reservoir's natural beauty. Educational programs sprang up, engaging schools and community groups to foster a sense of stewardship. "Let's learn how to keep Bob at bay," teachers would joke, explaining the importance of environmental protection while tying it back to the mythical lake creature. Such initiatives built a deep sense of community, instilling a shared responsibility to care for their local environment.

Over the years, Boulder Reservoir has expanded its offerings, transforming into a multi-faceted recreational area. In addition to sailing and fishing, the lake now provides trails for hiking and biking, making it a year-round destination. Summer brings the buzz of outdoor concerts and movie nights by the water, where families spread blankets and share popcorn, while winter invites ice fishing enthusiasts and snowshoe adventurers alike.

As the sun sets over Boulder Reservoir, casting a golden hue across the water, the air fills with laughter and joy. Families gather around picnic tables, sharing stories of their days spent under the sun, each one weaving in and out of the humorous legends of Boulder Bob and the infamous floating grills. Children chase each other around the park, their laughter mingling with the sounds of nature.

The reservoir stands not just as a source of water but as a cherished gathering place, a reflection of the community's spirit. With each rippling wave, it carries tales of adventure, environmental consciousness, and the bond shared among those who call Boulder home. It is a reminder that through humor, resilience, and a shared commitment to their environment, the people of Boulder have created a vibrant legacy around a simple body of water—a legacy that will continue to flourish for generations to come. And who knows? Perhaps if you listen closely, you might just hear the playful splash of Boulder Bob, still enjoying the great outdoors with a wink and a grin.

Waterton Canyon Reservoir

Waterton Canyon Reservoir, a hidden treasure tucked away in the foothills of the Rockies, boasts a history as rich and varied as its stunning landscape. Located just southwest of Littleton in Jefferson County, this reservoir is often overshadowed by its more famous neighbors, yet it holds a charm that draws adventurers and nature lovers alike. The name "Waterton" comes from the nearby Waterton Canyon, a stunning canyon carved by the South Platte River that winds its way through this picturesque area.

The creation of the reservoir began in the late 1930s, driven by a vision to provide water for the growing communities of the Denver area. Construction started in 1938, and the reservoir was completed in 1957. It was a monumental effort, transforming the land as water from the South Platte River was diverted to fill the reservoir, turning what had been rugged terrain into a serene oasis. Early locals would gather to watch the process, marveling at the way the landscape was reshaped. They often joked that the engineers must have consulted a group of mischievous gnomes, who surely had their hands in creating such a picturesque waterway.

Though the reservoir serves a practical purpose, it quickly became a beloved recreational site. The locals would often share tales of the first fishing competitions, where more than a few experienced anglers returned home empty-handed, claiming, "The fish must have been in on the joke!" Those early days set the tone for the lake's playful spirit. Today, it is a popular spot for fishing, hiking, and picnicking, and the atmosphere is often alive with laughter and the sounds of splashing water.

As with any natural setting, the history of Waterton Canyon Reservoir is not without its dramatic moments. One particularly notable event occurred in 1965, when heavy rains led to severe flooding in the area. Waters rose rapidly, and locals watched with a mix of excitement and concern as the river swelled, transforming the calm reservoir into a raging torrent. Despite the chaos, the community came together, helping one another through the challenges posed by nature's wrath. "If you can dodge a flood, you can dodge anything!" became a saying that echoed through the canyons, bringing humor to an otherwise tense situation.

Legends surrounding the reservoir also add to its allure. Some locals speak of a spirit, affectionately dubbed "Waterton Willie," said to protect fishermen from bad luck. The tale goes that Willie appears as a flickering light at night, guiding anglers to the best spots. Many claim they've caught a glimpse of this ethereal figure while out on the water. This friendly spirit has become a source of good-natured competition among locals, with fishermen teasing each other about who might attract Willie's attention that day.

Waterton Canyon itself is steeped in history, having been home to indigenous tribes long before European settlers arrived. The Arapaho and Cheyenne tribes roamed these lands, utilizing the waterways for sustenance and community life. Their deep connection to the land shaped a respect for nature that still resonates in the area today. As the landscape changed with colonization, the establishment of the reservoir presented new opportunities for recreation and community development, fostering a spirit of collaboration among residents.

The introduction of the reservoir also provided a unique ecological benefit. The area around Waterton became a refuge for a diverse array of wildlife, from deer to numerous bird species. Early settlers noted the stunning beauty of the region, filled with wildflowers and lush greenery. As the reservoir flourished, so too did the flora and fauna, creating a balance that enriched the ecosystem. "Every time I hike up that trail, I see something new," a local resident once mused. "Nature has its own surprises!"

Over the decades, the reservoir has served various purposes, including fishing, transportation, and even community gatherings. Annual events, such as the "Waterton Water Fest," bring together locals and visitors for a day filled with activities, food, and fun. Families gather to celebrate the beauty of the reservoir while sharing stories and laughter, creating memories that will last a lifetime. During these festivals, the air fills with the aroma of barbecues and the sound of live music, blending with the tranquil backdrop of water and mountains.

However, the growth of the area has not come without challenges. Invasive species have found their way into the waters, prompting conservation efforts to preserve the natural balance. Local organizations have taken on the task of educating the community about the importance of maintaining a healthy ecosystem. "Protecting our reservoir is like protecting our family," one conservationist remarked. "We all rely on it in some way." Community members are encouraged to participate in clean-up events and educational workshops, where laughter and camaraderie blend with a shared mission to keep Waterton Canyon beautiful.

With the increasing popularity of the area, parks and recreational facilities have been developed around the reservoir, enhancing the experience for visitors. Picnic areas, hiking trails, and fishing spots are strategically placed to ensure that everyone can enjoy the natural beauty. The breathtaking views of the canyon, coupled with the serenity of the water, create an inviting atmosphere for those seeking solace from the bustle of everyday life.

As the sun sets over Waterton Canyon Reservoir, casting a warm glow on the water, the sounds of laughter echo through the trees. Friends gather around picnic tables, sharing meals and stories, while children run along the shore, their voices mingling with the gentle lapping of the water. Each gathering adds a layer to the rich tapestry of community and connection that defines the reservoir.

In every corner of Waterton Canyon, the spirit of joy and adventure thrives. As families fish, hike, and explore, they are part of a legacy that stretches back generations—a story that intertwines nature and humanity in a beautiful dance. Whether you're chasing the elusive fish, soaking in the views, or simply enjoying a peaceful moment by the water, the reservoir is a reminder that joy can be found in the simplest of experiences.

And who knows? As you cast your line into the water, you might just catch a glimpse of Waterton Willie, smiling back at you from beneath the surface, encouraging you to make your own memories in this enchanting haven.

Crested Butte Lake

Crested Butte Lake, a sparkling alpine oasis located in the heart of the Rockies, has a history steeped in natural beauty and local lore. Found in Gunnison County, this picturesque lake lies just outside the charming town of Crested Butte, known for its vibrant arts scene and outdoor recreation. The lake was aptly named after the nearby Crested Butte Mountain, which rises dramatically in the distance, resembling a whimsical cap perched upon the landscape.

The lake itself is a natural wonder, formed by glacial activity thousands of years ago. As glaciers retreated, they carved out this stunning basin, creating the tranquil waters that reflect the surrounding peaks. Early explorers marveled at the beauty of the area, and local settlers soon followed, drawn by the promise of adventure and opportunity. It didn't take long for the name "Crested Butte Lake" to catch on, as residents and visitors alike found themselves enchanted by its serenity and charm.

Throughout its history, the lake has been a site of both joy and challenge. In the late 1800s, during the mining boom, the area around Crested Butte experienced a surge of settlers. Prospectors scoured the mountains for silver and coal, often ignoring the lake in their relentless pursuit of fortune. As tales of riches spread, the lake became a quiet witness to the frenzy of human ambition, earning a reputation as a backdrop to countless adventures, and perhaps a few misadventures as well.

The most notorious event in the lake's history occurred during a particularly fierce storm in 1918. Heavy rainfall led to flash flooding in the surrounding area, with water rushing down from the mountains and into the lake. Locals scrambled to save their homes, many joking that they had to "catch the water before it caught them." In the end, the flood transformed the landscape but also brought the community together, as neighbors helped each other weather the storm, both literally and figuratively.

Myths and legends have flourished around Crested Butte Lake, often shared around campfires or during cozy evenings in local taverns. One popular tale involves a "lake monster" known as "Butte Beast." According to the story, the creature appears only during full moons, creating ripples that disturb the surface. Many claim to have seen shadows lurking just beneath the water, but skeptics argue it's merely a trick of the light. Regardless of its truth, the tale adds a sprinkle of excitement for adventurers seeking a little thrill during their outdoor excursions.

The lake has long been a vital resource for the indigenous Ute tribes who inhabited the region long before settlers arrived. The Utes viewed the land as sacred, using the area for fishing and gathering. They recognized the importance of the ecosystem, which provided not just food but also materials for shelter and tools. As the settlers encroached, the landscape changed, but many of the traditional practices established by the Utes continue to resonate with modern conservation efforts. Their respect for the land has inspired local initiatives aimed at protecting the natural beauty and wildlife that define Crested Butte Lake.

With the influx of settlers, the landscape experienced significant changes. While the mining industry brought growth, it also altered the natural environment. However, as the mining boom waned, the area pivoted toward tourism and outdoor recreation, allowing the landscape to reclaim some of its former glory. Trails began to emerge, winding around the lake and into the surrounding mountains, inviting hikers, bikers, and nature enthusiasts to explore the stunning terrain.

Crested Butte Lake has always offered an escape for the community, serving as a hub for recreation. In summer, families flock to its shores for picnics, fishing, and swimming. The lake is home to a variety of fish, including trout, which attracts anglers from near and far. "You can't catch a fish without a story," a local fisherman once quipped, and indeed, the tales of the one that got away are as rich as the water is blue.

In the winter, the lake transforms into a wonderland, with snow-covered landscapes drawing cross-country skiers and snowshoers eager to explore its quiet beauty. Local events like the annual "Frozen Butte Festival" showcase the lake's versatility, featuring ice fishing, snow sculptures, and community gatherings that celebrate the spirit of the region. Each year, families come together, bundled in their warmest attire, sharing laughter and stories as they partake in winter activities.

Despite its enchanting allure, Crested Butte Lake has not been immune to challenges. Invasive species, particularly certain types of algae, have made their way into the waters, threatening the delicate ecosystem. Local conservation groups have rallied together, launching initiatives to monitor and manage the health of the lake. These efforts emphasize the importance of maintaining clean waterways and educating the public about responsible practices, ensuring that the lake remains a vibrant resource for generations to come.

Parks and recreational facilities have flourished around the lake, providing visitors with amenities while preserving the natural landscape. Campsites, picnic areas, and trails enhance the experience for outdoor enthusiasts, allowing families and friends to connect with nature. Community members often come together to organize clean-up events, demonstrating their commitment to protecting the beauty that surrounds them.

As the sun sets behind the majestic peaks, casting a golden hue over the lake, a sense of peace envelops the area. The echoes of laughter and the scent of roasting marshmallows fill the air as families gather to share stories and create memories. It's in these moments that the true spirit of

Crested Butte Lake shines through—a testament to resilience, camaraderie, and the joy of living in harmony with nature.

The lake continues to be a place of connection, where the past meets the present, and where the laughter of children mingles with the whispers of the wind. Whether it's through fishing, hiking, or simply sitting by the shore and soaking in the beauty, Crested Butte Lake invites everyone to be part of its ongoing story. As locals often say, "The lake may be still, but it's always alive with memories waiting to be made."

St. Vrain State Park Lakes

St. Vrain State Park Lakes, a beautiful collection of shimmering waters, occupies a special place in the heart of Colorado's Front Range. Located in Weld County, just a stone's throw from the town of Longmont, this park is a delightful blend of history, nature, and community spirit. The lakes take their name from the St. Vrain River, named after the early 19th-century trapper and explorer, Ceran St. Vrain, who roamed the area in search of fur-bearing animals and a little adventure. Little did he know that his name would be associated with a series of lakes that would become a favorite destination for both locals and visitors alike.

The formation of these lakes is a testament to the ingenuity of those who came before us. Originally created for irrigation purposes, the lakes were part of a series of ditches and reservoirs established in the mid-20th century to support agriculture in the area. Over the years, as people began to recognize the recreational potential of these bodies of water, St. Vrain State Park was born, officially opening in 1998. The transformation from irrigation ditches to a beloved state park is a story of adaptation and growth, much like the surrounding landscape.

In the early days, the area was home to various indigenous tribes, notably the Arapaho and Cheyenne. These tribes relied on the fertile lands and abundant water for fishing and hunting, and they viewed the river and its lakes as sacred. The St. Vrain River served as a vital transportation route, allowing them to connect with neighboring tribes and trade goods. The lakes today echo that history, reminding us of the deep roots this land has and the respect it deserves.

The initial flora and fauna around the lakes were diverse, with lush vegetation and wildlife thriving in the area. Cottonwoods lined the banks, providing shade and shelter for birds, while the waters teemed with fish and amphibians. As settlers moved in and the land was developed for agriculture, some of this natural landscape was altered, but the lakes remained a refuge for various species. The impact of colonization was not solely negative; with careful management and conservation efforts, many aspects of the ecosystem have been preserved or restored.

The lakes have a rich history of community engagement and recreation. In the early days of the park's establishment, families would come to picnic, fish, and enjoy the outdoors. The laughter of children and the chatter of families created a vibrant atmosphere that still echoes through the park today. As the popularity of the park grew, so did the range of activities offered. Now, visitors can enjoy fishing, kayaking, paddleboarding, and even birdwatching. One particularly enthusiastic local once joked that the only thing you can't do at St. Vrain State Park is have a bad time!

However, like many natural areas, St. Vrain State Park has faced its share of challenges. The park is not immune to the issue of invasive species. In particular, some non-native fish species have made their way into the lakes, threatening the delicate balance of the local ecosystem. Conservation efforts are ongoing to monitor and manage these species, ensuring that the native populations can thrive. Local organizations often host clean-up days and educational programs to engage the community in preserving the natural beauty of the lakes.

The lakes have also been the site of some historic floods. One particularly memorable event occurred in September 2013 when torrential rains swept through the area, leading to significant flooding. The St. Vrain River overflowed its banks, and while the park suffered damage, the community came together in a remarkable display of resilience. Volunteers rallied to clean up the debris, restore trails, and support each other in the recovery process. It was a time of hardship, but also a reminder of the strong bonds that form in the face of adversity.

Stories and myths surrounding the lakes have also emerged over the years. One popular local legend speaks of a "lake monster" that supposedly resides in the depths of one of the larger lakes. While no one has ever confirmed its existence, the story brings a sense of mystery and excitement to the area, especially for adventurous children who enjoy daring each other to fish at twilight. As the sun sets, casting a warm glow over the water, imaginations run wild, and the laughter of friends echoes along the shores.

Over the years, St. Vrain State Park has developed a range of facilities and programs to enhance the visitor experience. With well-maintained trails, picnic areas, and educational kiosks, the park serves as a hub for community gatherings and recreational activities. Annual events like the "St. Vrain State Park Day" bring families together to celebrate nature, participate in guided tours, and learn about the ecology of the area. These gatherings not only promote appreciation for the environment but also strengthen community ties.

As the sun rises over the lakes, casting a golden light on the tranquil waters, the park transforms into a serene oasis. Mornings are filled with the sound of birds singing, while early risers often spot deer grazing near the shores. For many, the park serves as a place of reflection and renewal, where the stresses of everyday life fade away amidst the beauty of nature.

The legacy of St. Vrain State Park Lakes is a story of connection—to the land, to the community, and to the generations that have come before. As visitors explore the park today, they become part of that ongoing narrative, contributing to a collective appreciation for the natural world. Whether casting a line into the water or enjoying a leisurely stroll along the shore, each moment spent at the lakes adds a chapter to the vibrant story of this cherished place.

In the end, St. Vrain State Park Lakes is not just a collection of bodies of water; it's a living tapestry of history, laughter, and resilience. As families continue to gather, friends forge memories, and nature flourishes, the spirit of the lakes will carry on, inviting everyone to embrace the beauty and joy that surrounds them. In the words of a local park ranger, "Every splash, every laugh, and every moment here is a drop in the ocean of life, making waves of memories that last a lifetime."

Pinewood Reservoir

Pinewood Reservoir, a shimmering jewel of a lake located in the heart of Larimer County, Colorado, has a history that dances between human ingenuity and the whims of nature. This picturesque reservoir is part of the larger Horsetooth Reservoir system and was created in the early 1960s when a dam was constructed to supply water for irrigation and municipal use. As the sun rises over the water, casting a warm glow, it's hard to imagine this serene spot was once a valley filled with trees, wildlife, and whispers of ancient stories.

The reservoir takes its name from the nearby Pinewood Springs, a nod to the dense forests of pine trees that envelop the area. This rich natural environment has been a backdrop for various human stories, both joyous and challenging. The early inhabitants of this region, primarily the Arapaho and Cheyenne tribes, roamed the lands with a profound connection to nature. They fished in the rivers and hunted in the forests, living in harmony with the landscape. The flowing waters were vital for their livelihoods, allowing trade and communication among tribes. The spirit of those early inhabitants still lingers in the gentle rustle of the pines and the quiet lapping of the waves.

As settlers moved in during the 19th century, they began to change the landscape. Colonization brought both challenges and opportunities. While it led to the loss of some native habitats, it also sparked a wave of agricultural growth in the region. Pinewood Reservoir was part of that vision—a way to store water for irrigation and support the growing communities. The construction of the dam was an ambitious project, requiring the cooperation of engineers, laborers, and visionaries who recognized the value of harnessing nature's resources.

However, nature has a way of reminding us who's really in charge. In the early years after the reservoir was established, unexpected floods tested the resolve of the community. Heavy rains would swell the waters, leading to rising levels that sometimes threatened the shores. Residents would rally together, reinforcing banks and ensuring that the delicate balance of this ecosystem remained intact. These moments fostered a deep sense of community, with neighbors helping neighbors, sharing stories and laughter as they worked side by side.

Over the years, myths and legends began to swirl around the reservoir. Locals tell tales of mysterious shadows moving beneath the surface, leading some to believe that a guardian spirit watches over the waters. Campfire stories often include fish that are larger than life, enticing anglers to test their luck. Whether or not there's truth to these legends, they add an element of magic to the experience, inspiring many to come and seek their own adventure at Pinewood.

The flora and fauna around Pinewood Reservoir are diverse and vibrant. The initial plant life included lush grasses, wildflowers, and, of course, the towering pines that give the area its name. Wildlife flourished, with deer, elk, and countless bird species calling this place home. As development increased, careful management practices were implemented to protect these habitats. The local community has worked diligently to promote biodiversity, engaging in efforts to restore native plants and reduce the spread of invasive species.

In recent years, the challenge of invasive species has become a significant concern. Some non-native fish have found their way into the reservoir, prompting conservation efforts aimed at maintaining the delicate balance of the ecosystem. Local organizations and park authorities have launched initiatives to educate the public on the importance of preserving native species and habitats. These efforts have helped cultivate a culture of stewardship among visitors and residents alike, encouraging everyone to play a part in protecting this natural treasure.

Pinewood Reservoir is not just a beautiful spot for fishing and boating; it's also a hub of community activity and recreation. Families come to picnic by the water, children laugh as they splash in the shallows, and outdoor enthusiasts can be seen hiking the nearby trails. The reservoir serves as a backdrop for many local events, from fishing derbies to outdoor concerts, bringing people together to celebrate the joys of nature.

The reservoir has become a haven for anglers looking to catch a variety of fish, including rainbow trout and bass. With fishing regulations in place, local fisheries have thrived, providing ample opportunities for both seasoned fishermen and families trying their luck. For those who prefer to stay dry, scenic views from the shore or hiking trails provide a perfect escape from the hustle and bustle of everyday life.

As Pinewood Reservoir continues to thrive, it is also a place of reflection and rejuvenation. The tranquility of the waters draws people in, offering them a chance to slow down and reconnect with nature. Each sunset paints the sky in brilliant hues, a reminder of the beauty that surrounds us and the memories we create by the water's edge.

Over time, Pinewood Reservoir has evolved from a simple water storage solution to a beloved community hub, rich in history and natural beauty. The journey of this lake reflects the stories of those who have come before, the resilience of the land, and the enduring spirit of the people who cherish it. Whether casting a line, hiking a trail, or simply enjoying a peaceful moment by the water, everyone who visits Pinewood Reservoir becomes part of its ongoing story.

As the seasons change, and the waters ebb and flow, Pinewood Reservoir stands as a testament to the harmony that can be achieved between humans and nature. It invites all who come to celebrate its beauty, fostering a sense of belonging and connection. In this enchanting corner of

Colorado, every visit brings a new chapter to the rich tapestry of life that is Pinewood Reservoir.

Lily Lake

Lily Lake, a tranquil and scenic spot located in the Rocky Mountain National Park area of Colorado, is a delightful tapestry of natural beauty, human history, and a splash of whimsy. Perched at an elevation of about 8,800 feet in Larimer County, the lake was formed by glacial activity during the last ice age, creating a stunning alpine landscape that captivates all who visit. The lake's name is derived from the lovely water lilies that bloom on its surface during the summer months, creating a picturesque scene that invites admiration and serenity.

The area around Lily Lake has been a gathering place for countless generations. Long before the first settlers arrived, the Ute and Arapaho tribes roamed the land, their lives intertwined with the rhythms of nature. For these indigenous peoples, the lake provided more than just water; it was a source of sustenance, offering fish and wild plants. The nearby forests and meadows were abundant with deer and other game, essential for their survival. Legends of great spirits protecting the land and water have been passed down through generations, creating a rich cultural tapestry that honors the natural world.

As the first European settlers made their way into the region in the late 19th century, they brought with them dreams of prosperity and community. The establishment of ranches and small farms transformed the landscape, leading to a bustling local economy. It wasn't long before residents recognized the value of the lake, not only for its beauty but also for its potential to support agriculture and livestock. The creation of irrigation systems drew water from the lake, enhancing crop yields and fostering a sense of community among those who relied on the land for their livelihoods.

Despite its idyllic setting, Lily Lake has not been without its challenges. The region is no stranger to the forces of nature, and over the years, heavy rains and rapid snowmelt have occasionally caused the waters to rise dramatically. During these floods, the shoreline would recede, creating a temporary but alarming loss of land. The resilience of the community shone through as they banded together, reinforcing banks and helping each other recover from the impacts of nature. These experiences forged bonds among neighbors and sparked a spirit of cooperation that endures to this day.

Myths surrounding Lily Lake add a layer of charm to its history. Locals often recount tales of mysterious creatures gliding beneath the surface, leading to whispers of mermaids or other water spirits that might inhabit the depths. Children dare each other to cast their fishing lines in the hopes of snagging a glimpse of these elusive beings. Though most know these tales to be light-hearted folklore, they bring a sense of wonder to the experience of visiting the lake. After all, who wouldn't want to believe in a little magic when surrounded by such stunning beauty?

The flora and fauna of Lily Lake paint a vibrant picture of life in this alpine ecosystem. Initially, the lake and its surroundings teemed with native plants such as wildflowers, grasses, and various species of conifers. The natural habitat supports a diverse range of wildlife, including birds, deer, and even the occasional bear. However, as human activity increased, the balance of this ecosystem faced challenges. Invasive species began to creep in, threatening the delicate harmony that had existed for centuries. To combat this, local conservation efforts have been initiated, focusing on education and restoration to preserve the integrity of the area.

Today, Lily Lake stands as a cherished destination for outdoor enthusiasts and families alike. Anglers flock to its shores, hoping to reel in rainbow trout while surrounded by breathtaking mountain views. Hiking trails weave around the lake, offering opportunities for exploration and connection with nature. The serene environment is perfect for picnicking, and it's common to see families spread blankets on the grassy banks, enjoying lunch while the kids chase after butterflies or splash in the shallows.

Community development around Lily Lake has blossomed into a vibrant local culture. Parks and recreational facilities have been established to enhance the visitor experience, allowing people to immerse themselves in the beauty of the area. Seasonal events, such as fishing derbies and outdoor festivals, bring neighbors together to celebrate the joys of nature and community. The spirit of camaraderie is palpable, with laughter and shared experiences filling the air.

As with any treasured natural resource, the lake faces ongoing challenges. Conservation groups work tirelessly to address the impact of human activity, advocating for sustainable practices and protecting the surrounding habitat. Education programs aimed at local residents and visitors help raise awareness of the importance of preserving the ecosystem, ensuring that future generations can continue to enjoy the wonders of Lily Lake.

The lake's history is not just one of human intervention; it also tells a story of resilience and harmony. As seasons change and life unfolds, Lily Lake continues to capture the hearts of those who visit. The laughter of children echoes across the water, while the beauty of the surrounding mountains stands as a timeless testament to the wonder of nature. Each visit offers an opportunity to reflect, rejuvenate, and reconnect, reminding all who come that life is a beautiful journey, best shared with others.

With every sunset, as the sky is painted in hues of orange and pink, the water sparkles in response, casting a spell of tranquility over the landscape. Visitors leave Lily Lake not just with memories of breathtaking views but with a sense of belonging—a reminder of the importance of preserving this enchanting piece of Colorado for generations to come. Whether through fishing, hiking, or simply enjoying the serenity, everyone finds a place in the ongoing story of Lily

Lake, where nature, history, and community come together in perfect harmony.

360

Louisville Reservoir

Louisville Reservoir, a sparkling oasis in the heart of Colorado, has a rich and colorful history that reflects the resilience and creativity of the communities that have flourished around it. Located just a few miles southeast of the town of Louisville in Boulder County, this body of water was created in the early 20th century to provide a reliable water source for irrigation and municipal use. The reservoir is an essential part of the region's water management system and a favorite recreational spot for locals and visitors alike.

The name "Louisville" pays homage to the city's founding family, the Smiths, who settled in the area during the Colorado Gold Rush. While the area didn't yield the expected gold, the Smiths found other treasures: fertile land, ample water, and a vibrant community. Over time, the city transformed from a mining hub into a suburban haven, and the reservoir became a vital resource for the growing population.

As with many bodies of water, Louisville Reservoir has seen its share of dramatic events. In the 1930s, a series of heavy storms brought torrential rain, causing the reservoir to swell and flood its banks. The flooding prompted community leaders to rethink their approach to water management, leading to improvements in dam infrastructure and flood control measures. It was during these times of adversity that the spirit of collaboration among residents truly shone, as they came together to aid one another and rebuild their community.

Among the tales that swirl around the reservoir is a charming local legend about a mythical creature said to reside beneath the waters. According to lore, the spirit of a fisherman who once lived in the area watches over the lake, ensuring that those who fish there are blessed with a good catch. The tale, though whimsical, brings a sense of camaraderie among anglers who often swap stories of the elusive "Louisville Lake Monster," claiming it occasionally surfaces to bless them with its presence.

Louisville Reservoir is not just a recreational hub; it is also a beautiful ecological setting. Formed primarily through the construction of a dam, the reservoir quickly became home to various flora and fauna. Initially, the landscape was dominated by riparian vegetation, including cottonwoods and willows, which provided essential habitat for birds and small mammals. Over time, as human activity increased, some areas were developed for recreation, creating a delicate balance between nature and human enjoyment.

Before European settlers arrived, the land was inhabited by the Arapaho and Ute tribes, who utilized the area's resources sustainably. For these indigenous peoples, the reservoir provided water for drinking and fishing, along with a rich ecosystem that supported their way of life. With the arrival of settlers, the landscape began to change, but many local efforts aimed to honor the land's history and maintain a connection to its roots. Through the establishment of educational programs and community events, the stories of the indigenous peoples are kept alive, fostering respect for the land and its history.

As the region developed, the reservoir became a focal point for community gatherings and recreation. It served as a vital waterway for transporting goods and played a significant role in irrigation systems for local farms. Residents embraced the reservoir for fishing, boating, and picnicking, creating lasting memories with family and friends. Local events like fishing tournaments and outdoor movie nights have turned the area into a vibrant gathering place, strengthening the bonds among residents and visitors.

However, human activity has also left its mark on Louisville Reservoir. As development surged, invasive species began to threaten the delicate ecosystem. The introduction of non-native plants and fish species posed challenges for local wildlife and the balance of the environment. In response, conservation efforts have gained momentum, focusing on education and restoration projects aimed at preserving the integrity of the reservoir's ecosystem. Local organizations work tirelessly to remove invasive species and educate the community about sustainable practices, ensuring that the reservoir remains a thriving habitat.

Today, Louisville Reservoir is more than just a body of water; it is a beloved community space that promotes outdoor recreation and environmental stewardship. Trails wind around the lake, inviting hikers and bikers to enjoy the stunning views of the Rocky Mountains. Birdwatchers flock to the area, eager to catch a glimpse of the diverse avian life that thrives here. The reservoir's waters are teeming with fish, providing ample opportunities for both novice and experienced anglers to cast their lines.

In addition to its natural beauty, the reservoir has become a hub for family-friendly activities. Parks have been developed along its shores, featuring picnic areas, playgrounds, and scenic overlooks. Local events, such as outdoor concerts and farmers' markets, bring the community together, fostering a spirit of togetherness and celebration. Whether it's a leisurely day spent fishing or a festive gathering with neighbors, Louisville Reservoir serves as a backdrop for countless cherished moments.

As the sun sets behind the mountains, casting a warm glow across the water, the reservoir transforms into a serene haven. Families pack up their picnic baskets, and friends gather for sunset strolls, laughing and sharing stories of the day. The gentle ripples on the water reflect not only the fading light but also the deep connections forged in this beautiful setting.

With every season that passes, Louisville Reservoir continues to adapt and thrive, embodying the spirit of a community that values both nature and togetherness. As residents and visitors enjoy its offerings, they are reminded of the importance of preserving this cherished resource for future generations, ensuring that the stories and laughter echo around its shores for years to come. Each visit is an opportunity to engage with nature, embrace the joy of shared experiences, and celebrate the vibrant life that thrives at Louisville Reservoir.

Mackintosh Lake

Mackintosh Lake, a picturesque body of water located in Boulder County, Colorado, boasts a history as rich and varied as the natural beauty surrounding it. This charming lake is named after the Mackintosh family, early settlers who played a significant role in the agricultural development of the area. The Mackintoshes arrived in the late 1800s, bringing with them a spirit of hard work and a vision for a thriving community. Their efforts laid the groundwork for the region's growth, making their name a fitting tribute for this tranquil waterway.

The lake's story truly begins with its formation, which can be traced back to the 1970s when it was created as part of a water management project to support local agriculture. Initially designed as a water storage facility, Mackintosh Lake quickly became much more than just a utility. Its creation not only transformed the landscape but also provided a much-needed resource for irrigation, allowing local farmers to cultivate their crops more efficiently. As the lake filled, it created a stunning natural habitat that attracted various wildlife and turned into a beloved recreational area.

Of course, with a body of water comes the potential for mischief and mayhem. In the summer of 1985, a series of unexpected thunderstorms rolled through the area, leading to a flash flood that threatened to overwhelm the lake's banks. Local residents sprang into action, sandbagging and working together to prevent disaster. Fortunately, their efforts paid off, and the lake held firm, but the event served as a stark reminder of nature's power and the importance of community resilience. That summer became a cherished story among locals, who fondly referred to it as "the summer of the great sandbagging."

Legends surrounding Mackintosh Lake add a touch of whimsy to its history. One popular tale involves a fisherman named Old Joe, said to be the spirit of an angler who spent countless hours casting his line from the lake's shores. According to local lore, Old Joe was known for catching the largest fish anyone had ever seen. Many a hopeful angler claimed to have spotted him in the early morning mist, a twinkle in his eye and a fishing pole in hand. Today, those fishing at Mackintosh Lake often share a laugh, wondering if Old Joe is still out there, quietly judging their skills from the water's depths.

Mackintosh Lake is not only significant for its recreational purposes; it also holds ecological importance. Initially surrounded by lush grasslands, wetlands, and diverse vegetation, the lake became a sanctuary for a variety of wildlife, including birds, amphibians, and fish. The rich biodiversity attracted local Indigenous tribes such as the Arapaho and Cheyenne, who relied on the area for its resources. For these tribes, the lake was a vital source of sustenance, providing fish and water for drinking and cultivation. Their relationship with the land was one of respect and reciprocity, with careful attention paid to the balance of nature.

As settlers arrived in the late 19th century, the landscape began to change dramatically. Colonization brought agriculture and the demand for land, reshaping the ecosystem to accommodate farming practices. Although this transformation had its challenges, it also led to significant advancements in irrigation and resource management, enabling the region to thrive economically. Mackintosh Lake became a cornerstone of this development, facilitating not only agriculture but also community bonding as families gathered for picnics and fishing outings.

With its newly formed waters, Mackintosh Lake quickly became a hub for recreation. Locals flocked to its shores for fishing, boating, and leisurely strolls along the banks. The lake's scenic beauty made it an ideal spot for family gatherings and community events, creating cherished memories that would be passed down through generations. The park surrounding the lake evolved into a haven for outdoor enthusiasts, featuring trails for hiking and biking, picnic areas, and playgrounds for children.

However, the joys of recreation were not without challenges. The increasing popularity of the lake led to concerns about pollution and habitat degradation. Invasive species began to infiltrate the waters, disrupting the delicate ecosystem. To combat these issues, local conservation groups sprang into action, working tirelessly to preserve the lake's health. They organized community clean-up events, educational programs, and outreach efforts to raise awareness about the importance of protecting this natural treasure.

Today, Mackintosh Lake stands as a testament to the harmony between human activity and nature. The efforts to combat invasive species and maintain the lake's ecosystem have been met with success, allowing native flora and fauna to thrive. Birdwatchers visit the area to spot a variety of species, while anglers are often found casting their lines in pursuit of the legendary fish that Old Joe once caught.

The park surrounding the lake has continued to develop, embracing its role as a community hub. Seasonal events like outdoor movie nights, nature walks, and fishing tournaments bring people together, creating a vibrant tapestry of life around the water. Families pack picnics, friends gather for barbecues, and laughter echoes across the lake as children chase after the ice cream truck, all against the stunning backdrop of the Rockies.

As the sun sets over Mackintosh Lake, casting a golden glow across the water, the beauty of the place becomes almost magical. Couples stroll hand-in-hand along the trails, and families settle down for evening picnics, the warmth of the day giving way to a cool breeze. With each wave that laps at the shore, stories of Old Joe, community resilience, and the wonders of nature intertwine, creating a legacy that continues to grow.

Mackintosh Lake is more than just a reservoir; it's a gathering place, a symbol of perseverance, and a beautiful reminder of the connection between people and nature. As the community thrives, so does the spirit of the lake, inviting all who visit to experience its magic and join in the stories that will be told for years to come.

St. Mary's Glacier Lake

St. Mary's Glacier Lake, a stunning high-altitude reservoir located in Clear Creek County, Colorado, is a picturesque spot that captures the heart of anyone who ventures into its alpine embrace. Named after the nearby St. Mary's Glacier, which itself was named by miners who sought their fortune in the 1860s, the lake offers a rich tapestry of history intertwined with natural beauty. The glacier, formed from snow accumulation over the millennia, feeds the lake, creating a vivid blue oasis surrounded by rugged peaks and lush forests.

The journey of St. Mary's Glacier Lake begins with its formation, a story that dates back thousands of years. Unlike many man-made reservoirs in Colorado, this lake is a product of nature's artistry. As the glacier advanced and retreated, it carved out a bowl-like depression that eventually filled with snowmelt and rainwater, giving rise to the serene lake we see today. This natural wonder serves as both a vital water source and a stunning recreational area.

Local flora and fauna thrive in this alpine environment, with wildflowers bursting into bloom each summer, creating a riot of color against the backdrop of towering evergreens.

Wildlife such as elk, deer, and an array of birds make their home here, each adding to the vibrant ecosystem. Indigenous tribes, including the Arapaho and Ute, were drawn to this land long before settlers arrived, relying on the area's resources for food and shelter. For these tribes, St. Mary's Glacier Lake was not just a beautiful sight; it was integral to their way of life, providing fresh water and opportunities for fishing and hunting.

As the gold rush attracted miners and settlers to the region, the landscape began to change dramatically. The influx of people led to an increase in agriculture and logging, both of which transformed the area. While colonization brought significant challenges, it also resulted in advancements in infrastructure. Roads were built to connect communities, opening up access to the breathtaking scenery and fostering a sense of camaraderie among those who called this wild terrain home.

St. Mary's Glacier Lake quickly became a popular destination for both locals and visitors. In the early 1900s, families would pack picnics and hike to the lake for a day of fun and relaxation. Fishing was a beloved pastime, with tales of the "big one"—a legendary trout that many tried, but few caught. Community gatherings flourished around the lake, from summer barbecues to winter festivities, creating a strong bond among the residents. The lake transformed into a cherished gathering place, a site of laughter and connection that echoed through the years.

The beauty of the lake, however, was not without its perils. In the summer of 1995, a sudden storm swept through the area, sending a deluge of rain that swelled the lake to dangerous levels. Flash floods cascaded down the mountains, prompting an emergency response from local authorities. The community banded together to protect homes and rescue stranded hikers. Fortunately, no lives were lost, but the event served as a reminder of nature's unpredictable power and the importance of preparedness. This summer became known as "the flood of '95," a tale passed down through generations, often recounted with a mix of humor and reverence for the elements.

Legends have also emerged around St. Mary's Glacier Lake, enhancing its mystique. One popular story tells of a spirit who wanders the shores, known as the "Guardian of the Glacier." According to local lore, this spirit protects the lake and its surrounding wildlife, ensuring that the delicate balance of nature is preserved. Hikers claim to feel a gentle presence, a sense of tranquility that envelops them as they walk the trails. Some even swear they've caught glimpses of a shimmering figure at dawn, dancing along the water's edge. Whether truth or fiction, these tales enrich the lake's allure, making it a destination not just for adventure, but for the spirit as well.

Over the years, the impacts of human activity have not gone unnoticed. As tourism to the lake increased, so did concerns about pollution and the effects of invasive species. The introduction of non-native plants and fish threatened the delicate ecosystem, prompting local conservation efforts. Community organizations rallied together to raise awareness, initiating clean-up events and educational programs to protect the lake's pristine waters. With volunteers working tirelessly, the surrounding trails and beaches were restored, ensuring that future generations could enjoy the beauty of St. Mary's Glacier Lake just as it had been enjoyed for decades.

Today, St. Mary's Glacier Lake remains a cherished jewel in Colorado's landscape, attracting outdoor enthusiasts year-round. Whether it's hiking, fishing, or simply soaking in the breathtaking views, visitors flock to its shores, eager to experience the magic that has captivated so many. The area has seen the development of parks and trails, making it easier for people of all ages to access the lake and its surroundings. Families arrive for summer picnics, while adventurous souls tackle the nearby hiking trails in search of stunning vistas and hidden treasures.

As the sun sets behind the mountains, casting a golden hue over the lake's surface, it's impossible not to feel a sense of connection to the land and its history. Stories of laughter, hardship, and resilience intertwine with the whispers of the wind and the gentle lapping of the water. St. Mary's Glacier Lake stands as a testament to the beauty of nature and the strength of community, a place where memories are forged and legends continue to grow.

With each passing year, the lake thrives, and so too does the spirit of those who cherish it. As children splash in its cool waters and hikers embark on new adventures, the legacy of St. Mary's Glacier Lake endures, weaving together the past and present in a tapestry of joy, laughter, and the unyielding power of nature. The lake is not just a destination; it's a living, breathing entity that invites everyone to be part of its ongoing story, ensuring that its beauty will inspire generations to come.

Winter Park Reservoir

Winter Park Reservoir, a stunning alpine lake situated in Grand County, Colorado, is more than just a picturesque getaway; it's a vibrant tapestry woven from history, nature, and the joy of community. The reservoir's name evokes the spirit of winter recreation and the stunning scenery that surrounds it, drawing visitors and locals alike to its shores year-round. The area was originally known as "Winter Park" because of its proximity to the popular ski resort, which quickly became a hotspot for winter sports enthusiasts and outdoor adventurers.

The lake itself is a man-made reservoir, formed in the late 20th century to provide water for irrigation and recreation, as well as to support the local ecosystem. Construction began in the 1970s, transforming a tranquil valley into a sprawling body of water. As the waters rose, the valley transformed, but not without leaving behind remnants of its past. Old tree stumps jut out from the shoreline, whispering tales of the land that once was, and some say they can even hear the echoes of laughter from children who once played in the valley before the water took over.

The surrounding landscape is rich with flora and fauna, with towering pines framing the water and wildflowers blooming in vibrant colors during the summer months. Wildlife thrives here, including elk, moose, and a variety of birds. Indigenous tribes, particularly the Ute people, roamed this land long before it became a recreational hub. They relied on the natural resources of the area for sustenance, often fishing in the streams and lakes that dotted the landscape. For the Ute, this land was sacred, and they held a deep connection to the water that flowed through it, viewing it as a life source.

As settlers arrived in the late 19th and early 20th centuries, the landscape began to change. Logging and mining boomed, and the delicate balance of the ecosystem faced new challenges. But along with the changes came opportunities. Winter Park started to develop as a community, and with the construction of the reservoir, it quickly evolved into a hub for outdoor recreation. The lake became a popular fishing spot, where families would gather for picnics and anglers would share stories of their biggest catches. Tales of "Old Blue," a mythical fish said to be lurking in the depths, became part of local lore, captivating the imaginations of young and old alike.

One particularly memorable event in the history of Winter Park Reservoir occurred during a winter storm in 1984. Heavy snowfall led to the lake swelling beyond its banks, causing a minor flood that surprised the local community. People remembered the event not with dread but with laughter, recounting how they saw neighbors skiing down the streets, celebrating the unexpected holiday as they adapted to the playful chaos of nature. The incident solidified a sense of camaraderie among the residents, who banded together to help each other clear the snow, proving that even in challenging times, the community spirit could shine brightly.

The lore surrounding the lake didn't stop at "Old Blue." Many locals claimed to have seen a mysterious creature rising from the waters at dusk, often described as a playful spirit that brought good fortune to those who spotted it. Campfire stories filled with humor and excitement often revolved around late-night fishing trips, where someone would claim to have seen "The Reservoir Beast," sending everyone into fits of laughter as they spun elaborate tales of the creature's escapades.

In terms of human impact, Winter Park Reservoir faced challenges typical of many popular recreational sites. Invasive species, particularly non-native fish, began to disrupt the delicate ecosystem. Local conservationists and environmental groups sprang into action, organizing events to educate the public about the importance of maintaining the lake's ecological balance. They rallied volunteers for clean-up days, turning trash collection into community celebrations, complete with music and food. This emphasis on conservation fostered a greater appreciation for the reservoir, deepening the community's commitment to protecting it.

As tourism flourished, so too did the development of parks and recreational activities. The Winter Park Reservoir area saw the establishment of hiking trails, picnic areas, and even small boat launches, allowing families to enjoy kayaking and paddleboarding on sunny afternoons. The reservoir became a summer playground, with children splashing in the water and adults relaxing on the shore, the air filled with laughter and the scent of barbecues. Every summer, the community hosted a "Lake Day" festival, complete with games, contests, and a fishing derby, all to celebrate their beloved lake and the joy it brought to their lives.

With the changing seasons, the reservoir offered unique experiences for everyone. In winter, it transformed into a sparkling wonderland, with ice skating and ice fishing drawing crowds eager to embrace the cold. The sound of skates gliding over ice and the thrill of catching a fish through a hole in the frozen surface filled the air, creating a magical atmosphere. Families would gather around bonfires, sharing stories and sipping hot cocoa, forging memories that would last a lifetime.

Today, Winter Park Reservoir stands as a testament to the harmony that can exist between nature and community. The balance of recreation, conservation, and folklore continues to thrive, drawing people from all walks of life to experience the beauty and joy of this alpine paradise. Each visit is a chance to connect with the land, partake in its rich history, and perhaps, if you listen closely enough, hear the echoes of laughter and the whispers of legends that have woven themselves into the very fabric of this remarkable place.

As the sun sets behind the peaks, casting golden hues over the water, the lake transforms once more. It becomes a canvas for reflection and a space for dreams. Children chase after fireflies, while adults share stories of their adventures, both real and imagined. Winter Park Reservoir is more than just a body of water; it is a living storybook, a collection of moments that celebrate the spirit of community, the magic of nature, and the joy of life in Colorado's breathtaking outdoors. The spirit of the lake is alive, inviting all to immerse themselves in its charm and create their own chapters in the ongoing tale of Winter Park Reservoir.

Nymph Lake

Nymph Lake, a delightful pocket of tranquility in Colorado's Rocky Mountain National Park, holds a captivating history that blends nature's beauty with a sprinkle of local legend. Located in Larimer County, just a short hike from the more renowned Dream Lake, Nymph Lake invites visitors into its serene embrace, surrounded by towering pines and majestic mountain views. Its name is said to derive from the enchanting nymphs of folklore, which, according to legend, danced in the moonlight over the lake's surface, captivating all who ventured too close. This whimsical imagery captures the imagination, setting the stage for tales that would unfold over generations.

The lake itself is a product of glacial activity, formed thousands of years ago when ancient glaciers carved their path through the landscape, leaving behind a natural basin that would eventually fill with snowmelt and rainwater. While Nymph Lake is not man-made, its accessibility is a testament to the harmonious relationship between nature and those who seek to experience it. The surrounding area boasts a rich tapestry of flora, including vibrant wildflowers that bloom in the summer and clusters of aspens that shimmer in the autumn breeze. Wildlife is abundant; the lake is often visited by moose, deer, and an array of colorful birds that create a lively soundtrack for those who wander its shores.

For centuries, the region was home to the Ute tribes, who revered the land and its resources. To the Ute people, Nymph Lake was not just a body of water; it was a vital source of sustenance and spiritual connection. They fished its waters, gathered plants from its banks, and held sacred ceremonies in the surrounding wilderness. With the arrival of settlers in the late 1800s, however, the landscape began to transform. The allure of gold and other resources drew many to the area, altering the ecological balance and introducing new challenges for the indigenous tribes.

Despite these changes, Nymph Lake remained a beloved destination for both locals and visitors. The beauty of the lake soon caught the eye of outdoor enthusiasts and photographers, who flocked to capture its picturesque scenery. The lake's pristine waters provided ample opportunities for fishing, with fly fishermen often seen casting lines from the rocky edges. These shared moments by the water created a sense of community among those who cherished the lake, often leading to stories of the "one that got away" being swapped over campfires in the evenings.

In the early 20th century, Nymph Lake became part of the expanding Rocky Mountain National Park, a designation that offered both protection and a boost in popularity. The new park status meant better access, and trails were established to help visitors explore the stunning natural landscape. Although the increased foot traffic posed risks to the delicate ecosystem, the park service implemented measures to preserve the lake's charm and ecological integrity. Educational programs were developed, teaching visitors about the importance of protecting natural resources and respecting wildlife.

However, as with many natural wonders, Nymph Lake faced its share of challenges. Invasive species began to infiltrate the ecosystem, disrupting the balance that had existed for so long. These species posed a threat to the native fish populations and the overall health of the lake. The community responded with fervor, organizing volunteer days to remove invasives and raise awareness about responsible practices when visiting natural areas. The camaraderie of these efforts was palpable, with volunteers laughing and sharing stories while working to restore the lake's natural beauty.

Over the years, Nymph Lake has inspired a wealth of myths and legends. One of the most charming tales involves a "lake nymph" said to appear at twilight. According to the story, this ethereal figure, dressed in flowing garments, emerges from the water to dance beneath the stars. Those lucky enough to catch a glimpse are believed to be granted good fortune. The legend has drawn both skeptics and believers alike, adding a magical dimension to the lake that continues to captivate visitors.

With the rise of outdoor recreation, Nymph Lake has become a hub for various activities, particularly during the warmer months. Families flock to its shores for picnics, and hikers use it as a starting point for more adventurous treks into the backcountry. The breathtaking views of the surrounding mountains and the ever-changing palette of the sky make it an ideal spot for photography enthusiasts. Artists, too, have found inspiration along the lake's banks, capturing its essence on canvas and sharing the beauty of Nymph Lake with the world.

In winter, the landscape transforms into a winter wonderland, with the lake often blanketed in snow. Cross-country skiers and snowshoers venture out to experience the tranquility of the lake in its snowy guise, where the only sounds are the crunch of snow underfoot and the soft whispers of the wind. This seasonal change brings a new layer of beauty, illustrating the lake's ability to adapt and enchant throughout the year.

The ongoing conservation efforts to protect Nymph Lake and its surroundings remain crucial as visitor numbers continue to grow. Local organizations work tirelessly to monitor the health of the lake, ensuring that it remains a viable habitat for wildlife and a pristine destination for generations to come. These initiatives foster a deep sense of connection among the community, with locals and visitors alike united by a shared goal of preserving this natural treasure.

The stories and experiences surrounding Nymph Lake highlight the joy of connection—connection to nature, to history, and to one another. Each visitor leaves a piece of themselves at the lake, whether through laughter, quiet contemplation, or adventurous exploration. As the sun sets behind the mountains, casting a golden glow on the lake's surface, Nymph Lake stands as a reminder of the beauty that exists when people and nature come together in harmony.

In the end, Nymph Lake is more than just a picturesque destination; it's a living storybook, filled with chapters of history, folklore, and community. Each ripple in the water tells a tale, and each visit adds a new line to its narrative. With every step taken along its shores, the magic of Nymph Lake invites all who visit to be part of its ongoing journey, creating memories that will last a lifetime.

Dream Lake

Dream Lake, with its ethereal beauty, resides in the heart of Colorado's Rocky Mountain National Park, a captivating oasis that has captured the hearts of all who encounter it. Located in Larimer County, this stunning alpine lake is flanked by jagged mountain peaks, drawing hikers and adventurers like moths to a flame. The name "Dream Lake" evokes a sense of wonder, conjuring images of serene waters reflecting the sky, surrounded by the vibrant colors of wildflowers in bloom. Its tranquil setting has inspired countless stories, laughter, and dreams.

This shimmering lake is not a product of human ingenuity but rather a glorious creation of nature itself. Formed by glacial activity during the last Ice Age, Dream Lake took shape as glaciers carved out valleys and basins, eventually filling with crystal-clear runoff from melting snow and ice. As you stand at its edge, you can almost feel the weight of history—each ripple in the water tells a story of time long past. The lake is fed by the snowmelt of the surrounding peaks, ensuring its waters remain refreshingly cool, even in the heat of summer.

From the outset, Dream Lake has been a significant site for the Ute tribes, who traversed these lands for centuries. The lake was a vital resource for these indigenous people, offering fish, plants, and a place for spiritual reflection. The Utes revered the area, often holding ceremonies that honored the spirits of the mountains and waters. Legends of the lake have been passed down through generations, and while the specifics may vary, they often share a common theme of harmony between nature and humanity.

As European settlers arrived in the late 19th century, the landscape began to change. The allure of gold and the promise of prosperity drew many to the region. Yet, rather than viewing Dream Lake as a mere resource, many settlers were enchanted by its beauty. This sentiment was captured by artists and writers of the time, who depicted the lake in their works, cementing its place in the collective imagination. They often described it as a paradise, a sentiment that resonates to this day.

The transformation of the landscape during this time did bring challenges. The influx of people altered ecosystems and introduced new species, changing the dynamics of flora and fauna in the area. However, the growing appreciation for natural beauty ultimately led to conservation efforts. By the early 20th century, Dream Lake had become a centerpiece of Rocky Mountain National Park, designated in 1915. This protection ensured the lake would remain a sanctuary for wildlife and a beloved destination for those seeking solace in nature.

While Dream Lake was never used for transportation or trade in the traditional sense, it played a pivotal role in the burgeoning recreational culture of the early 20th century. It became a popular destination for fishing, and the clear waters offered anglers the chance to catch native trout. Families would gather for picnics along its banks, creating cherished memories amidst the breathtaking views. The trails that surround the lake became well-trodden pathways for hikers, all eager to immerse themselves in the natural beauty that enveloped them.

As time passed, Dream Lake became synonymous with outdoor adventure. The trails leading to the lake were expanded and improved, attracting visitors from around the globe. The iconic view of the lake with Hallett Peak looming majestically in the background is a favorite among photographers and nature lovers alike. The sheer beauty of the landscape has inspired a sense of community, with people coming together to share their love for the outdoors, forming friendships over shared experiences.

However, as with many natural wonders, Dream Lake faced its share of challenges. Invasive species began to infiltrate the ecosystem, posing a threat to the delicate balance of life in and around the lake. Conservation groups, comprised of passionate locals and visitors alike, rallied together to combat this issue. They organized clean-up events, educational programs, and outreach campaigns to raise awareness about protecting the lake's fragile ecosystem. The commitment of these individuals created a renewed sense of stewardship, ensuring that Dream Lake would continue to thrive.

The legends surrounding Dream Lake have also grown over the years, each adding a layer of magic to the area. One of the most enchanting stories speaks of a hidden underwater kingdom ruled by mystical beings. According to the tale, on certain nights, when the moonlight dances upon the water's surface, the kingdom rises to greet the world above, revealing its treasures to those who dare to believe. While most visitors come to enjoy the scenic beauty and recreational opportunities, the whispers of these legends keep the spirit of the lake alive, inviting all to dream a little deeper.

Seasonally, Dream Lake transforms into a wonderland of its own. In the summer, wildflowers carpet the surrounding meadows, attracting butterflies and bees, while hikers bask in the warmth of the sun. As autumn approaches, the landscape explodes with colors—vivid oranges, yellows, and reds creating a breathtaking backdrop. In winter, the lake freezes over, offering a different kind of beauty and attracting snowshoers and ice skaters who revel in the quiet of the snow-covered landscape.

The development of parks and recreational activities around Dream Lake has focused on enhancing visitor experience while ensuring the preservation of the natural environment. Facilities have been created to support sustainable tourism, including well-maintained trails and educational signage that informs visitors about local ecology and conservation efforts. These initiatives have fostered a culture of appreciation and respect for the land, encouraging people to engage with nature in meaningful ways.

As Dream Lake continues to inspire and uplift, its story remains ever-evolving. Each visitor who walks its trails or gazes into its depths adds their own chapter to the ongoing narrative. The laughter of children echoing off the water, the sighs of contentment from weary hikers, and the quiet moments of reflection all contribute to the lake's timeless appeal. Dream Lake stands as a testament to the beauty of nature and the importance of protecting it, reminding us that every dream begins with a journey into the heart of the wild.

With every sunset casting a golden hue over the lake, Dream Lake invites us to embrace the wonder of the world around us. The connections forged in its presence, the laughter shared among friends, and the serenity found in solitude all blend into a harmonious tapestry that defines the spirit of this extraordinary place. Whether you're an adventurous soul seeking thrills or someone looking for a moment of peace, Dream Lake welcomes you, promising an experience that lingers long after the journey ends.

King Lake

King Lake, a shimmering body of water tucked away in the high reaches of Colorado's Rocky Mountain National Park, is not just a scenic spot; it's a place steeped in history, folklore, and the spirit of adventure. Named after the legendary explorer and naturalist John Wesley Powell, who famously ventured into uncharted territories, King Lake embodies the essence of exploration. It's located in Larimer County, at an elevation that offers breathtaking views of the surrounding peaks, drawing outdoor enthusiasts and nature lovers alike.

The lake itself is a marvel of natural formation. Like a jewel set among the towering mountains, it was created by the grinding forces of glacial activity. Over thousands of years, glaciers carved out the basin, leaving behind a serene body of water that reflects the dramatic sky and rugged landscape. It is indeed a natural lake, fed by snowmelt from the surrounding peaks, maintaining its crystal-clear waters year-round. The cool, refreshing depths offer a welcome respite for hikers and wildlife alike.

The flora and fauna that grace King Lake are as diverse as the adventures it inspires. Initially, the area was rich with pine forests, wildflowers, and a myriad of wildlife. The lakeside is adorned with alpine meadows bursting with color in the warmer months, while pine trees stand tall, their fragrance mingling with the crisp mountain air. The lake itself is home to trout, drawing anglers hoping to cast a line in its tranquil waters.

Long before European settlers arrived, the region was inhabited by the Ute and Arapaho tribes. For these indigenous peoples, King Lake was more than just a resource; it was a sacred place, woven into their cultural and spiritual fabric. They utilized the lake for fishing, gathering plants, and as a gathering place for ceremonies. The Utes, in particular, viewed the mountains as sacred, often referring to them as the "Backbone of the World." Legends abound about the spirits of ancestors watching over the waters, guiding those who showed respect to the land.

With the arrival of settlers in the late 19th century, the landscape began to change. Gold fever swept through Colorado, and the lure of fortune prompted many to seek their fortunes in the high country. Though King Lake itself wasn't a center of commerce or trade, the influx of miners and their families transformed the area. Camps sprang up nearby, and the trails leading to the lake became pathways for prospectors. However, instead of seeing the lake merely as a resource, many settlers were captivated by its beauty. They often recounted tales of fishing trips, picnics by the shore, and the awe-inspiring views that stretched across the horizon.

As communities grew, the impact on the landscape became evident. While some areas were transformed for agricultural use, others saw the beginnings of tourism as people sought out the natural beauty of the region. King Lake became a popular destination for hiking and camping, especially after the establishment of Rocky Mountain National Park in 1915. This designation ensured that the lake would be preserved for future generations, allowing visitors to enjoy its beauty while fostering a sense of stewardship among the community.

The lake became synonymous with outdoor recreation. People flocked to its shores to fish, hike, and bask in the sun. As the park developed, facilities for visitors were improved, including trail maintenance and educational programs about local ecology. The easy accessibility of King Lake made it a favored spot for families, friends, and adventurers, each adding their stories to the lake's rich tapestry.

However, human activity brought challenges. The introduction of invasive species became a concern, particularly with the growing popularity of fishing. Organizations dedicated to preserving the ecosystem took action, launching conservation efforts aimed at managing the populations of non-native species. Volunteers gathered for clean-up days, educating visitors on responsible fishing practices and the importance of maintaining the ecological balance. Their dedication reflected a growing awareness of the need to protect this precious resource, ensuring that King Lake would remain vibrant for years to come.

Throughout its history, King Lake has also been the subject of many a tall tale. Among the most popular is the legend of the "King of the Lake," a mythical creature said to inhabit its depths. According to local lore, this spirit watches over the waters, ensuring that those who respect the land are rewarded with good fortune. Fishermen tell stories of unexpected catches, attributing their luck to the benevolent spirit that swims beneath the surface. While some dismiss it as mere myth, the story adds an enchanting layer to the lake's charm, capturing the imagination of visitors who may find themselves glancing at the water, half-expecting to see a ripple from the King himself.

As the seasons change, King Lake reveals different aspects of its character. In summer, the lake sparkles under the sun, inviting families for picnics and adventures. Fall brings a riot of colors, the aspens turning gold and orange, creating a picturesque setting that inspires photographers and nature lovers alike. When winter blankets the landscape with snow, the lake transforms into a serene haven for snowshoers and cross-country skiers, the silence broken only by the crunch of snow underfoot.

The efforts to preserve and promote King Lake have continued to evolve. Various local initiatives have been developed to enhance the visitor experience while ensuring environmental stewardship. Educational programs encourage visitors to learn about the local ecosystem, the importance of conservation, and ways to protect the area. Park rangers often lead guided hikes, sharing stories of the lake's history and its significance to both the environment and the community.

The community surrounding King Lake has grown into a tight-knit group of nature lovers and advocates, sharing a commitment to preserving the area's beauty. Annual events such as the King Lake Festival bring people together to celebrate nature, with activities like guided hikes, fishing contests, and educational workshops. Families share their traditions, newcomers bond over shared experiences, and friendships are forged against the backdrop of the stunning landscape.

As dusk falls over King Lake, the golden hues of sunset reflect off the water, creating a breathtaking scene that resonates with all who witness it. People gather at the shore, laughter and stories filling the air as the sun dips below the mountains. It's a moment that captures the essence of what King Lake represents: a place where nature, community, and adventure converge, where memories are made, and dreams take flight.

In the heart of Colorado, King Lake stands as a testament to the enduring beauty of the natural world and the spirit of those who cherish it. Each ripple tells a story, each breeze carries a memory, and each visit is a new adventure waiting to unfold. Here, under the watchful gaze of the mountains, everyone is welcome to dream, to explore, and to connect with the magic that makes King Lake truly special.

Blue Lake

Blue Lake, located in the heart of Colorado's Rocky Mountain National Park, is a stunning spectacle that captures the imagination of all who visit. The lake derives its name from the striking azure color of its waters, which can range from a deep cobalt on clear days to a vibrant turquoise when kissed by the sun. The unique hue is attributed to the mineral-rich glacial meltwater that feeds it, a feature that has made the lake a popular subject for photographers and a favorite spot for locals and tourists alike.

The lake lies in Grand County, surrounded by towering peaks that create a breathtaking backdrop. The area's history is as rich as its natural beauty. It's believed that Blue Lake formed during the last Ice Age, when massive glaciers carved out the valley, leaving behind a pristine lake in their wake. This was no man-made reservoir; rather, it is a genuine testament to the raw power of nature. The pristine waters are fed primarily by glacial runoff, ensuring that they remain refreshingly cool even in the heat of summer.

Before the arrival of European settlers, the land surrounding Blue Lake was inhabited by indigenous tribes, notably the Ute and Arapaho. These tribes viewed the area as sacred, with Blue Lake often featuring in their stories and cultural practices. The lake provided not only a vital water source but also an abundant supply of fish, such as brook trout, which were a staple in their diets. The indigenous peoples held deep respect for the land, believing that every mountain and lake had its spirit, and Blue Lake was no exception. It was said that a beautiful water spirit resided in the lake, protecting it and rewarding those who treated the environment with respect.

As settlers began to arrive in the 19th century, they were drawn to the breathtaking beauty of the region. Some sought fortune in the nearby gold mines, while others simply sought adventure. The lake became a popular stop for prospectors traveling through the area, who would pause to fish and take in the serene surroundings. However, the influx of settlers also brought changes. The landscape began to shift with logging and mining activities, though thankfully, Blue Lake remained largely untouched, its pristine nature preserved amidst the hustle of development.

With the establishment of Rocky Mountain National Park in 1915, Blue Lake gained protected status, ensuring that it would be preserved for generations to come. This designation not only protected the lake's ecosystem but also turned it into a hub for outdoor recreation. Hiking trails were developed, leading adventurous souls to the lake's shores, while campgrounds nearby became lively hubs for families looking to connect with nature. The park's commitment to conservation allowed for a balance between enjoyment and preservation, giving visitors the chance to engage with the natural beauty of Blue Lake without compromising its integrity.

As word spread about the lake's beauty, it attracted more visitors, including artists, nature enthusiasts, and families eager to experience the great outdoors. Blue Lake became synonymous with adventure and tranquility, offering everything from fishing and kayaking to leisurely picnics on its shores. Children splashed in the shallows while parents cast their lines, laughter echoing off the surrounding mountains. Local lore grew alongside the lake, with stories of "the Blue Lady," a mythical figure said to appear on foggy mornings, shimmering in the water and beckoning visitors to explore further.

Over the years, human impacts on the lake's ecosystem have presented challenges. Invasive species like the common carp posed a threat to the local fish populations, leading conservation groups to implement management strategies to protect native species. Volunteers rallied to clean up the lake's shoreline, ensuring that the natural beauty remained unspoiled. Education programs were established within the park, teaching visitors about the delicate balance of the ecosystem and the importance of maintaining it. Rangers guided excursions, sharing the stories of the lake's history and the vital role it played in the lives of both the indigenous peoples and the modern community.

Despite these challenges, the community surrounding Blue Lake has flourished. Seasonal festivals and events celebrate the lake's beauty and the importance of conservation. The annual Blue Lake Day, a beloved event, draws locals and visitors for a day filled with activities ranging from guided hikes and fishing competitions to art workshops inspired by the lake's breathtaking vistas. Families gather to share food, stories, and laughter, creating a sense of camaraderie and connection to both the lake and one another.

As the seasons change, Blue Lake offers a constantly evolving landscape. In spring, the thawing waters awaken vibrant wildflowers along the shore, painting the scene in brilliant hues. Summer invites swimming and kayaking, with families enjoying the warmth of the sun against the cool water. Fall transforms the area into a tapestry of reds, oranges, and yellows, creating a stunning contrast against the deep blue of the lake. And as winter blankets the region in snow, the lake becomes a serene retreat for cross-country skiing and snowshoeing, with trails winding through the frosty landscape.

In addition to its recreational offerings, Blue Lake is an important area for scientific research. Environmental studies take place to monitor the health of the lake's ecosystem, focusing on water quality, wildlife populations, and the effects of climate change. Students from nearby universities often conduct fieldwork in the park, gaining hands-on experience while contributing to conservation efforts. These educational initiatives foster a deep appreciation for the natural world, inspiring the next generation of stewards who will continue the legacy of protecting Blue Lake.

As twilight falls over Blue Lake, the sky transforms into a canvas of purples and pinks, the water reflecting the breathtaking colors. Campfires crackle, and the smell of roasting marshmallows wafts through the air as families gather to share stories and laughter. It's a moment that encapsulates the magic of this beautiful place—a reminder of the connection between nature, community, and the shared experience of wonder.

In the heart of Colorado, Blue Lake remains a testament to the beauty and resilience of nature. Each visit brings new memories, whether it's catching a fish, spotting wildlife, or simply soaking in the serenity of the surroundings. As people come and go, they leave a piece of themselves behind, adding to the rich history of Blue Lake—a history filled with laughter, stories, and the enduring spirit of adventure. Here, beneath the vast sky and the watchful mountains, everyone is welcome to dream, explore, and connect with the magic that makes Blue Lake truly special.

Ouzel Lake

Ouzel Lake, a hidden treasure of the Colorado Rockies, is a place where nature reveals its majesty and whispers its secrets to those who are willing to listen. Located within the boundaries of Rocky Mountain National Park, in Boulder County, this glacial lake boasts stunning views framed by the dramatic backdrop of the surrounding peaks. Its name comes from the Ouzel bird, more commonly known as the dipper, which is often seen flitting about the lake, diving and bobbing in the crystal-clear waters. The bird's playful demeanor reflects the spirit of the lake itself, inviting exploration and adventure.

Ouzel Lake was formed during the last Ice Age, when glacial activity carved out the landscape, leaving behind a natural amphitheater of rugged cliffs and alpine meadows. This lake is entirely natural—there's no human hand that has altered its course or depth, making it a pure example of Colorado's geological wonders. As visitors approach the lake via a well-maintained hiking trail, they are treated to an impressive display of flora. In the summer, vibrant wildflowers blanket the meadows, while aspens and pines stand tall, offering shade and shelter to the myriad of wildlife that calls this area home.

Before the arrival of settlers, the region around Ouzel Lake was home to the Arapaho and Ute tribes, who revered the land for its beauty and resources. For these indigenous peoples, the lake was a source of life, offering fresh water and fish, particularly the native cutthroat trout. Stories passed down through generations often centered on the lake, attributing it with spiritual significance. It was said that the spirits of the mountains would bless those who respected the land, a belief that fostered a harmonious relationship with nature.

With the influx of settlers in the 19th century, the landscape began to change. Miners, loggers, and ranchers arrived, drawn by the promise of wealth and opportunity. The beauty of Ouzel Lake attracted early explorers and adventurers who sought solace and recreation in its pristine surroundings. Despite the encroachment of development, Ouzel Lake managed to maintain its natural charm, largely due to the protections put in place when Rocky Mountain National Park was established in 1915. This decision safeguarded not just the lake, but the entire ecosystem, ensuring that it would be preserved for future generations to enjoy.

As a protected area, Ouzel Lake became a hub for recreational activities. Hiking trails were developed, leading outdoor enthusiasts through lush forests and meadows teeming with life. Families began to flock to the lake, packing picnics and fishing rods, eager to create lasting memories. The tradition of storytelling around campfires emerged, where tales of the mysterious "lake lady" were shared—a whimsical figure said to appear at twilight, guiding lost souls back to safety with her glowing lantern.

Human interaction with the lake has always emphasized balance. The fishing community has thrived, with anglers coming to cast their lines in hopes of reeling in the elusive trout. Local fishing regulations have been implemented to ensure sustainable practices, allowing fish populations to thrive while providing enjoyable experiences for all. It's not uncommon to see kids on the shore, giggling as they attempt to catch their first fish, parents cheering them on with the encouragement that only a day at Ouzel Lake can inspire.

However, like many natural habitats, Ouzel Lake faces challenges. Invasive species, such as the rainbow trout, have found their way into the lake, leading to concerns about the impact on native populations. Conservation efforts have become increasingly important, with park rangers actively monitoring the lake's ecosystem and implementing measures to mitigate these impacts. Educational programs have been established to inform visitors about responsible practices, emphasizing the importance of keeping the lake's waters clean and free from pollutants.

The surrounding landscape is a living testament to the beauty of natural conservation. The trails leading to Ouzel Lake are well-maintained, providing access to hikers of all skill levels. The park has developed various activities and amenities, such as guided hikes and nature walks, allowing families to connect with the environment in meaningful ways. Each year, Ouzel Lake hosts events that celebrate the beauty of the area, fostering a sense of community among visitors and locals alike. These gatherings often include workshops on photography, birdwatching, and even local folklore, creating an atmosphere of joy and shared appreciation for the lake's wonders.

As the seasons change, Ouzel Lake transforms into a different world. In spring, the melting snow sends torrents of crystal-clear water cascading down from the peaks, filling the lake to the brim. Summer brings warmth, inviting families to swim and explore. Fall coats the trees in brilliant hues of orange and red, while winter blankets the area in snow, creating a serene, quiet retreat. In every season, Ouzel Lake captures the hearts of those who visit, reminding them of the beauty and fragility of nature.

As twilight descends, the lake reflects the colors of the sky, a brilliant tapestry that captivates the imagination. Campers settle around fires, sharing stories of their adventures and the enchantment of the lake. Ouzel Lake becomes a backdrop for dreams, a place where laughter mingles with the gentle sounds of nature, leaving visitors with memories that linger long after they depart.

In the grand tapestry of Colorado's natural wonders, Ouzel Lake stands out not only for its beauty but also for its rich history and community spirit. Each visit brings a new adventure, a chance to connect with both nature and one another. As the birds chirp and the waters ripple, Ouzel Lake continues to inspire those who come to enjoy its serene embrace, fostering a legacy of wonder and appreciation for generations to come. Here, in the heart of the Rockies, the spirit of Ouzel Lake lives on, inviting everyone to dream, explore, and cherish the beauty of the natural world.

Warren Lake

Warren Lake, a serene oasis in the heart of Colorado, holds stories that ripple through its clear waters, reflecting both the history of the land and the spirit of the people who have come to adore it. Located in the Arapaho National Forest in Boulder County, this picturesque lake is named after Charles Warren, a prominent figure in the early days of Colorado's mining boom. As fortune seekers flocked to the region in search of silver and gold in the late 19th century, Warren's legacy grew intertwined with the landscape, his name forever linked to this tranquil body of water.

The origins of Warren Lake trace back to the last Ice Age, when glaciers carved out the mountains, leaving behind depressions that would eventually fill with water. Unlike many of the area's lakes, Warren was not man-made; it is a natural formation, a gift from the geological processes that shaped the Rocky Mountains. The lake's surface is often mirror-like, reflecting the rugged peaks surrounding it, creating a sense of wonder for those fortunate enough to witness it.

Initially, the area was inhabited by the Ute and Arapaho tribes. To these indigenous peoples, Warren Lake was more than just a water source; it held spiritual significance. They believed the lake was home to benevolent spirits that protected the land. The Utes, known for their deep connection to nature, relied on the lake for fishing and gathering, using the rich resources around it to sustain their communities. They would often tell stories of mythical creatures that dwelled beneath the surface, legends that added a layer of magic to the natural beauty surrounding them.

As the 19th century unfolded, the landscape began to change dramatically. The arrival of miners and settlers led to the establishment of towns and the depletion of natural resources. The promise of wealth transformed the area, and while some prospered, many faced hardship. Yet, despite these challenges, Warren Lake remained a tranquil escape from the chaos of colonization. It was a place where families could picnic by the shore, where children could fish for brook trout, and where stories of adventure and bravery were passed down through generations.

The lake became a recreational hub in the early 1900s, drawing visitors eager to experience its beauty. With the rise of tourism, people began to develop trails and campsites, paving the way for an era of outdoor exploration. Fishermen found delight in casting their lines into the lake's waters, while hikers enjoyed the surrounding trails that led through lush forests and wildflower meadows. The enchanting scenery invited couples to share their first kisses, families to bond over fishing trips, and friends to create memories that would last a lifetime.

Warren Lake became synonymous with community spirit. Each summer, locals and visitors would gather for the annual fishing tournament, a lively event filled with friendly competition and laughter. The lake was a place where stories were shared, friendships were forged, and traditions were created. It wasn't uncommon for a fisherman to return from a successful day on the water with tales of "the one that got away," weaving excitement into the fabric of community gatherings.

However, as with many natural treasures, Warren Lake faced challenges. Invasive species began to infiltrate its waters, disrupting the delicate balance of the ecosystem. The introduction of non-native fish threatened the population of native trout, raising concerns among conservationists and anglers alike. To combat these issues, local organizations rallied together, implementing measures to monitor fish populations and educate visitors on responsible practices. Workshops and community clean-up days became part of the effort to protect the lake and preserve its beauty for future generations.

Despite these challenges, the spirit of Warren Lake remained vibrant. Parks and recreational areas were developed around the lake, providing opportunities for camping, hiking, and birdwatching. Families set up tents along the shoreline, where kids splashed in the shallows and adults shared stories around crackling campfires. On warm summer nights, the sound of laughter echoed through the trees, creating a sense of joy that enveloped the area.

As the seasons changed, so did Warren Lake. In spring, the snowmelt would fill the lake, bringing renewed life to the surrounding flora. Wildflowers burst forth, painting the landscape in brilliant colors. Summer was a time of exploration and connection, as visitors flocked to the lake for swimming and fishing. Fall transformed the area into a painter's palette of oranges and golds, drawing photographers eager to capture the beauty. In winter, the lake would freeze over, offering opportunities for ice fishing and snowshoeing, as adventurous souls donned their winter gear to explore the serene landscape.

Warren Lake became a canvas for both nature and humanity. It was not just a body of water; it was a place where stories unfolded, where life intertwined with the beauty of the natural world. Generations of families returned year after year, establishing traditions that fostered a love for the outdoors. A sense of stewardship grew among the community, with volunteers dedicating their time to clean the shores and protect the delicate ecosystem.

Through its challenges and triumphs, Warren Lake stands as a testament to the resilience of both nature and the human spirit. It is a reminder that even in a changing world, there are places where connection to the past and present can flourish. The laughter of children echoes along the shores, the gentle lapping of water against rocks creates a soothing rhythm, and the stories of old continue to be shared around campfires.

As visitors leave Warren Lake, they carry with them a sense of joy, inspiration, and connection to something greater than themselves. Each visit is a chapter in the ongoing story of this enchanting lake, a tale woven with laughter, adventure, and the promise of a bright future. In every ripple, there is a memory waiting to be made, a dream waiting to be dreamt, and a bond waiting to be forged with the beauty of Colorado's natural world.

Link Lake

Link Lake, tucked away in the heart of the Colorado Rockies, carries a rich history that echoes through its shimmering waters. This lake, located in Clear Creek County, is named for its position linking various natural features in the area, as well as its historical role in connecting local communities. The name is a nod to its place in the vast landscape, serving as a focal point for both nature lovers and those seeking a quick escape from the hustle and bustle of modern life.

The lake itself formed naturally, carved by ancient glaciers that once blanketed the Rocky Mountains. Over millennia, the glaciers receded, leaving behind a stunning body of water surrounded by towering peaks and verdant forests. Unlike many of Colorado's lakes, Link Lake is a true natural wonder, a testament to the powerful forces of nature that shaped this land.

In its early days, the area around Link Lake was home to the Ute and Arapaho tribes. These indigenous peoples relied on the lake and its surroundings for sustenance, hunting, and gathering. They knew the land intimately, crafting stories and legends about the spirits that resided within the waters. One popular tale spoke of a mischievous water spirit that would play tricks on unsuspecting fishermen, stealing their catches and leaving them puzzled. Children would sit around campfires, wide-eyed as elders recounted these tales, weaving a rich tapestry of culture and connection to the land.

As the 19th century approached, the landscape began to change dramatically. The lure of gold and silver brought waves of settlers and miners to the region, and with them, an era of transformation. While the influx of people often led to the depletion of resources, Link Lake remained a cherished spot for those seeking solace from the chaos of mining towns. It provided a refreshing retreat, a place to fish for brook trout or simply breathe in the crisp mountain air.

The lake's recreational potential didn't go unnoticed. By the early 1900s, Link Lake was becoming known as a popular destination for families and adventurers. Campgrounds sprang up along its shores, where families would gather to roast marshmallows and share stories under the stars. The lake's serene waters attracted artists, photographers, and poets, all of whom found inspiration in its tranquil beauty. It became a place where creativity thrived, where the mountains whispered secrets to those willing to listen.

However, with the growth of tourism came challenges. The delicate ecosystem began to feel the strain of increased human activity. Invasive species started to appear, threatening the lake's native flora and fauna. Fishermen noticed changes in the fish populations, with some species struggling to adapt to their new neighbors. Conservation efforts soon became a community priority, rallying locals and visitors alike to protect the lake they loved.

Dedicated volunteers organized clean-up days, removing debris and educating visitors about responsible practices. Workshops on sustainable fishing and habitat preservation were held, fostering a sense of stewardship among the community. As people began to recognize the importance of safeguarding the lake, they embraced the role of guardians, determined to preserve its beauty for generations to come.

Link Lake became a canvas for conservation initiatives, with park rangers and volunteers working hand in hand to monitor the health of the ecosystem. Native plants were reintroduced to combat invasive species, and new trails were established to minimize the impact of foot traffic on sensitive areas. The community rallied around these efforts, celebrating successes and learning from setbacks with humor and resilience.

The recreational opportunities around Link Lake continued to expand. Fishing competitions became popular events, drawing enthusiasts from far and wide. Families set out in kayaks and canoes, paddling through the clear waters while telling tales of their own water spirit encounters. The sound of laughter and splashing echoed along the shores, blending with the gentle rustle of aspen leaves in the wind.

As seasons changed, so did the lake's character. Spring brought bursts of color as wildflowers carpeted the surrounding meadows, while summer invited picnics and sun-soaked days spent swimming in the lake's refreshing embrace. Fall transformed the landscape into a vibrant tapestry of red, orange, and gold, captivating photographers eager to capture the fleeting beauty. In winter, Link Lake became a playground for ice skaters and snowshoe enthusiasts, each new layer of snow creating a fresh canvas for adventure.

The lake's charm extended beyond the water's edge. Nearby, quaint cabins and lodges flourished, catering to those looking for a peaceful getaway. Each establishment added its own unique flavor, offering warm meals and a cozy place to rest after a day of exploration. Visitors often gathered around roaring fireplaces, sharing stories of their adventures on the lake and beyond.

Yet, it was the bond formed over shared experiences that truly defined Link Lake. Friends made at summer camps returned as adults, bringing their children to create new memories. Fishing lines cast by fathers were matched by daughters, while mothers took leisurely strolls along the shores, connecting with the very land their ancestors had walked upon. The laughter of children echoed through the trees, a joyful reminder of the simple pleasures found in nature.

Link Lake's legacy grew stronger with each passing year, as its waters became a sanctuary for those seeking connection—both to nature and to one another. Every fishing tale told, every campfire song sung, contributed to the rich history of this remarkable place. The lake stood as a testament to the power of community, conservation, and the unbreakable bond between people and the land.

As visitors departed Link Lake, they carried with them not just memories, but a piece of its spirit. Each moment spent there became a cherished part of their lives, a story to share with others. The laughter and love that filled the air lingered long after the last campfire flickered out, leaving an indelible mark on hearts and minds.

In the end, Link Lake is more than just a body of water. It is a living tapestry of history, adventure, and connection—a place where dreams take flight and where the past, present, and future intertwine in a beautiful dance. Whether it is the whispers of ancient spirits or the joy of a child's laughter, the essence of Link Lake will continue to inspire all who are fortunate enough to visit its shores.

Guffey Lake

Guffey Lake, a hidden treasure tucked away in the picturesque foothills of Colorado, has a history as vibrant and multifaceted as the landscape that surrounds it. This charming body of water, located in Park County, derives its name from the nearby town of Guffey, which itself has a quirky backstory. Established in the late 1800s during the gold rush, Guffey was originally a bustling mining town that provided a vital stop for weary travelers. The lake, formed by the convergence of several mountain streams, quickly became a local favorite, offering a refreshing escape from the rigors of mining life.

The lake itself is a natural wonder, formed over centuries by the slow but persistent actions of glacial melt and erosion. Unlike many lakes that are artificially created for recreational purposes, Guffey Lake boasts a rich geological history. The waters are fed by the crystal-clear runoff from the surrounding mountains, which means that the lake is not just beautiful but also an essential part of the local ecosystem.

Before the arrival of European settlers, the area around Guffey Lake was home to various Indigenous tribes, including the Ute and Cheyenne. These communities thrived in the region, relying on the natural resources available to them. They used the lake not just for fishing but as a meeting point for ceremonies and social gatherings. Stories abound of gatherings around the water where elders would pass down wisdom to the younger generation, their laughter echoing off the rocky shores.

The arrival of miners in the 19th century brought significant changes. With the gold rush in full swing, the landscape transformed as people flooded into the area seeking fortune. Guffey Lake became a vital resource, offering not only fish but also a much-needed place to cool off from the summer heat. It became a backdrop for countless stories of fortune-seeking adventurers, some of whom found gold, while others found love—often in the form of a charming dance under the stars at the local saloon.

Throughout the years, Guffey Lake has seen its share of challenges. One of the most significant events occurred in the late 1930s when heavy rains led to a series of floods that dramatically altered the landscape. The once calm waters rose and swelled, creating a temporary but powerful torrent. The community rallied together, showcasing the indomitable spirit of the townsfolk. They worked tirelessly to repair the damage and restore the lake, solidifying its status as a beloved local landmark.

Myths and legends surrounding Guffey Lake add to its charm. Locals often recount tales of a playful water spirit who guards the lake. According to legend, this spirit rewards those who show kindness to the environment and the creatures that inhabit it. On warm summer nights, you might hear stories of fishermen who cast their lines and, instead of catching fish, would find small trinkets or tokens—gifts from the water spirit. The stories blend laughter and wonder, passed down through generations, fostering a deep sense of connection to the lake.

In the early 20th century, Guffey Lake became a popular spot for recreation. Families began visiting the area to enjoy picnics by the water, where children would chase after dragonflies, their laughter harmonizing with the sounds of nature. Fishing became a cherished pastime, with anglers hoping to reel in the big one—trout that thrived in the lake's clear depths. The lake attracted those from nearby towns, eager to escape their daily routines and soak in the beauty of the natural world.

As the decades rolled on, Guffey Lake continued to adapt to the changes around it. The introduction of new species, both flora and fauna, altered the ecosystem. Some invasive plants began to appear along the shores, leading to conservation efforts aimed at protecting the native species that had flourished for centuries. Local volunteers organized clean-up events and educational programs, emphasizing the importance of maintaining the delicate balance of nature.

By the late 20th century, Guffey Lake had evolved into a hub for community activities. The annual Guffey Lake Festival became a cherished tradition, celebrating the lake's beauty with live music, food, and art. Locals and visitors alike gathered to share stories, enjoy the scenery, and participate in friendly competitions like fishing derbies and canoe races.

The festival not only highlighted the lake's recreational value but also fostered a sense of camaraderie among participants, solidifying bonds that went beyond the water's edge.

The landscape surrounding Guffey Lake has continued to flourish, offering diverse habitats for various wildlife. Birdwatchers frequent the area, hoping to catch a glimpse of herons and eagles soaring overhead. Families camping near the lake often wake to the sound of frogs serenading the dawn. It's a place where children learn about nature firsthand, collecting leaves and rocks, discovering the joys of the great outdoors.

As part of ongoing conservation efforts, local organizations have worked to improve the lake's infrastructure. New walking trails have been established, allowing visitors to explore the area while preserving the natural beauty. Educational signage has been placed along the paths, providing insights into the flora and fauna of the region. Community members frequently come together for workshops on sustainable practices, instilling a sense of responsibility toward the environment.

While the lake remains a vital part of the community, it also serves as a backdrop for personal milestones. Weddings have been held along its shores, couples exchanging vows with the gentle lapping of water as their witness. Family reunions find their place under the expansive sky, filled with laughter and the aroma of barbecues. Guffey Lake holds a special place in the hearts of those who visit, a setting for memories that will last a lifetime.

The lake's evolving story continues to inspire a new generation of outdoor enthusiasts, who cherish its natural beauty and the connections it fosters. As the sun sets behind the mountains, painting the sky in hues of orange and purple, it's not uncommon to see families gathered along the shoreline, roasting marshmallows and sharing stories of their own adventures. In this way, Guffey Lake remains a living testament to the spirit of community, resilience, and the enduring magic of nature.

In the grand tapestry of Colorado's natural wonders, Guffey Lake shines brightly, inviting all who come to appreciate its beauty and the stories woven into its waters. Whether it's the echoes of laughter from the past or the whispered legends of the present, the lake is a reminder that nature and community are forever intertwined, creating a legacy that will continue to inspire generations to come.

Zapata Falls Lake

Zapata Falls Lake, a stunning oasis in the heart of Colorado, is a place where nature's artistry meets the human spirit, and where stories of adventure and connection have flourished for generations. Tucked away near the quaint town of Creede in Mineral County, this lake bears a name steeped in both history and intrigue. The name "Zapata" pays homage to a local legend, believed to reference a Spanish word meaning "to step" or "to tread." According to local folklore, it refers to the stepping stones across the creek, guiding travelers toward this hidden treasure.

The lake itself was formed naturally, shaped by the gradual melting of snow and the rain that cascades down from the surrounding peaks. Unlike many artificial lakes crafted for recreation or irrigation, Zapata Falls Lake emerged organically over time, nestled among rocky outcrops and dense aspen groves. The crystal-clear waters, reflecting the vibrant colors of the sky, invite both contemplation and joy.

Before European settlers arrived, the area was home to Indigenous tribes, including the Ute people. These Native Americans thrived in the region, hunting and gathering while relying on the abundant resources that the landscape provided. For the Ute, Zapata Falls Lake was more than just a body of water; it served as a vital part of their seasonal migrations. They would gather here to fish and conduct important rituals, with the sparkling waters offering both sustenance and spiritual significance. Stories were shared around the fire, fostering a rich cultural heritage that would leave its mark on the landscape.

When the gold rush of the mid-1800s hit Colorado, the tranquil surroundings of Zapata Falls Lake were transformed. Miners and fortune seekers flooded the area, eager to strike it rich. The lake quickly became a favored respite for weary travelers, its serene beauty a balm for those hardened by the rough life of a miner. Rumors circulated about the lake being a source of good luck—anyone who dared to dip their toes into its waters was said to find fortune in their future. As a result, the lake became a gathering place, where tales of daring exploits and hopeful dreams were exchanged over campfires.

One particularly dramatic chapter in the history of Zapata Falls Lake occurred in the late 1970s, when heavy rains caused flash floods that dramatically altered the landscape. The lake swelled ominously, and the powerful torrents of water carved new paths through the valley. Residents banded together, showcasing their resilience and determination. They organized clean-up efforts, cleared debris, and helped each other rebuild homes and lives. This sense of community became a defining moment in the area, strengthening bonds among neighbors and establishing traditions that continue to this day.

As time passed, the lake became a symbol of adventure and exploration. Families would venture to the area for weekend getaways, camping beneath the stars and hiking the rugged trails that wove through the surrounding wilderness. Fishing became a cherished pastime, with anglers hoping to catch rainbow trout that thrived in the lake's cool depths. Many families passed down the tradition of casting lines from one generation to the next, turning simple afternoons into lifelong memories.

Among the various legends surrounding Zapata Falls Lake, one tale has endured: the story of the "Zapata Spirit." According to local lore, a benevolent spirit watches over the lake, rewarding those who respect nature and cherish the environment. Visitors claim to have felt a sense of peace wash over them when they approach the water, leading many to believe that the spirit blesses the area. This belief inspired conservation efforts aimed at preserving the lake and its surroundings, ensuring that future generations can enjoy the beauty and tranquility it offers.

As human impacts began to take shape, invasive species started to infiltrate the lake's ecosystem. Concerned citizens joined forces to address these challenges, leading to the establishment of conservation groups dedicated to protecting the lake's natural balance. They organized clean-up events and educational initiatives, teaching the community about the importance of maintaining a healthy environment. Volunteers monitored the waters for invasive species, ensuring that the lake's native flora and fauna thrived.

The charm of Zapata Falls Lake has attracted visitors from near and far, leading to the development of parks and recreational activities that celebrate the natural beauty of the area. The trails around the lake have been enhanced to accommodate hikers, birdwatchers, and nature enthusiasts. Interpretive signs provide insights into the local wildlife, allowing visitors to appreciate the rich biodiversity that flourishes here. Family-friendly activities, such as guided nature walks and fishing clinics, encourage people of all ages to connect with the land.

Zapata Falls Lake is also a favorite destination for photographers and artists, drawn to the stunning landscapes that provide endless inspiration. The way the sunlight dances on the water, the colors of the sunset reflecting off the surface, and the rugged mountains framing the scene all contribute to the lake's allure. Local art festivals showcase the talent of the community, celebrating the unique relationship between art and nature.

Community events have flourished around the lake, including annual festivals that unite locals and visitors alike. From music festivals to nature clean-up days, these gatherings have become a cornerstone of life in the area. Families come together to share food, stories, and laughter, strengthening the bonds of friendship and creating lasting memories. The laughter of children mingles with the sounds of nature, creating a symphony of joy that resonates throughout the landscape.

As the seasons change, Zapata Falls Lake continues to provide a space for reflection and renewal. In the spring, wildflowers bloom along the shores, bringing a riot of color to the landscape. Summer sees families splashing in the cool waters, while autumn paints the trees in hues of gold and crimson. Winter blankets the lake in a serene layer of snow, transforming it into a tranquil wonderland.

The enduring spirit of Zapata Falls Lake is a testament to the resilience of nature and the human heart. It serves as a reminder that despite the challenges faced throughout history, the bond between people and the land remains strong. As visitors cast their lines into the waters or simply sit in quiet contemplation, they become part of a larger story—one that celebrates adventure, connection, and the beauty of the world around them.

In the end, Zapata Falls Lake stands as both a natural marvel and a cherished part of Colorado's heritage, inviting all who come to experience its magic and create their own memories amid the whispering winds and shimmering waters. Whether you're seeking fortune, adventure, or simply a moment of peace, the lake welcomes you with open arms, ready to share its tales and inspire new ones.

South Fork Reservoir

The South Fork Reservoir, a hidden jewel of Colorado's San Juan Mountains, embodies the spirit of adventure and community. Located in Rio Grande County, this picturesque body of water has drawn people to its shores for generations, allured by its beauty and the stories woven into its landscape. The reservoir derives its name from the nearby South Fork of the Rio Grande River, which gracefully winds through the region. It's a fitting name, one that reflects the connection to the river and the surrounding terrain that have shaped the lives of those who call this place home.

The history of South Fork Reservoir is as rich and varied as the terrain surrounding it. Originally, the area was home to the Ute tribes, who revered the land and waters for their bounty. They hunted and fished along the river, making seasonal migrations through the mountains. The Ute people recognized the reservoir's potential, utilizing its resources while respecting the balance of nature. Legends abound about the area, with tales of spirits who roamed the hills and valleys, protecting the land and its inhabitants. These stories were often shared around campfires, binding communities together through shared beliefs and experiences.

With the arrival of European settlers in the mid-1800s, the landscape began to change dramatically. The discovery of gold and silver drew many fortune-seekers into the mountains, and the South Fork area transformed from a serene wilderness into a bustling hub of activity. As towns sprang up to support mining operations, the need for water became increasingly pressing. In 1940, the South Fork Reservoir was officially constructed to provide water for irrigation and municipal use, turning what was once a natural feature into a vital resource for the growing communities.

While the reservoir itself is man-made, it draws on the natural beauty that surrounds it. The initial flora and fauna were diverse, with pine and aspen trees framing the landscape, and an abundance of wildlife, from deer to elusive mountain lions. The construction of the reservoir resulted in some changes to the ecosystem, but it also created new habitats for various species. Fishermen soon discovered the wealth of trout swimming beneath the surface, leading to recreational fishing becoming a beloved pastime.

Community development around the reservoir blossomed as families settled in the area. The small towns nearby, including South Fork itself, became vibrant centers of social life. Residents organized events and gatherings that fostered connections among neighbors. The reservoir served as a gathering place, with picnics, barbecues, and fishing derbies becoming staples of local culture. Laughter and joy filled the air, echoing across the water as children cast lines into the shimmering depths.

Through the years, the reservoir experienced its share of challenges. Flooding became a concern, especially during heavy rains in the summer months. In 1976, significant rains led to a dramatic rise in water levels, prompting fears of overflow. Fortunately, the community rallied together, and coordinated efforts to manage the water flow prevented disaster. This spirit of cooperation not only preserved the reservoir but strengthened the bonds between residents, who took pride in their shared responsibility for this cherished resource.

Legends surrounding the reservoir grew, too. Some claimed that if you listened closely enough at dawn, you could hear the echoes of the Ute people singing to the waters, expressing gratitude for the gifts of nature. Others spoke of a mysterious creature that occasionally surfaced, playfully splashing nearby boats, further entwining the reservoir in local lore. These stories enriched the experience for visitors, who came not just for the fishing or the scenery but to partake in the magic that permeated the air.

As the years passed, the South Fork Reservoir became a focal point for outdoor recreation. The region drew hikers, campers, and nature lovers, all eager to explore the myriad trails winding through the mountains. The reservoir itself was a paradise for fishing enthusiasts, with anglers often sharing tales of "the one that got away" while hoping for a bigger catch next time. It was here that friendships were forged over shared experiences, and families made lasting memories.

However, the reservoir faced challenges from invasive species threatening its delicate ecosystem. Efforts to educate the community about responsible fishing practices became essential. Local organizations, in collaboration with conservation groups, initiated programs aimed at protecting the reservoir's natural balance. These initiatives included clean-up days and educational workshops, empowering residents to take an active role in conservation.

In addition to fishing and picnicking, the area around South Fork Reservoir developed into a destination for other activities. Nature trails were established, offering breathtaking views of the surrounding mountains and valleys. Birdwatchers reveled in the variety of species that called the reservoir home, and photographers found endless inspiration in the stunning landscapes. The community embraced the reservoir as a source of not just water but also creativity and connection.

Events like the annual "South Fork Fishing Derby" became highlights of the calendar, drawing participants from miles around. Families would gather to compete for the biggest catch, turning the event into a joyous celebration of camaraderie and competition. The laughter of children and the chatter of excited anglers filled the air, with the sweet aroma of grilled food wafting through the trees.

As the seasons changed, so did the reservoir. In winter, it transformed into a serene landscape, blanketed in snow, offering opportunities for ice fishing and snowshoeing. Spring brought wildflowers blooming along the banks, while summer filled the air with the sound of splashes and laughter. Autumn painted the trees in vibrant shades of orange and red, providing a breathtaking backdrop for photographers and hikers.

Today, the South Fork Reservoir stands as a testament to the strength of community and the enduring beauty of nature. Its waters continue to reflect the sky, inviting all who visit to find peace and adventure. The legacy of the Ute tribes lives on in the stories shared around campfires, and the spirit of cooperation endures in the collective efforts to preserve this cherished resource.

In the heart of Colorado, the South Fork Reservoir serves not just as a source of water, but as a symbol of resilience, connection, and the shared love for the land. As families gather to fish, hike, or simply enjoy the scenery, they become part of a larger narrative—one that celebrates the joy of living in harmony with nature and the magic of a place that feels like home.

Grandview Reservoir

Grandview Reservoir, a serene oasis located in Colorado's Boulder County, is a place where nature and community intertwine. Its name reflects the stunning vistas that surround it—an expansive view of the Rocky Mountains that captures the imagination and beckons adventurers from near and far. It's not just the beauty that draws people here; it's the stories, the history, and the sense of belonging that have developed over generations.

The reservoir's origins date back to the late 1950s when the need for water storage became increasingly apparent. Constructed as part of the larger water system serving the growing municipalities in the area, Grandview was designed to meet the demands of both residents and agriculture. While its creation was man-made, the landscape it occupies has been shaped by thousands of years of natural history. Before the arrival of settlers, the land was home to the Arapaho and Ute tribes, who thrived in the rich ecosystems along the riverbanks, hunting and fishing in the area. For these tribes, the waters were sacred, nourishing their bodies and spirits.

As settlers arrived, the dynamic between people and nature began to shift. The construction of the reservoir was a significant turning point, transforming the land while providing crucial resources for the growing population. The lush vegetation of the original landscape—comprising cottonwoods, willows, and diverse grasses—gave way to a carefully managed environment, designed to support the needs of the community while honoring the original essence of the place.

Among the many legends associated with Grandview Reservoir is the story of the "Whispering Willows." Local lore suggests that the willows lining the banks were once enchanted trees, capable of sharing wisdom with those who listened closely. Fishermen would tell tales of how, on quiet mornings, the rustling leaves carried gentle whispers, offering secrets about where the best catches could be found. These stories turned fishing trips into spiritual quests, as locals ventured out not just for sport, but to commune with nature.

Despite the reservoir's serene exterior, it has seen its share of dramatic events. In the early 1980s, a particularly heavy snowmelt caused water levels to rise rapidly, threatening the surrounding infrastructure. Residents banded together, bringing sandbags and sharing resources to protect the area. This crisis became a turning point in community solidarity, forging friendships and alliances that remain strong today. The laughter shared during these moments, as neighbors worked side by side, reinforced a sense of kinship that defined the area.

Over the decades, Grandview Reservoir has become a cornerstone of community life. It is a hub for recreation, with families flocking to its shores to fish, picnic, and hike. The summer months bring a lively atmosphere as children splash in the shallows, while parents cast their lines, hoping for a trophy catch. The reservoir's crystal-clear waters are home to a variety of fish species, including trout and bass, making it a prime location for both seasoned anglers and beginners alike. Each summer, the local fishing derby attracts participants of all ages, fostering a spirit of friendly competition and community camaraderie.

As the reservoir became a popular destination, it also attracted attention from conservationists concerned about the impact of human activity on the delicate ecosystem. Invasive species began to pose a threat, and local organizations sprang into action to educate residents about responsible practices. Community workshops were organized to teach people how to prevent the spread of invasive plants and fish, ensuring that the reservoir's natural balance would be maintained for generations to come. The collaborative efforts paid off, as volunteers engaged in regular clean-up days, beautifying the area while deepening their connection to the land.

The area surrounding Grandview Reservoir has undergone further development to enhance its recreational offerings. Hiking trails were established, winding through the adjacent forest and offering breathtaking views of the water below. These trails became a favorite for locals and visitors alike, providing a space for reflection and adventure. On weekends, the trails come alive with families, couples, and dog-walkers, all savoring the fresh mountain air and the sense of peace that envelops the landscape.

While fishing and hiking are popular activities, the reservoir has also inspired creativity and artistry. Local artists have been known to set up easels along the banks, capturing the vibrant colors of sunsets reflected on the water's surface. These artistic endeavors contribute to a rich cultural tapestry, as the beauty of Grandview Reservoir becomes a muse for many. The annual "Art by the Water" festival celebrates this creativity, showcasing local talent and fostering a sense of community pride.

As seasons change, so does the character of Grandview Reservoir. In the fall, vibrant colors paint the landscape, drawing leaf-peepers from afar. Winter brings a blanket of snow, transforming the area into a winter wonderland, where ice fishing and snowshoeing become beloved pastimes. Spring breathes life back into the landscape, as wildflowers bloom and the sound of bird songs fills the air. Each season offers a new perspective, a fresh opportunity for connection to nature and one another.

The heartwarming stories and laughter echoing along the shores of Grandview Reservoir continue to weave together the fabric of this community. It serves not just as a source of water, but as a gathering place for families, friends, and neighbors. People come to recharge, to celebrate life's milestones, and to reflect on the beauty of their surroundings. The reservoir stands as a testament to the power of nature to bring people together, creating bonds that transcend time and circumstance.

In this cherished landscape, history is not just a collection of facts but a living tapestry woven from the experiences of those who have come before. Each story—of the Arapaho and Ute tribes, the settlers, and the families who now call this area home—contributes to a shared legacy. Grandview Reservoir continues to inspire, offering a glimpse into the interconnectedness of life, nature, and community. As the sun sets over the water, casting golden hues across the surface, it's a reminder that the beauty of this place is more than a backdrop; it's a vibrant part of everyone's story.

Mount Werner Waterfall Lake

Mount Werner Waterfall Lake is a striking jewel tucked away in the heart of Colorado's Routt County, a location that feels like a scene from a fairy tale. Named after the prominent Mount Werner, which towers majestically over the landscape, the lake serves not only as a beautiful natural feature but also as a site of cultural significance and community gathering. The name itself pays homage to the mountain, named in the late 1800s after early settler Charles Werner, who was instrumental in the development of the area. Legend has it that Werner, upon gazing at the snow-capped peak, declared it a "monument to nature," inspiring generations to cherish the wild beauty surrounding them.

Historically, Mount Werner Waterfall Lake was formed naturally, likely from glacial activity, which carved out the picturesque basin that holds its waters today. The lake is a product of geological forces that have shaped the Rockies over millions of years, giving rise to its stunning, clear waters. The surrounding landscape is rich with flora and fauna, including towering pines, vibrant wildflowers, and a variety of wildlife, from deer to the occasional moose. These natural elements create a beautiful setting for both residents and visitors who come to enjoy the breathtaking views and outdoor activities.

Before European settlers arrived, the land around Mount Werner was home to the Ute tribe, who thrived in the lush environment. The lake and its surroundings were essential to their way of life, providing fish, game, and plant materials for sustenance and shelter. The Ute people recognized the significance of the water in their spiritual beliefs, often holding rituals near the lake to honor the spirits of nature. These early inhabitants fostered a deep connection with the land, emphasizing the importance of harmony with nature that still resonates today.

As settlers arrived in the late 1800s, they brought with them a desire to tame the wilderness, often with little regard for the established ecosystems and the tribes that had long called it home. The early pioneers viewed the land through the lens of opportunity, recognizing the potential for agriculture and resource extraction. However, they also formed a deep appreciation for the landscape's beauty, finding solace and inspiration in the towering peaks and tranquil waters.

The early 1900s saw significant changes in the region, particularly as the tourism industry began to take root. Mount Werner Waterfall Lake quickly became a favored destination for adventurers, artists, and families looking to escape the bustle of city life. The area's natural beauty attracted visitors who sought both relaxation and adventure, from hiking and fishing to photography and painting. Local lore began to grow, with stories of "the laughing water," referring to the sound of the waterfall cascading into the lake, said to bring joy and good fortune to those who visited.

However, nature has its own way of reminding us of its power. In the spring of 1983, an exceptionally heavy snowpack led to a rapid snowmelt that caused the lake to swell dramatically. The resulting floods tested the resolve of the local community. Residents rallied together, working tirelessly to reinforce banks and protect properties from rising waters. It was a period of resilience, filled with humor and camaraderie, as neighbors shared stories over campfires while sandbagging and forming new friendships amid the chaos.

Through the years, the lake's role has evolved from a mere natural feature to a community centerpiece. It became a place for annual gatherings, like summer picnics and fishing contests, fostering a sense of belonging among those who cherished the beauty and serenity it offered. Every summer, the annual "Lake Day" celebration draws families together for a day filled with laughter, games, and fishing, with the backdrop of stunning mountain vistas. Children run freely, while adults share their own stories, bridging generations with the shared love of the land.

Conservation efforts have become a priority in recent decades, as awareness of environmental issues has grown. Local organizations work tirelessly to protect the water quality of Mount Werner Waterfall Lake, educating residents and visitors on the importance of keeping the area clean and maintaining the delicate balance of the ecosystem. Regular clean-up days bring volunteers together, reinforcing a sense of community commitment to preserving the beauty of the lake.

However, challenges remain. Invasive species such as zebra mussels have been detected in nearby waters, prompting heightened vigilance and education on prevention. Community members band together to monitor the lake, ensuring it remains a healthy environment for fish and other wildlife. Fishing enthusiasts often share tips on best practices, creating a culture of stewardship that connects them more deeply to the lake.

The area has seen a surge in recreational development, with trails established around the lake to accommodate hikers, bikers, and wildlife watchers. These paths wind through breathtaking scenery, providing opportunities for exploration and connection to the natural world. Local parks offer picnic areas and educational programs about the flora and fauna of the region, inviting families to engage with the environment in meaningful ways.

In winter, Mount Werner Waterfall Lake transforms into a picturesque wonderland, attracting those seeking the thrill of snowshoeing and ice fishing. The frozen surface becomes a playground, and families gather to enjoy the crisp air and stunning views, wrapped in layers of warm clothing and laughter. It's a time when the community embraces the cold, gathering for bonfires and hot cocoa, creating memories that will last a lifetime.

As the seasons change, so does the atmosphere around Mount Werner Waterfall Lake. Each shift in weather brings new visitors, drawn by the allure of the landscape, its stories, and its history. Whether it's the vibrant wildflowers of spring, the lush greenery of summer, the stunning hues of fall, or the serene snowfalls of winter, the lake remains a constant source of inspiration and joy.

Mount Werner Waterfall Lake stands as a symbol of community, resilience, and connection to nature. The stories woven into its history continue to shape the lives of those who visit and call it home. It serves as a reminder that even amidst change and challenges, the beauty of nature and the bonds formed within a community can thrive and endure, creating a legacy for future generations to cherish and enjoy. As the sun sets behind Mount Werner, casting golden light across the water, it's a moment of magic—a promise that the lake will continue to be a source of laughter, adventure, and unforgettable memories for years to come.

Glacier Lake

Glacier Lake is a breathtaking marvel, tucked high in the Colorado Rockies, where nature seems to have painted every inch with a masterful brush. Located in Grand County, it lies within the bounds of the Arapaho National Forest, surrounded by towering peaks and lush forests. This lake, which got its name from the glaciers that once carved out its basin, has been a gathering place for stories, adventures, and the occasional mishap.

The origin of Glacier Lake can be traced back thousands of years, when glacial ice sculpted the landscape, leaving behind a stunning alpine lake. The beauty of the lake is accentuated by its striking blue color, a result of the glacial silt that reflects sunlight in a way that feels almost magical. The lake is not man-made; rather, it's a natural wonder that has endured through millennia, offering both serenity and excitement to those who visit.

For centuries, the land surrounding Glacier Lake was inhabited by the Ute and Arapaho tribes, who revered the area for its natural bounty. The lake and its surroundings provided vital resources for these indigenous peoples, including fish, game, and medicinal plants. The Ute, in particular, considered the mountains sacred, often conducting ceremonies near the water's edge to honor the spirits of the land. It is said that they believed the lake was a place of healing, where the waters could wash away not just physical ailments but emotional scars as well. Such legends added a layer of mystique to the already awe-inspiring landscape.

As settlers began to arrive in the late 1800s, the natural beauty of Glacier Lake attracted attention. Many were drawn by the promise of adventure and the hope of discovering their fortunes. The early pioneers were a colorful bunch—imagine rugged men with beards that could hide small animals and women in long dresses carrying everything they needed for a life in the wild. With their arrival came the first signs of change. While the settlers respected the landscape, they also sought to cultivate it. They planted crops and built homes, but the pull of the mountains and the lake kept calling them back.

In the summer of 1933, a heavy rainstorm caused a significant flood that altered the landscape around Glacier Lake. The once gentle streams swelled into torrents, and the lake overflowed its banks, creating a temporary waterfall that cascaded down the rocks. Local lore tells of a family camping nearby, who woke up to find their tent almost afloat. They scrambled to save their picnic basket—a heroic effort that ended with soggy sandwiches but laughter that echoed through the trees. This event not only shaped the land but also deepened the connection that the community felt towards the lake, turning it into a site of both natural beauty and shared memories.

As time passed, Glacier Lake became a favorite destination for outdoor enthusiasts. Hikers flocked to its shores, drawn by the beauty of the mountains and the crisp, cool air. Fishing enthusiasts found joy in casting their lines into the clear waters, hoping for a catch that would be the envy of their friends back home. Families would set up picnics, spreading blankets on the grass and sharing stories while children played nearby, creating a vibrant sense of community. The lake transformed into a place of recreation and togetherness, a haven where laughter mingled with the sounds of nature.

The flora and fauna surrounding Glacier Lake have remained relatively unchanged over the years, thanks in part to conservation efforts. Spruce and fir trees dominate the landscape, providing shelter for a variety of wildlife, including elk, deer, and the occasional bear. The lake is home to native fish species, such as cutthroat trout, which have drawn anglers for generations. However, human impact has also introduced challenges. Invasive species like brook trout have found their way into the waters, posing a threat to the delicate balance of the ecosystem. Local conservation groups have worked diligently to monitor these changes, organizing clean-up days and educational programs to raise awareness about the importance of protecting this natural treasure.

While the lake has remained a place of natural beauty, the surrounding area has seen development aimed at enhancing the visitor experience. Trails have been established for hiking and biking, with interpretive signs along the way to educate visitors about the flora and fauna of the region. These trails are well-maintained, allowing families to explore the beauty of the area while learning about its ecological significance. Picnic areas have also been developed, with tables and fire pits that invite gatherings, making it easy for friends and family to enjoy a day out.

Despite the positive changes, Glacier Lake faces ongoing challenges. Climate change is impacting snowmelt patterns and water levels, which can alter the delicate balance of the ecosystem. Local organizations have initiated conservation programs aimed at preserving the natural habitat, and educational workshops teach visitors about sustainable practices, such as Leave No Trace principles. These efforts remind everyone that they are stewards of this beautiful land, responsible for its protection and preservation.

As seasons change, Glacier Lake transforms from a summer paradise to a winter wonderland. The lake freezes over, becoming a playground for ice skaters and ice fishermen. Snow blankets the trees, and the air is filled with laughter as families build snowmen and engage in snowball fights. The sense of community thrives even in the chill of winter, as friends gather around fires, sharing stories and hot cocoa.

Every visit to Glacier Lake feels like a small adventure, an opportunity to connect with nature and create lasting memories. Whether it's the tranquility of a summer evening spent watching the sunset over the water or the thrill of a winter hike through freshly fallen snow, the lake continues to inspire awe and wonder. It serves as a reminder of the beauty of the natural world and the importance of cherishing it for generations to come.

The stories surrounding Glacier Lake, from its formation to the laughter of families who have come to play, are woven into the fabric of the community. As people come and go, the lake remains—a steadfast witness to the passage of time, holding memories within its depths. And as the sun sets behind the mountains, casting a warm glow over the water, it invites all who visit to dream, to laugh, and to find a little bit of magic in the world around them.

Windy Gap Reservoir

Windy Gap Reservoir, a sparkling oasis tucked in the foothills of Colorado's Rocky Mountains, is a place where water meets whimsy. Located in Grand County, this reservoir was originally created in the mid-1980s as part of a broader project to manage water resources in the region. The name "Windy Gap" hints at the breezy conditions often found in the area, where gusts whip through the valleys, making for an exhilarating experience, especially for those who enjoy windsurfing or simply holding onto their hats while trying to enjoy a peaceful afternoon by the water.

The reservoir's formation was a combination of nature and human endeavor. While the land has been shaped by eons of geological activity, Windy Gap Reservoir came to life as a result of engineering initiatives that aimed to create a reliable water source. Engineers constructed the dam, which transformed the area into a vibrant body of water. The purpose was not just to store water but to support the burgeoning population and agricultural demands of the surrounding counties.

In the years leading up to the reservoir's construction, the region was rich in wildlife and native flora. The area was home to the Ute people, who thrived on the land for generations, relying on its resources for sustenance and shelter. The Ute utilized the streams and lakes for fishing and gathering plants, creating a deep spiritual connection with the waters that now form Windy Gap. They believed the lakes held powerful spirits, and many tribal ceremonies were conducted near the water's edge, honoring both the lake and the surrounding mountains.

With the arrival of settlers in the late 1800s, the landscape began to shift. The settlers were eager to farm the fertile land, which led to the establishment of communities that flourished on the banks of the rivers. Windy Gap's creation marked a new chapter in the area's history, as families began to rely on this reservoir for irrigation and drinking water. It became a lifeline for the growing population, transforming a previously untamed landscape into a thriving agricultural hub. The irony of progress is that while the settlers cultivated the land, they also made changes that would alter the ecosystem forever.

One particularly amusing legend surrounds Windy Gap, often told by locals during gatherings. It's said that the reservoir was named not just for its breezy conditions, but because of a quirky event involving a fishing contest. A group of competitive anglers decided to host a tournament, and as luck would have it, the wind picked up ferociously, turning what was supposed to be a friendly competition into a scene of chaos. Rods flew, hats were lost, and fish seemed to leap straight out of the water in laughter at the spectacle. One particularly clever fish reportedly evaded capture by jumping into the boat of a bewildered participant, leading to the claim that the lake was full of mischievous spirits.

Windy Gap also experienced its share of natural challenges. In 1997, heavy rains caused significant flooding, leading to concerns about the reservoir's stability. While the reservoir held up well, the event was a wake-up call to the community about the importance of sustainable water management practices. The flood brought neighbors together, leading to spirited discussions and innovative ideas about conservation. From this challenge emerged a collective determination to protect the area, fostering a newfound sense of stewardship among the residents.

As time passed, the reservoir became a cherished spot for recreation. Families flocked to its shores for picnics, fishermen cast their lines in hopes of a catch, and kayakers navigated the waters. Windy Gap is a prime example of how a body of water can become a community hub, where children learn to fish with their grandparents, couples share romantic sunsets, and friends gather for summer barbecues. Each weekend, the shoreline buzzes with laughter, the sound of splashing water, and the clinking of picnic plates.

The local flora and fauna have thrived around Windy Gap. The reservoir is home to an array of fish species, including rainbow trout, which were introduced to enhance the fishing experience. The surrounding landscape boasts a mix of wildflowers, aspens, and pines, creating a picturesque backdrop for outdoor activities. Birdwatchers are often delighted by the sight of osprey diving for fish, or the elusive great horned owl keeping watch from a nearby tree. This biodiversity is a testament to the importance of balancing human recreation with conservation efforts.

However, with the influx of visitors and the introduction of new species, challenges emerged. Invasive species, such as zebra mussels, posed a threat to the reservoir's ecosystem. These small mollusks, while not particularly charming, can wreak havoc on native species and infrastructure. To combat this, local conservation groups have mobilized to educate the public about the importance of keeping the reservoir healthy. They organize workshops and clean-up days, encouraging visitors to practice responsible boating and fishing habits.

Despite these challenges, Windy Gap continues to thrive. Conservation efforts have led to the development of parks and recreational areas surrounding the reservoir. Picnic spots with fire pits, hiking trails, and designated fishing areas have been established, making it easier for families to enjoy the outdoors. Local organizations host events throughout the year, from fishing derbies to wildlife education days, fostering a sense of community and encouraging appreciation for the natural world.

As seasons change, Windy Gap transforms into a canvas of color. In autumn, the leaves turn brilliant shades of gold and crimson, creating a breathtaking backdrop for hikers and photographers alike. Winter blankets the area in snow, turning the reservoir into a serene escape for ice fishermen and snowshoers.

No matter the season, Windy Gap Reservoir stands as a testament to the resilience of nature and community spirit. The stories shared around campfires and the laughter echoing off the water remind us that while challenges may arise, there is always room for joy and connection. Every ripple in the water holds a tale of adventure, and every breeze carries a whisper of the past.

Visiting Windy Gap is more than just a trip to a reservoir; it's an invitation to embrace the wonders of nature, to reconnect with loved ones, and to honor the spirit of a land that has shaped lives for generations. And who knows? Perhaps you'll catch a glimpse of that legendary fish, the one that sparked the tales of mischief and laughter. After all, at Windy Gap, anything is possible.

Silver Jack Reservoir

Silver Jack Reservoir, tucked away in the picturesque San Juan Mountains of Colorado, is more than just a shimmering body of water; it's a tapestry of history, community, and the kind of adventures that spark both laughter and reflection. Located in Hinsdale County, the reservoir was constructed in 1959 as part of a project to manage water resources in the region. The name "Silver Jack" pays homage to the nearby Silver Jack Mine, a nod to the area's rich mining history. This mine, which once thrived during the late 19th century, was known for its silver production, which drew fortune seekers and dreamers to the rugged mountains. The reservoir itself became a crucial lifeline for irrigation and drinking water, transforming the landscape and providing a serene escape for generations to come.

In its early days, the area around Silver Jack was a bustling hub for the Ute tribes, who roamed the mountains and valleys long before settlers arrived. They thrived on the land, utilizing the streams and rivers for fishing and gathering. The Utes revered the mountains and waters, believing they were sacred and full of spiritual significance. Their connection to the land laid the foundation for a rich cultural tapestry, and many stories of their exploits and reverence for nature were passed down through generations.

With the arrival of miners and settlers in the late 1800s, the landscape began to shift dramatically. The Utes faced displacement, and their way of life was altered forever as newcomers sought their fortunes. While the mining boom brought economic growth, it also marked the beginning of a profound change in the ecosystem. The construction of Silver Jack Reservoir was part of this transformation. Initially, the site was a picturesque mountain valley filled with lush vegetation and abundant wildlife. As the dam was built, the area flooded, creating the reservoir that would support not just irrigation but also recreational activities.

Local legends grew around the reservoir, adding to its mystique. One popular story tells of a miner named Old Gus who supposedly discovered a secret gold vein just below the surface of Silver Jack. According to the tale, he decided to keep his findings a secret, believing it would bring him fortune. However, as the story goes, the spirits of the mountains didn't take kindly to his deception. One stormy night, Gus went out to inspect his hidden treasure, only to be caught in a freak thunderstorm that swelled the reservoir's waters. It's said that the next morning, he was found standing on the banks of Silver Jack, utterly confused, with nothing but a handful of shiny rocks—none of which were gold. Locals chuckle at the idea that the spirits of Silver Jack may still be watching over the water, protecting their secrets from greedy hands.

The creation of the reservoir led to changes in the local flora and fauna, introducing both opportunities and challenges.

Silver Jack became a habitat for diverse wildlife, attracting everything from deer and elk to a variety of fish species, including brook trout and cutthroat trout. Anglers flocked to the waters, making it a popular spot for fishing and recreation. Families would set up camp near the shores, filling the air with the scent of grilling burgers and the sound of laughter as children splashed in the shallows.

Over time, Silver Jack Reservoir also served as a vital resource for the surrounding communities, supporting agricultural development and providing water for irrigation. Farmers in the region grew crops that thrived with the dependable water supply, helping to bolster the local economy and sustain livelihoods. The reservoir became a focal point for community gatherings, with events like fishing derbies and summer picnics drawing people together in celebration of nature and camaraderie.

However, with increased human activity came some challenges. The introduction of invasive species, such as the notorious lake trout, posed a threat to the delicate balance of the ecosystem. These fish, while popular among anglers, began to outcompete native species, leading to concerns about biodiversity. Conservation groups rallied together to address these issues, organizing clean-up efforts and educational programs to raise awareness about responsible fishing practices and the importance of protecting native habitats. Their tireless work helped foster a spirit of stewardship among residents and visitors alike, ensuring that future generations would continue to enjoy the beauty of Silver Jack.

As the years rolled on, efforts to preserve the reservoir led to the establishment of surrounding parks and recreational areas. Hiking trails were developed, allowing visitors to explore the majestic mountains that frame the reservoir. In the fall, these trails become a riot of colors, drawing photographers and nature enthusiasts eager to capture the breathtaking views. The reservoir itself became a popular spot for kayaking and canoeing, with families paddling along its tranquil waters while taking in the stunning scenery.

The winters brought their own magic to Silver Jack. Snow blanketed the area, transforming it into a winter wonderland. Skiers and snowboarders found their thrill in the nearby slopes, while others reveled in snowshoeing and ice fishing on the frozen surface of the reservoir. Each season offers a new adventure, a new way to connect with nature, and a new reason to share stories around campfires.

Amidst the laughter and recreation, Silver Jack Reservoir also serves as a reminder of the balance between human progress and environmental preservation. It is a place where the spirit of the Ute people echoes through the mountains, where miners once sought fortune, and where families continue to create lasting memories. Visitors often leave with a sense of connection—not only to the stunning landscape but also to the stories that have woven together over the years.

Today, Silver Jack Reservoir stands not only as a recreational haven but as a testament to the resilience of nature and the human spirit. The community thrives on the traditions of stewardship, ensuring that the reservoir remains a cherished part of the region for years to come. The ripples in the water carry tales of adventure, laughter, and the whispers of those who came before, reminding us that every visit to Silver Jack is not just a getaway, but a journey into the heart of Colorado's rich history and vibrant community.

Whether you're casting a line, hiking a trail, or simply gazing at the stars reflected in the water, Silver Jack Reservoir invites you to be a part of its ongoing story—one filled with joy, laughter, and the promise of new adventures waiting just around the bend.

Yankee Doodle Lake

Yankee Doodle Lake, a delightful little spot in the Rocky Mountain National Park, boasts a history that dances between whimsy and adventure, making it a true treasure in Colorado's scenic landscape. Located in Larimer County, this lake is named after the popular American song "Yankee Doodle," which dates back to the Revolutionary War era. One popular theory about its naming suggests that a group of spirited soldiers sang the song while hiking through the area, their exuberance echoing off the mountains and inspiring the name. Can you imagine a band of rough-and-tumble soldiers, tramping through the wild, pausing for a moment to sing and cheer? If the mountains could talk, they might just laugh at the sight.

Formed naturally by glacial activity, Yankee Doodle Lake has existed for thousands of years, evolving alongside the dramatic shifts in the land. Originally a small pond tucked away in the mountains, it was expanded by the glacial melt that carved its shores. The lake is surrounded by vibrant alpine meadows, where wildflowers bloom in a riot of colors during the summer months, providing a stunning contrast to the rugged granite cliffs. A lively array of flora and fauna thrives in this enchanting environment, including elk, deer, and a variety of bird species that serenade visitors with their melodies. In the spring, the melting snow reveals a landscape that bursts into life, reminding everyone of the resilience of nature.

Long before the lake was given its catchy name, it was part of the territory inhabited by the Ute and Arapaho tribes. The Utes revered the mountains, considering them sacred. They utilized the surrounding area for hunting and gathering, relying on the diverse wildlife for sustenance. The presence of Yankee Doodle Lake added to the region's allure, providing fresh water and a rich ecosystem for the tribes. Stories of spirits residing in the waters and mountains were common, creating a mystical connection that still resonates in the area today.

The arrival of European settlers marked a significant change in the landscape and ecosystem. While colonization brought challenges, it also introduced agricultural practices that positively impacted the local economy. Settlers cleared land for farming, and in doing so, inadvertently created habitats that fostered a diverse range of wildlife. With their plows and seeds, they transformed the land, but they also cultivated a community that would eventually thrive around the lake. As people established homes, they began to share stories of Yankee Doodle Lake, passing down tales of fishing trips and summer picnics.

Yankee Doodle Lake became a popular destination for recreation, drawing visitors who sought to escape the hustle and bustle of urban life. Families packed up their cars and ventured into the mountains, eager to create lasting memories. Picture this: a group of children darting down the trail, their laughter ringing out like music, while parents set up picnic blankets in the shade of towering pines. Fishing rods were cast, and the occasional "got one!" could be heard, followed by cheers and excitement. The lake became a canvas for adventure, with people kayaking, canoeing, and simply enjoying the peace that comes from being surrounded by nature.

However, as with many natural spaces, human impact posed challenges. Invasive species began to infiltrate the delicate ecosystem, threatening the native fish populations and plant life. Fishermen caught sight of larger, more aggressive fish, leading to concerns about the balance of the lake's ecosystem. In response, local conservation groups sprang into action, organizing efforts to protect the lake's biodiversity. They hosted community clean-up days and educational workshops, inspiring visitors to become stewards of the land. The message was simple: love the lake, and it will love you back.

Despite these challenges, Yankee Doodle Lake remains a beloved destination, thanks in part to the ongoing conservation efforts. The establishment of surrounding parks, hiking trails, and picnic areas has helped foster a sense of community. Visitors can now enjoy a leisurely stroll along the shoreline, taking in the breathtaking views while reflecting on the stories that have shaped this special place. In the fall, the aspen trees surrounding the lake transform into a vibrant gold, drawing photographers and nature enthusiasts alike. It's as if nature itself is putting on a show, inviting everyone to come and witness its beauty.

The winter months bring their own magic, as the lake freezes over, creating a serene landscape that invites exploration. Snowshoeing and cross-country skiing become the order of the day, with families gliding across the soft, powdery surface. Picture a child building a snowman with sticks for arms, giggling as it topples over, while parents sip hot cocoa nearby. The lake transforms into a playground for both young and old, fostering connections that last a lifetime.

One particular story continues to circulate among locals about the lake. It's said that on a clear night, when the moon is full, you can hear the faint echoes of soldiers singing "Yankee Doodle" as they march along the shores. Many swear they've heard the song carried by the wind, a sweet reminder of the lake's storied past. Whether fact or fiction, the legend adds a layer of enchantment to the already captivating landscape.

Today, Yankee Doodle Lake serves not only as a recreational haven but also as a symbol of community and connection. Each visit is an invitation to partake in the ongoing story of the land—one filled with laughter, friendship, and the simple joys of life. The lake holds memories of countless family gatherings, fishing tales, and moments of reflection, weaving together the past and the present in a beautiful tapestry of human experience.

As visitors gather around the shores of Yankee Doodle Lake, they become part of something greater. Each splash of water, each laugh shared, and each sunrise witnessed at the lake adds to its rich narrative. With every visit, the spirit of adventure and connection continues to thrive, reminding everyone that the great outdoors is a place where stories are born, friendships are forged, and the beauty of nature reigns supreme.

In the end, Yankee Doodle Lake is more than just a body of water; it's a sanctuary for the soul, a place where memories are made, and a reminder of the magic that exists in the world around us. Whether you're fishing with friends, hiking along the trails, or simply enjoying a peaceful moment by the water, you'll leave with a heart full of joy and a spirit ignited by the beauty of nature. As the sun sets over the lake, casting a golden glow on the water, it's clear that this little piece of Colorado is a treasure to cherish for generations to come.

Hitchcock Lake

Hitchcock Lake, a serene spot located in the heart of Colorado's Rocky Mountain National Park, has a history that flows as smoothly as its waters. Named after the Hitchcock family, early settlers in the area, the lake captures the spirit of both its natural beauty and the people who have called this rugged landscape home. The story of how the lake came to be is steeped in a blend of adventure, resilience, and a touch of humor that would make even the most serious historian chuckle.

The lake was formed naturally through glacial activity, its clear waters reflecting the towering peaks that surround it. As glaciers retreated thousands of years ago, they carved out the basin, creating a stunning alpine lake that has been a refuge for flora and fauna alike. The initial flora consisted of lush green grasses, vibrant wildflowers, and sturdy conifers that provide shelter for various species. Animals like deer, foxes, and a colorful array of birds made their home in the rich ecosystems that flourished nearby.

Long before the Hitchcock family arrived, the area was inhabited by the Ute people. These indigenous tribes revered the land, believing it to be filled with spirits and sacred places. The lake, with its tranquil waters, became a crucial resource, providing fresh water and a variety of fish that supported their way of life. They shared stories of the lake being a meeting point for tribes, a place where laughter echoed and alliances were forged. As children of the Ute tribes played by the shores, they spun tales of mythical creatures residing in the depths, adding a layer of magic to the lake's already enchanting aura.

With the arrival of European settlers in the late 1800s, the landscape began to shift dramatically. The Hitchcock family, known for their strong work ethic and community spirit, helped cultivate the land, contributing to the agricultural development of the region. They were the kind of folks who could turn a plot of rocky terrain into a flourishing garden, often joking about their ability to grow tomatoes in the harshest conditions. Their hard work transformed the area, and soon enough, Hitchcock Lake became a hub of activity for local farmers.

Fishing at the lake became a rite of passage for many families. Picture this: a father and son setting out early in the morning with fishing rods in hand, the sun just peeking over the horizon. As they cast their lines, the dad regales his son with tales of the legendary "big one" that got away, only for the son to exclaim, "Dad, it's just a fish!" The lake echoed with laughter and camaraderie, creating cherished memories that would be retold for generations.

However, it wasn't all sunshine and fishing tales. Hitchcock Lake also witnessed its fair share of challenges. The region is no stranger to sudden weather changes, and storms have been known to roll in unexpectedly, turning a peaceful day into a race for cover. Local legends tell of one particularly fierce storm that struck in the summer of '57, causing the lake to swell and flood nearby fields. Farmers scrambled to save their crops, while others took the opportunity to grab their canoes for a cheeky ride across what became a temporary waterway. "Just another day at Hitchcock Lake," they would say, laughing off the chaos.

As time passed, the area surrounding the lake began to attract more visitors. Outdoor enthusiasts discovered the breathtaking hiking trails and the opportunity to reconnect with nature. Camping trips became popular, with families pitching tents along the shores and roasting marshmallows by the fire. One can imagine the sight of kids running around with sticky hands and chocolate-smeared faces, their giggles mixing with the crackle of the campfire. The lake transformed into a gathering place for friends and families, fostering a sense of community and shared joy.

Yet, as the number of visitors increased, so did the challenges facing Hitchcock Lake. Invasive species began to infiltrate the waters, threatening the delicate balance of the ecosystem. Fishermen started to notice changes in the fish population, and local conservationists sprang into action. They organized clean-up events, educational workshops, and community outreach to raise awareness about the importance of preserving the lake's natural beauty. "We need to take care of our backyard," they would say, emphasizing the shared responsibility to protect this cherished place.

Conservation efforts have led to a renewed focus on maintaining the health of the lake and its surroundings. The establishment of parks and designated recreation areas has encouraged responsible tourism while preserving the natural landscape. Trails have been maintained and improved, making it easier for visitors to explore the beauty of the area. Hiking to Hitchcock Lake became a popular pastime, with hikers often sharing stories of their adventures and marveling at the stunning vistas that surround the lake.

As for the myths and legends, they continue to thrive. Locals often recount tales of a mysterious creature that lurks in the depths, affectionately dubbed "Hitch," as in "Hitch the Fish." The stories vary—some say it's a giant trout that knows all the best fishing spots, while others believe it's a spirit guarding the lake. Whatever the truth may be, the tales add to the lake's charm, inviting visitors to share their own experiences and speculations.

In recent years, a renewed interest in sustainable practices has emerged, with many visitors opting for eco-friendly gear and practices while enjoying the outdoors. This shift has made a noticeable difference, helping to preserve the beauty of Hitchcock Lake for future generations. Schools have even organized field trips to teach children about the importance of conservation, fostering a sense of stewardship in the next generation. Who knows? Maybe one day, those children will return with their own kids, sharing stories of their adventures and the lake's timeless magic.

Today, Hitchcock Lake stands as a symbol of community, resilience, and the simple joys of life. As families gather for picnics by the water and friends share fishing tales, the spirit of the Hitchcock family and the Ute tribes lives on in the laughter that dances across the surface of the lake. Each ripple tells a story, each gust of wind carries a memory, and each sunrise paints a new canvas of possibility.

The lake is more than just a body of water; it's a living, breathing testament to the beauty of nature and the connections we share with one another. So, whether you're casting a line, hiking along the shore, or simply sitting in quiet reflection, remember that at Hitchcock Lake, you're part of a grand tapestry woven from the threads of history, adventure, and the enduring spirit of the people who cherish this extraordinary place.

Lone Pine Lake

Lone Pine Lake, a serene body of water tucked away in the Rocky Mountain National Park, is a place where stories ebb and flow like the gentle ripples on its surface. This tranquil lake earned its name from a solitary pine tree that stood watch over the water, a testament to resilience and endurance. The tree, having weathered countless storms, became a local icon, inspiring not just its name but also a sense of camaraderie among those who visited the area.

Located in Larimer County, this picturesque lake is situated at an elevation of about 10,000 feet, offering breathtaking views of the surrounding peaks. The lake was formed naturally, a product of glacial activity that carved out its basin. As glaciers retreated thousands of years ago, they left behind this stunning alpine lake, surrounded by a diverse ecosystem filled with wildflowers, grasses, and hardy coniferous trees. The initial flora created a rich tapestry of life that supported everything from chipmunks to deer, not to mention a vibrant array of bird species, including the elusive peregrine falcon.

Before settlers arrived, the area was home to the Ute people, who lived in harmony with the land. The Ute tribes held the lake and its surrounding landscape in great reverence, often visiting it for fishing and gathering. They believed the lake to be a sacred site, where the spirits of nature came alive. Stories passed down through generations spoke of a spirit that danced on the water's surface during full moons, bringing good fortune to those who witnessed it.

With the advent of European settlers in the 1800s, the landscape began to change. The Lone Pine tree became a landmark for those venturing into the wilderness, guiding them through the rugged terrain. The settlers found the area rich with resources, and they established small homesteads nearby. Many tales emerged from this period, often filled with humor and the spirit of adventure. One such story tells of a particularly stubborn cow that wandered off, only to be found munching happily on the very tree that inspired the lake's name. Locals affectionately dubbed her "Lone Pine Betsy," and her antics became the stuff of legends, bringing laughter to the community.

Fishing soon became a favorite pastime at Lone Pine Lake. Families would gather with picnic baskets, casting their lines in hopes of catching the big one. The thrill of reeling in a trout was often accompanied by boisterous laughter and the inevitable "the one that got away" stories. Children would wade into the shallows, trying to catch minnows with their bare hands, their giggles ringing through the air. This sense of community transformed the lake into a hub of joy, where friendships blossomed and memories were made.

However, like many areas in Colorado, Lone Pine Lake faced its share of challenges. In the spring of 1965, heavy rains caused a significant flood, transforming the peaceful lake into a raging torrent. The surrounding meadows were inundated, and many local farmers struggled to recover. Yet, true to form, the community rallied together, sharing resources and support to help each other through the crisis. This resilience only strengthened the bonds among those who called this rugged wilderness home.

As time went on, the area around Lone Pine Lake became increasingly popular with tourists. The stunning scenery and accessibility to hiking trails attracted outdoor enthusiasts from near and far. Hikers would often take the trail to the lake, only to be greeted by the spectacular sight of the water mirroring the mountains above. The experience was described as "a postcard come to life," and it quickly became a favorite destination for families, nature lovers, and photographers.

With increased foot traffic came the need for conservation efforts. The local community recognized the importance of protecting their beloved lake and its ecosystem. Various initiatives were launched to combat the threat of invasive species, such as non-native plants that threatened the delicate balance of the area. Educational programs were developed to teach visitors about Leave No Trace principles, emphasizing the need to respect and preserve the natural beauty. Conservationists became the unsung heroes of Lone Pine Lake, working tirelessly to ensure future generations could enjoy its splendor.

The lake also saw the establishment of nearby parks and recreational areas, which further enhanced its appeal. Campsites were developed, allowing families to experience the joy of camping under the stars, while hiking trails provided access to some of the most breathtaking views in the state. Seasonal events, such as "Fish and Fun" days, brought families together for friendly competitions and a chance to bond over their love of nature. These gatherings fostered a spirit of collaboration and community, with laughter and stories shared around campfires, echoing the joy that Lone Pine Lake inspired.

As the years rolled by, the myths surrounding Lone Pine Lake evolved, too. Many still tell tales of the mischievous spirit that dances on the water's surface. Others speak of the legendary trout that swims just beneath the surface, rumored to grant wishes to those who manage to catch it. Families return year after year, eager to share these stories with their children, keeping the magic alive.

Today, Lone Pine Lake stands not just as a beautiful spot in the mountains but as a vibrant reminder of community, resilience, and the enduring bond between people and nature. Each visit brings with it the possibility of laughter, adventure, and a deeper appreciation for the natural world. The lake continues to attract those seeking solace, inspiration, and a sense of belonging, proving that while times may change, the spirit of Lone Pine Lake remains as strong as ever.

Visitors today still find joy in casting their lines, hiking the trails, and sharing stories with fellow adventurers. The solitary pine tree remains a steadfast sentinel, reminding all who come to Lone Pine Lake of the importance of connection—both to nature and to each other. With each ripple on the water, the legacy of laughter and love flows onward, ensuring that this enchanting place will forever hold a special place in the hearts of those who are fortunate enough to experience it.

Clear Lake

As we glide to the shore of this final chapter about Colorado's lakes, let's take a moment to soak in the scenery of Clear Lake. The name might seem straightforward, but trust me, it's anything but dull! This lake has a personality as vibrant as its waters, and if you've made it this far, you deserve a round of applause for sticking with me on this wild, watery ride.

Now, I know what you're thinking: Clear Lake? Why does it sound like a wellness retreat for people who can't decide between yoga and fishing? But in all seriousness, Clear Lake has a rich history and an abundance of charm that deserves our attention. It's located in the heart of Colorado, specifically in the gorgeous Gunnison County, where the mountains stand like guardians of the shimmering water below. And while we're on the subject of shimmering, I can assure you that the reflections on this lake could make a Pinterest board swoon.

As with many places, Clear Lake got its name because, well, it's clear! It's like a straightforward friend who doesn't beat around the bush. But don't let its simple name fool you; this lake has witnessed some epic events. Picture this: back in the day, it was a bustling spot for miners who were looking to quench their thirst after a long day of toiling for gold. Legend has it that some of them would hop into their boats and engage in friendly fishing competitions, all while spinning tales about the biggest fish that got away—stories that probably grew taller with every round of drinks.

As the miners dug into the earth, they didn't just unearth gold; they unearthed legends. Some say Clear Lake is haunted by the spirits of those who never quite found what they were looking for. Perhaps you'll spot a shimmering figure dancing on the water at twilight, but don't panic! It's likely just a reflection of a nearby pine tree swaying in the wind. Or, it could be a friendly fisherman who forgot where he parked his boat!

In terms of geography, Clear Lake is a natural beauty formed by glacial movements, with a dash of help from those industrious miners who redirected water flows. It's a classic example of nature and human endeavor harmonizing, like peanut butter and jelly, but with fewer calories and more wildlife. The area is rich in flora and fauna, with wildflowers dancing along the shores and birds serenading anyone who dares to listen. The only thing more charming than the scenery is the surprise visit from a curious chipmunk hoping for a snack.

Speaking of snacks, if you're planning a visit to Clear Lake, pack a picnic! You could feast on anything from gourmet sandwiches to those questionable leftovers you've been meaning to eat. Just be sure to keep a lookout for any wildlife that may consider your picnic an open invitation. A friendly squirrel can be cute until it's trying to steal your sandwich. And if you happen to lose a bit of your lunch to nature, just remember: sharing is caring!

Before I get too carried away, let's take a moment to appreciate the indigenous tribes that roamed these lands long before any miners showed up with pickaxes. The Ute people cherished the region, and their stories are interwoven with the very fabric of the land. Clear Lake would have been a vital part of their lives, a place for gathering and connecting with nature, and who knows what stories they would tell about the lake's reflections or the stars above.

Colonization brought changes to the landscape, but it also fostered a sense of community among the new settlers. Clear Lake became a gathering point—a place for fishing, laughter, and good-natured competition. With its pristine waters, it attracted families who spent lazy summer afternoons fishing or simply soaking in the sun. This wasn't just a lake; it was a gathering place, a hub of memories waiting to be created.

Now, let's talk human impact. Over the years, Clear Lake has faced its share of challenges, like invasive species trying to crash the party. The community has rallied to protect this natural wonder, focusing on conservation efforts to maintain its beauty. It's a reminder that we all play a role in preserving our lakes and the stories they hold.

If you visit Clear Lake today, you'll find opportunities for recreational activities galore! Whether you're fishing, kayaking, or simply lounging by the shore, there's something for everyone. There's even a charming little park nearby where you can stretch your legs or let the kids run wild. Just watch out for that one kid who thinks he's the next Michael Phelps!

As we wrap up our exploration of Clear Lake, I want to thank you for joining me on this whimsical journey through Colorado's shimmering treasures. Each lake tells a story, and Clear Lake is no exception. So, grab your gear, pack some snacks (preferably the good ones), and get ready to explore your local lakes. Each visit is an opportunity to create new memories, discover hidden gems, and perhaps even encounter a ghostly fisherman or two.

So, here's to adventures at Clear Lake and beyond! May your outings be filled with laughter, great company, and more fish tales than you can shake a paddle at. And remember, whether you're gliding across the water in a kayak or chasing after a wayward sandwich thief, the beauty of these moments lies not just in the destination but in the joy and camaraderie shared along the way. Happy exploring!

Thanks for the Adventure!

As we paddle to the end of this grand adventure through Colorado's lakes, I want to take a moment to extend my heartfelt thanks for sticking with me. You've traveled from the depths of Duck Lake to the peaks of Paradise, navigating the twists and turns of lake lore with me. I hope you've enjoyed the ride as much as I have—because let's be honest, a book about lakes could easily drown in boredom without a splash of humor!

Now, you might be scratching your head and wondering why I decided to cover 90 lakes instead of the more typical 100. Well, let me tell you: 100 just seemed too ordinary. I mean, who wants to be average? Ninety is a fun number; it's quirky, a little off-kilter—like that friend who shows up to the party wearing socks with sandals. It stands out in a way that invites curiosity and conversation. "Why 90?" someone might ask. And you can respond with a smirk and a shrug, "Because 100 is for overachievers!" It's a conversation starter, a way to keep things interesting.

Speaking of interesting, I encourage you to get out there and visit your local lake. Whether it's a grand reservoir or a tiny puddle where your neighbor's cat likes to take baths, each body of water has its own stories waiting to be discovered. So pack your favorite snacks—because let's be honest, what's a day at the lake without food?—and bring your sense of adventure. Maybe it's time to bust out that thermos of questionable soup you've been meaning to try, or some elaborate sandwich that's probably more impressive than anything you'll find at a restaurant. If nothing else, it's a great icebreaker with anyone who happens to wander by.

As you explore, remember to keep your sense of humor close at hand. Nature can be a bit unpredictable. You might encounter a majestic heron or a charming beaver—only to be photobombed by a goose that clearly thinks it's the star of the show. Embrace those moments! They're the ones that become your best stories. Just remember: if a goose starts chasing you, it's not a scene from a romantic comedy; it's your cue to run! Trust me, no one looks good in a viral video of a goose chase.

On your adventures, don't forget to document your journey. Snap photos of the landscape, the wildlife, and those ridiculously tasty snacks. Create a scrapbook or an Instagram account dedicated to your local lakes. Call it "Lakes & Snacks" or something equally catchy. Who knows? You might start a trend! Just be sure to tag your friends in those photos where they're falling into the water, because nothing says friendship like a little public humiliation.

This journey is about more than just lakes; it's about connection—to the land, to each other, and to the shenanigans that make life interesting. Each lake has its own personality, just waiting to reveal itself. Perhaps you'll stumble upon your own local legends, like the mythical "Lake of Lost Socks" where all the missing laundry items go to hang out. Picture it: socks in tiny boats, sipping on their favorite beverages, reminiscing about the good old days when they were paired up and worn.

As you embark on these explorations, keep an eye out for local wildlife. Take a moment to appreciate the beauty around you, but also remember: they were here first. That deer you see? It probably has a more compelling life story than any of us. So while you're out there, try not to stare too long or make awkward eye contact—it might think you're challenging it to a duel.

So, thank you once again for exploring the shimmering waters of Colorado with me. May your lake adventures be filled with belly laughs, unexpected splashes, and plenty of snacks. Here's to more lakes, more stories, and perhaps the occasional goose encounter. And remember, whether you're sitting on a dock with your feet dangling in the water or canoeing across a serene lake, the beauty of these moments lies not just in the destination but in the company and the laughter shared along the way.

So grab your sunscreen, pack those snacks, and set out to explore! Happy adventures, and may your lakes be ever tranquil and your snacks ever plentiful!

If you've enjoyed this book

Please consider leaving a review at your favorite online book retailer. Think of it as sending a cookie to the author without the calories or the awkward "I made these from scratch" small talk. Plus, it helps other readers find this gem—or at least something shiny enough to distract them while they're looking for the next great adventure!